Melungeon Portraits

CONTRIBUTIONS TO SOUTHERN APPALACHIAN STUDIES

1. *Memoirs of Grassy Creek: Growing Up in the Mountains on the Virginia–North Carolina Line.* Zetta Barker Hamby. 1998

2. *The Pond Mountain Chronicle: Self-Portrait of a Southern Appalachian Community.* Edited by Leland R. Cooper and Mary Lee Cooper. 1998

3. *Traditional Musicians of the Central Blue Ridge: Old Time, Early Country, Folk and Bluegrass Label Recording Artists, with Discographies.* Marty McGee. 2000

4. *W.R. Trivett, Appalachian Pictureman: Photographs of a Bygone Time.* Ralph E. Lentz II. 2001

5. *The People of the New River: Oral Histories from the Ashe, Alleghany and Watauga Counties of North Carolina.* Edited by Leland R. Cooper and Mary Lee Cooper. 2001

6. *John Fox, Jr., Appalachian Author.* Bill York. 2003

7. *The Thistle and the Brier: Historical Links and Cultural Parallels Between Scotland and Appalachia.* Richard Blaustein. 2003

8. *Tales from Sacred Wind: Coming of Age in Appalachia. The Cratis Williams Chronicles.* Cratis D. Williams. Edited by David Cratis Williams and Patricia D. Beaver. 2003

9. *Willard Gayheart, Appalachian Artist.* Willard Gayheart and Donia S. Eley. 2003

10. *The Forest City Lynching of 1900: Populism, Racism, and White Supremacy in Rutherford County, North Carolina.* J. Timothy Cole. 2003

11. *The Brevard Rosenwald School: Black Education and Community Building in a Southern Appalachian Town, 1920–1966.* Betty J. Reed. 2004

12. *The Bristol Sessions: Writings About the Big Bang of Country Music.* Edited by Charles K. Wolfe and Ted Olson. 2005

13. *Community and Change in the North Carolina Mountains: Oral Histories and Profiles of People from Western Watauga County.* Compiled by Nannie Greene and Catherine Stokes Sheppard. 2006

14. *Ashe County: A History; A New Edition.* Arthur Lloyd Fletcher. 2009 [2006]

15. *The New River Controversy; A New Edition.* Thomas J. Schoenbaum. Epilogue by R. Seth Woodard. 2007

16. *The Blue Ridge Parkway by Foot: A Park Ranger's Memoir.* Tim Pegram. 2007

17. *James Still: Critical Essays on the Dean of Appalachian Literature.* Edited by Ted Olson and Kathy H. Olson. 2008

18. *Owsley County, Kentucky, and the Perpetuation of Poverty.* John R. Burch, Jr. 2008

19. *Asheville: A History.* Nan K. Chase. 2007

20. *Southern Appalachian Poetry: An Anthology of Works by 37 Poets.* Edited by Marita Garin. 2008

21. *Ball, Bat and Bitumen: A History of Coalfield Baseball in the Appalachian South.* L.M. Sutter. 2009

22. *The Frontier Nursing Service: America's First Rural Nurse-Midwife Service and School.* Marie Bartlett. 2009

23. *James Still in Interviews, Oral Histories and Memoirs.* Edited by Ted Olson. 2009

24. *The Millstone Quarries of Powell County, Kentucky.* Charles D. Hockensmith. 2009

25. *The Bibliography of Appalachia: More Than 4,700 Books, Articles, Monographsand Dissertations, Topically Arranged and Indexed.* Compiled by John R. Burch, Jr. 2009

Melungeon Portraits

Exploring Kinship and Identity

Tamara L. Stachowicz

Contributions to Southern Appalachian Studies, 44

McFarland & Company, Inc., Publishers
Jefferson, North Carolina

All photographs are from the author's collection.

LIBRARY OF CONGRESS CATALOGUING-IN-PUBLICATION DATA

Names: Stachowicz, Tamara L., 1963– author.
Title: Melungeon portraits : exploring kinship and identity / Tamara L. Stachowicz.
Other titles: Contributions to southern Appalachian studies ; 44.
Description: Jefferson, North Carolina : McFarland & Company, Inc., Publishers, 2018 | Series: Contributions to southern Appalachian studies ; 44 | Includes bibliographical references and index.
Identifiers: LCCN 2018004430 | ISBN 9781476669793 (softcover : acid free paper) ∞
Subjects: LCSH: Melungeons—Ethnic identity.
Classification: LCC E184.M44 S73 2018 | DDC 305.800975—dc23
LC record available at https://lccn.loc.gov/2018004430

BRITISH LIBRARY CATALOGUING DATA ARE AVAILABLE

ISBN (print) 978-1-4766-6979-3
ISBN (ebook) 978-1-4766-3163-9

Front cover image © 2018 Shutterstock; *inset* Addie Gibson, about 15 years old, circa 1938

Printed in the United States of America

McFarland & Company, Inc., Publishers
Box 611, Jefferson, North Carolina 28640
www.mcfarlandpub.com

To my husband of 30 years, Dr. David Stachowicz

In memory of my brother,
James "Jimmy" Michael Campbell (1967–2011),
and my dear friend Mrs. Lucille Johnson (1920–2016)

Acknowledgments

Sylvia Ray, Arlene Walsh, Kateri Petrie, Josef Stachowicz,
Angela Blankenship, Connie Smith, Logan Johnson, Keith Johnson,
Rachel Bray, Wilma King, Katie Hillison, Shirley Ellis, Anna Partin,
William Isom, Joanne Pezzullo, Jack Goins, Darlene Wilson,
Katherine VandeBrake, Wayne Winkler, Brent Kennedy,
Anita Puckett, Paul Johnson, Carolyn Kenny,
Lize Booysen, and Dara Culhane.

Table of Contents

Preface

In this book, I lay out a foundation based on the historical and academic writings that have so far informed research on Melungeons. Some of these are older sources that have been often recounted, at times like a children's game of telephone: with slight changes and reinterpretations as the time or cultural context demands. The "portraits" included are specifically and intentionally created to empower those who might not otherwise have the power to enter the conversation about their own thoughts on a Melungeon identity. They are called portraits as they are to preserve the "essence" of an individual in the manner of painting with words.

The journey ultimately started with my own mother and her desire to understand her parents, grandparents, and some of the things they said and did. She believed the stories she was told, but realizes she has more questions now than she thought to ask as a child. I do not claim to abandon all bias or to work from a point of certain objectivity. I do intend to share the information as truthfully as I can. I especially want to give as accurate of a portrayal of my interviews and experiences as possible. You, the reader, will know my questions and thoughts as I co-construct portraits with individuals. The process was a collaborative one that required many hours of discussions, back and forth interpretations and reflections, until the co-researcher was satisfied that we had an accurate portrait.

I see the individuals portrayed as my peers, collaborators and co-researchers. Their explanations of their experiences are sometimes harsh, their opinions of others rather angry and demeaning, and their emotions strong and often raw. They are sharing their lives—truly they are opening themselves up for judgments and critiques of their very identity and often their life's work. It is a vulnerability I do not take lightly. I will also not patronize them by sanitizing their comments.

You will find that there is no interpretation of the various "portraits" because the point is to empower the reader or audience as well. You are encouraged to interpret the information and come to your own under-standing. I have been intentional in choosing this methodology and rec-ognizing these participants as co-researchers. Together we explored meaning, experiences, and thoughts, and reflected on them. These people do not intend to speak for anyone but themselves, to share their ideas on their own identity and by what means of understanding they came to those conclusions. You will find family members who experienced the same event with different points of view. We are not trying to determine *the* truth, but to understand an individual's experience as *their* truth.

I'd like to give credit to Antioch University's Leadership and Change program that works to "empower students with the knowledge and skills to lead meaningful lives and to advance social, economic, and environ-mental justice... that fosters innovation and inspires social action." To that end, I hope this work inspires others to believe the stories they are told—to believe that all of us have the right to author our own lives and be accepted for who we are.

Introduction

"I think if I had to put a finger on what I consider a good education, a good radical education, it wouldn't be anything about methods or techniques. It would be loving people first."

—Myles Horton, *We Make the Road by Walking: Conversations on Education and Social Change*

I recall the first time I encountered the word *Melungeon*. I was researching my family's genealogy on my mother's side. I began by consulting internet sources available in the late 1990s and discovered what was then considered a multi-racial group, comprised of white, black, and Indian, called Melungeons. Mom had shared several stories of her childhood with us. Her stories consisted of family members working in the coal mines, harvesting lumber, and hunting up ginseng. In particular she described her maternal grandmother, Arline Campbell Gibson, as Saponi, with very long black hair, and healing methods that included herbs and poultices.

I started by searching county historical records in Bell County, Kentucky, Lee County, Virginia, and Claiborne County, Tennessee, for Campbells and Gibsons. Often putting those names together with the counties and then searching for records of Native Americans would lead to a likely Melungeon connection. At the beginning of my personal research, I understood the term to mean people from the area close to the Cumberland Gap. Eventually I found research that described physical characteristics and socioeconomic status that more narrowly defined Melungeons.[1] Mom's stories and recollections about Cherokee and Saponi ancestors, as well as photographs and my own memories, began to support these explanations. I recalled a "tan" grandmother, aunts, and uncles as well as first and second cousins with accented speech and exciting musical gifts. Oft repeated tales of living on the mountain, hunting herbs, and living in tar paper shacks nudged their way into my consciousness. It was as if someone had completed

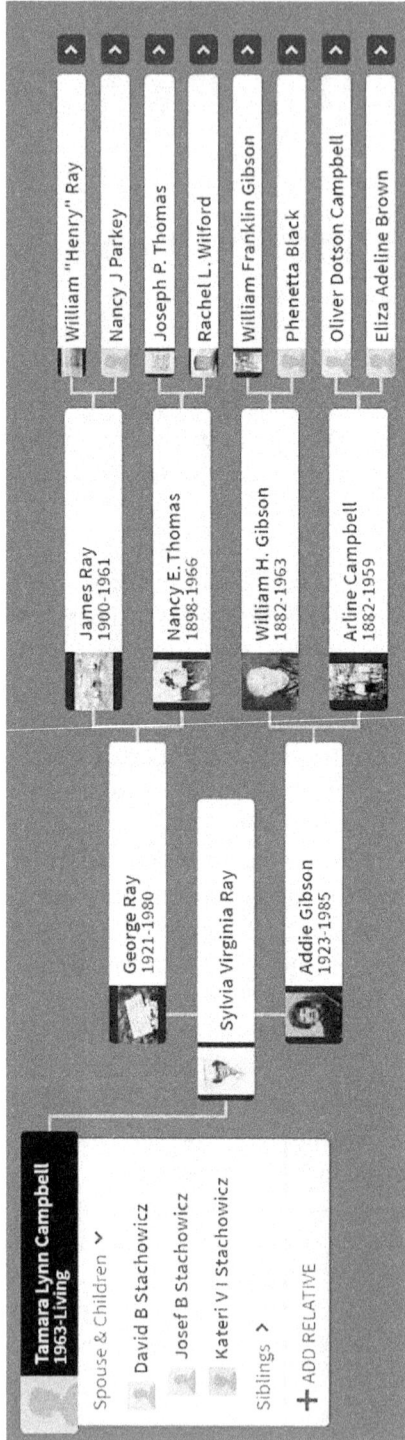

Author's family tree: mother is Sylvia Virginia Ray, maternal grandmother Addie Gibson, etc.

the outside edges of a jigsaw puzzle and placed the inside pieces into likely sections. Every now and then I would look at my life and discover another piece to the puzzle, but I had no idea where the piece belonged or what the finished picture was "supposed" to look like. Pieces were coming fast and furious from the internet, books, and mom's memories.

As most children do, I had listened to the stories of my mother's family members with fascination—similar to how a child might respond to legends and myths. Running off to play with cousins, I only caught snippets of grown-up talk that had little to do with the present reality. Now I wish I had asked more questions back then or that my relatives had lived longer. For many years I wondered how much of what I remembered or what my mother recalled could be substantiated. Questions about my heritage nagged me:

- How would I sift through stories and memories to find my place within a family we didn't often visit?
- What evidence would I need to convince myself that I was of this southern culture, and who else did I want to believe it?
- Do I belong to my mother's family, and if so, what does that mean?

Many of my mother's kin had moved north during the diaspora of Appalachian natives to find industrial jobs that provided a more stable living in places like Detroit, Chicago, and Kokomo, Indiana. The practices that defined their mountain culture were rarely still visible, seen only in family stories, at impromptu family reunions when we would share music and food, and during the few times when my grandmother or uncle lived with us in Michigan. Later I would discover that remnants of southern living and hints of mountain culture surrounded much of my upbringing.

This project is born from these experiences, memories, and questions. I want to have a cultural heritage that I can explain and pass down to my children and grandchildren. I want to be accepted and welcomed into a group. Ultimately, while I entertain a possible Melungeon ancestral identity for myself, I am hoping to understand how people learn to live their cultural identity, how they come to know and accept the definition of that identity, and what evidence or support they would need to accept or reject a particular cultural identity.

The Purpose of This Project

Additional background information on the author might help the reader understand how and why I chose to research my mother's people.

I went to college later in life as a non-traditional college student. I had personal reasons for seeking a degree and by the time this interest came along I was hoping to complete a master's degree in anthropology, the study of human societies and cultures and their physical characteristics. This project includes evidence supporting the value in the search for identity and belonging. Exploring the relevant literature, I decided that portraiture as the methodology of choice would offer the greatest amount of empowerment to those who were helping me. It would also allow the greatest amount of transparency and authenticity since I knew that true objectivity would be a challenge. I present findings that illustrate the process of ethnic, social, and individual identity development as positioned in familial, historical, and geopolitical contexts.

The answers to my research question and sub-questions can help co-researchers (those whom I interviewed and helped me research their families and their own identity) understand the family values, behaviors, and unspoken rules passed on to them. Once understanding the rules of behavior and the values that spawned them, descendants can then determine if the rules are still useful in supporting their individual values or if other traditions and behaviors might better serve that purpose. Furthermore, understanding the value of identity in other contexts might help us understand the challenges that have faced other systems besides the Melungeon Identity Movement, such as leadership, family studies, anthropology, psychology, and sociology.

Any change in behaviors first requires an understanding of self. The answers to the research questions can help further define the difference between chosen and ascribed identity and the options an individual has for each; this can be empowering and transformative. Once our identity is accepted and integrated into our sense of self, we can move forward to empower and advocate for those with whom we identify. We can then become change agents, pushing and prodding, acting and protesting, transforming what is into what can be.

In the Beginning

In my hand is a picture of my mother, Sylvia, sitting on the ground in an overgrown cemetery on the side of a mountain near Middlesboro, Kentucky, next to the headstones of her maternal grandparents, William and Arline Gibson. My sister Arlene is standing nearby, looking at the tangled jumble of family plots and vegetation that seems to be clinging to the mountain while her three-year-old son naps in his car seat just a few feet away. We are searching for answers, explanations for questions we have not formed. It is September 10, 2001. Race, culture, meaning, genealogy, belonging—it is all jumbled up in my mind together: the personal quest we were on to find meaning in my mother's past, along with the bombing of the twin towers in New York City the day after the picture is taken. I hold another picture. This one is our brown conversion van, which we had driven from Michigan to Kentucky. There are American flags duct-taped to both side mirrors, patriotic slogans painted with poster paint on the sides, including "United We Stand" above the back bumper. Current literature regarding the politics of racial identity explains the collective identity that forms during movements, such as that of patriotism in the U.S. following 9/11.[2]

It is precisely this cultural homogeneity, outlined by racial markers, which allowed "us" to define "them" both in Appalachia and after the attacks of 9/11. This book discusses Melungeon cultural markers and identity, as well as social belonging, through the lens of my own and my co-researchers' personal identity journeys.

Racial Identification and Politics

Some of the answers my family and I sought during our trip to Kentucky were explanations or validation of narratives shared through generations. Stories of Grandmother Arline Campbell, allegedly purchased by William H. Gibson to be his wife, and of a black Irish aunt who had dark skin and kinky hair lived on in the personal narratives of the family, further defining cultural if not racial identities. My mother was interested in genealogy and wanted to know more about her race and ethnicity, including possible Native American and Melungeon heritage. The family history of multi-racial ethnicities and practices demanded our attention, if not appreciation.[3]

Armed with names, birth dates, and residences, we began with family narratives and then moved on to federal census records. We noted changes from white to mulatto to black and back again. These labels, nothing more than checkmarks in delineated boxes on forms, illustrate currently accepted scholarship that explains race as both a "social structure and cultural representation," which is based on historical context.[4] The changes on the census forms also illustrate the dichotomy between race as something "fixed, concrete, and objective" or as "a mere illusion, a purely ideological construct." Omi and Winant (1994) note the importance of understanding race "as an unstable and 'decentered' complex of social meanings constantly being transformed by political struggle."[5] It was disconcerting to note direct application of systemic and political marginalization to my own ancestors that enabled government agents to reclassify them and effectively deny them the rights of full citizenship. Remember that this was the Jim Crow era, a way of life that legitimized racism.

The historical context during the early 1900s includes the eugenics movement prevalent in Southern Appalachia; this movement influenced the scientific and sociopolitical thought and policies in Europe and the United States.[6] The policies intended to keep the races pure. In 1924 the state of Virginia, with help from Walter Plecker, the Virginia State Registrar, and Earnest S. Cox, an ethnologist, author, and white supremacy activist, passed the Racial Integrity Act with the intention of preserving the white gene pool. Their definition of *whiteness* allowed only those of Caucasian descent to be classified white. Eventually, however, some Virginian aristocracy who prided their connections to Pocahontas wrangled a modification to include 1/16th percent Native American lineage to be permitted a white identity.[7] Cox and Plecker, along with John Powell, a noted musician and also a white supremacist, remained concerned that blacks would claim to be Indian and infiltrate the white race. The three waged a largely successful campaign to reclassify Virginia Indians as Negro. "Subsequently, the absence of African-American ancestry became the sine qua non of Amerindian identity and many Indians began to deny their African heritage."[8]

The stories of a black Irish great aunt, or Saponi grandmother, seemed to make more sense in the context presented above and through the writings and scholarship of Goldberg and Essed (2005) regarding the politics of race, or racial states. As Essed points out, it becomes evident how "factors of privilege and risk are distributed across population groups historically tied to racial conception and condition in radically uneven and inequitable ways."[9] The risks inherent in acknowledging any African ancestry proved too much for my ancestors, who then found acceptable euphemisms to explain appearances or migration to another state where the laws were easier to navigate. Tracing family genealogy from the late 1800s and early 1900s is complicated by family structure, racial ascription, and political policies of documentation, including that of oppression.

Eliza Adeline Brown, born in Virginia around 1855, is my maternal great-grandmother. As I looked through census records, I came across a document where I saw the racial classifications had been changed on many individuals, including Eliza. These documents appear to confirm Goldberg's 2002 suggestion that "racial arrangement is ... inherently an imposed mode of controlling governance and self-surveillance."[10] The federal census records from 1880 and 1900 document contradictions about where Eliza's parents were born (U.S. Census, 1880). One can assume that the self-surveillance included evading authorities because the risks of identification as a person of color could be quite costly, even life threatening.[11] Roediger (1999) points to this fear, or terror, that has made for a very early and complete creation of the white race.[12] While the distance between poor whites and Native Americans was distinctive, the polarity of black America is the stick by which Melungeons (and other Southern whites) measured their whiteness.

As evidenced by strategic moving, contradictory answers to census takers, and lack of education (and thus school records), one can discern a condition of being in accordance with a *racial state* for Eliza Brown, Arline Campbell, Addie Gibson, and, ultimately, my mother—Sylvia Ray. Five generations later the invisibility of everyday racism has insidiously framed cultural values, identity, and family structures where the effects are sad, if not tragic. Even through interviews with second cousins, their responses revealed a fear of acknowledging any African admixture in the family gene pool.[13]

I think of the questions my mother and I first pondered on our trip to Kentucky and my mother's desire to uncover any evidence of her Mamaw's Native heritage. Addie's delayed birth certificate was applied for after my mother (Sylvia) moved to Detroit and wasn't issued until 1954. At the time Addie was 31, Sylvia 11, and Walter Plecker had only been out of office for 8 years. Plecker, the Vital Records Registrar of Virginia from 1912 to 1946, "was exceedingly proud of his efforts to track racially suspect persons and families' pedigrees, proudly referencing these researches of racial integrity."[14]

> For Melungeons, migration held the distinct advantage of evading the full impact of Plecker's assault on multiethnic groups. Melungeon individuals who were suspect, by virtue of their genealogical and geographic associations, could escape the denotations of their last names by leaving the region. Often their identity choices changed with their move to the North; their opportunities to pass as white expanded, and, in general, the stigma associated with their names and histories was diluted as they joined a working force whose priority was production instead of ethnic gatekeeping.[15]

Clearly, applying for a birth certificate in Virginia and the surrounding counties contained great risk of discrimination, loss of legal rights, segregation in church, schools, employment, medical care, and housing. Considering the questions and explanations we were looking for, along with documenting through census records where family members resided or migrated to and from, I believe that at least circumstantially we understood why my ancestors moved from Virginia to Kentucky: in Kentucky, they were white.

Social Influence on Melungeon Ethnicity

It is important to note that identity work is a "group accomplishment as well as an individual one and can therefore be examined at a group or subcultural level."[16] Also, identity construction includes anything that participants do either individually or collectively to give meaning to themselves or others. A movement such as the Melungeon Identity Movement not only constructs an identity but determines how it will function as a point of context and motivation for participation and action. For the purposes of this book and project, an examination of identity allows us to explore at an individual level one's motivation for integrating a collective identity. Many believe the movement started with N. Brent Kennedy and Robyn Vaughan Kennedy's 1997 book *The Melungeons: The Resurrection of a Proud People: An Untold Story of Ethnic Cleansing in America.*

As of 1997, it was estimated that 75,000 individuals, including N.B. Kennedy, had participated in internet listservs, user groups, websites, and written printed publications associated with Melungeon identity. While most members living outside the Cumberland Gap area have little to lose by claiming a Melungeon identity, those whose lives and constructions of identity are more likely to include experiences of local racial discrimination are not so fortunate. Where the stigmatization of being Melungeon is not yet fully erased in the rural South, the population of white, middle-class, educated Melungeons further explores their own experiences at the expense of the former.[17]

Given the romanticized notion of a mysterious ancestry, many middle-class whites are seeking what Omi and Winant (1994) propose as a notion of ethnicity rather than one of race. In fact, long-term Melungeon researcher and local activist Jack Goins says as much: "I don't look at them as a race. It's an ethnic group." The rising awareness of white privilege has led also to white guilt, and people may be looking for a distinction or heritage that distinguishes them from the masses of middle-class whites.[18] Claiming oppression and marginalization in one's ancestry may operate to assuage guilt and discomfort in dialogues about race and culture. However, ethnonyms, such as Melungeon, interconnect in discussions like those on social media and can "acquire value that enhances or erases the collective identity of the group referenced by them."[19]

The need for validation complicates notions of privilege and power as one attempts to prove his ancestry and claim his cultural identity. Authenticity as defined by one group effectively marginalizes those whose claim is based on a different measure. Just ask Rachel Dolezal, past president of the National Association for the Advancement of Colored People (NAACP) chapter in Spokane, Washington. Born to white parents, Dolezal began acquiring what some might call an "affiliative" or "trans" racial identity with African Americans. From kinship with adopted siblings to relationships at a predominantly black college, Dolezal began to identify as black herself. The following controversy is very much the same argument over nature vs. nurture that we have been exploring for decades. Is she black by birth/biology? Could she be black by culture/affiliation?

Admonished by Garroutte (2003) in writings about Native American identity and authenticity, we are called to recognize that while it is one thing to claim an ethnic identity, "it is quite another for that claim to be received by others as legitimate."[20] Yet in the wake of Dolezal's unmasking, another scholar stepped forward to tell her story and suggested it is time to reexamine racial experience and "see if we can entertain the possibility of authentic transracial identity."[21] The collision of identity and legitimacy is making its way into our consciousness with cases like that of Rachel Dolezal and Caitlyn Jenner. Whatever the outcome of their respective identifications and acceptance, we do know the outcome of systematically denying someone the right to identify as he sees fit evidenced by the Racial Purity Act. It legitimizes oppression, marginalization, segregation, and even discrimination.

These attempts to claim an ethnicity (or identity) may also be in response to an institutional and systemic political movement towards multiculturalism where ethnic difference is something to be recognized and celebrated.[22] Educational institutions throughout the 1990s supplied a myriad of ethnic cultural experiences and influences to meet the growing demand for ethnic difference: a way to stand out from the masses and to construct an ethnicity that can be recognized and celebrated. This desire for ethnic difference and distinction was clearly evident in a pilot project I did prior to the larger research study, and expressed by my sister, nephew, daughter, and mother. My nephew, Devon, explained it as "bragging rights."[23] Until the focus on multiculturalism, most whites did not pursue a racial identity. Those who were members of a dominant or advantaged group took that element of their identity for granted.[24]

In 2001, my mother was 57 years old and navigating her own life's journey. She was doing considerable identity work with autobiographical memory and the construction of a narrative self-identity.[25] Think of the stories we tell about our memories, our childhoods, or even vacations. We shape them according to the audience, but we also refine our identity by the words we choose and how we narrate our actions, thoughts, and conversations. With family members, we make smaller incremental changes in our identification in the story, or narrative, because often these family members have also authored a story around the event and we sometimes need our mother/daughter to confirm/corroborate our identity/story. We were traveling the path together, mother and daughter, challenging the political significance of mothering on identity and on public policies.[26]

For generations census records and other legal documents have privileged a patriarchal system; we were seeking to empower our grandmothers' voices as a part of our sense of self. This searching by my mother, coupled with a growing body of biosocial group identities, exploited her desire for belonging and need for identifying a cultural or ethnic group with which to affiliate. The explosion of commercial providers of genetic services has "initiated what has been referred to as a genetic revolution in identity politics."[27] As Jack Goins suggested about the requests he gets from people wanting to be in his DNA study, "They feel left out, I guess.... It was a derogatory name, Melungeon ... which they hated, now everybody wants to be one," he said, laughing.[28]

Identity work has included reflections and the need for congruence between how individuals see themselves and how they perceive others see them. This kind of reflection can be significantly impacted by leaders, both formal and informal, as evidenced in the "Not my president" protests that followed the 2016 U.S. election and following inauguration. Leadership research regarding social identity theory confirms that group members support group prototypical leaders (the leader that fits group norms of what the leader should be) more strongly than non-prototypical leaders. However, the support for the prototypical leader weakens when group members have rising levels of uncertainty due to support of a non-prototypical leader.[29]

As the Melungeon Identity Movement's informal leader, Brent Kennedy, became unable to fulfill the expected role of uniting and empowering his followers, the movement began to disintegrate and splinter. The resultant uncertainty of the group in defining a Melungeon identity encouraged many individuals to search for support or evidence of their belonging to alleviate the discomfort. The subsequent search for a variety of evidence to legitimize their claim of identity has splintered a once cohesive group as they struggle to determine who is a "real" Melungeon, and who is a wannabe.

Research on authentic leadership has identified "such leaders as having followers who increasingly identify with, as well as who feel more psychologically empowered to take on greater ownership for their work."[30] Kennedy's openness with his own journey and purpose in studying his family genealogy (and possible ethnic ancestry) connected with many other researchers and family historians as authentic. It has been a common pursuit to identify and document one's roots. From writing names and dates in a family Bible, to computer searches on genealogy sites, Kennedy's observations were easy for many to relate to.

A chosen, rather than ascribed, "affiliative ethnic identity" serves an important role. While affiliative ethnics do not identify with the ancestral details of ethnicity, their knowledge, "consumption, and regular use of an ethnic culture are central to how they identify themselves and how others identify them."[31] Their allegiance to social and political causes also affords them membership with ancestral ethnics, allowing them to distinguish themselves from a mainstream. This affiliative ethnicity is enacted through use of language; expressed through art, activities, and food; or through academic study. However, once again ethnic identity has "currency only to the degree that others deem it authentic," which may explain the desire for genetic testing to authenticate membership in the ancestral ethnic group.[32]

As demonstrated by the outpouring of interest among people with roots in southern Appalachia and the activity in online and physical locations, descendants are eager to hear and comprehend a variety of "family mysteries that were hushed, insults that were suffered, and humiliation endured."[33] It remains to be seen how the discussions will further shape the cultural artifacts of Melungeons, including meaning placed on the label itself. Further, legitimizing experiences and narratives adds much to the scholarship and exploration of Melungeonness rather than taking away from it.

Melungeon Identity

Recently I have recorded the stories of my mother's childhood and the meaning she attributes to her geographic and kinship roots. We go through pictures doing genealogy as she describes various relatives and shows me the picture of her Black Irish aunt, Susie. The pictures are almost all black and white so the telltale darkening of skin indicative of Melungeons is hard to make out. I hear stories I have not heard before, explanations I did not think to ask about, and meanings she assigns to several family traditions. While I have never lived in the Appalachian South, research delved into the construction of a geographic identity through family narratives. I feel Southern, but I am not sure about Melungeon—nor is she.

We look at a picture of my maternal grandmother, Mamaw Addie. In later pictures that are developed in color, they reveal a darker skin. Her hair is coarse and kinky, dyed dark brown, and she sits casually on the floor, smoking a cigarette and wearing white bell-bottom pants. Her eyes are small and black, flashing defiance. Her skin is lined pleasantly, but the set of her jaw reveals strength. I used to think I looked like her.

We look next at my mother's paternal grandmother, her Mamaw Ray. The old grainy photograph reveals a heavy woman in a dark dress with a large white apron. She is sitting in a straight-back chair, holding a toddler in training pants. Her feet are bare and large, as are her hands. She is smil-

Left: **Addie Gibson, about 15 years old, circa 1938.** *Right:* **Addie (Gibson) Ray Robinson, circa 1970.**

ing and relaxed, her long hair pulled into a bun at the back of her head. The floors are wide wood planks; there is nothing on the walls, and the paint around the baseboards is chipping. She, too, has small black eyes. I look back at the hands. My mother's hands and feet are tiny; she is petite and small boned. I always wondered about my strong stocky hands with their short fingers and fleshy palms. I wonder what else I can glean about myself by looking at these pictures.

This is my heritage, my culture, my ethnicity. What does it mean? I reflect on the years of teaching diversity and the lectures I gave on white privilege, racism, and colonialism. I often conduct an exercise with my students during which we explore the difference among race, ethnicity, and nationality. Although I am white and my nationality is United States American, I struggle with the question: But just what *is* my ethnicity? Can I choose an ethnic identity that will be accepted as authentic? And, whose acceptance am I longing for?

The cultural traditions and ways of life have been relegated to memory.[34] They have been rearticulated by cosmopolitan values and consumption practices. I think back to my thoughts about the peeling paint and lack of aesthetics in my ancestor's picture. I reflect on the meaning I have assigned to the bare feet and half-naked toddler. I am reminded of Fivush's (2009) work on memory, and its link to autobiographical self, that remembering and sharing are vital to individuals and systems in defining and making sense of our experiences and our lives.[35]

Besides the politicized uses of history, we are living in an information and edutainment culture that fosters a longing for pasts that have the potential to create a genetic bio-culture that is commercialized, one in which genetic histories are implemented and appropriated. Individuals desire a collective self-verification that is consistent with their social identities.[36] This desire for congruence between one's personal identity and acknowledgment by others, coupled with technology available to verify one's genetic identity, explains the large participation in the Melungeon Identity Movement along with available genetic testing and genealogical websites. This membership also provides opportunities to practice the ethnic identity markers espoused by Jimenez (2010) that include language, arts, food, and research.[37] Delicately navigating the cultural norms and mores, mitigating sanctions and identity threats, one can construct an ethnic identity in relative obscurity. Yet in an age of social media and advanced technologies, is it worth the risk of being called a fraud should one choose to pursue a particular identity publicly?

This need for evidentiary data provided by current DNA studies encouraged by some Melungeon activists is driven by the "growing sense of many individuals that genetics in some ways holds the key to their 'identities.'"[38] The commercialization of genetic history is filling a void in the market for tracing ancestry, recording history, and linking to one's past: "Half a million people are said to have bought the services."[39] Understanding the brick wall common to genealogy researchers of African American history and the relative youth of this nation, it should come as no surprise that the consumption of DNA technologies for ancestry is most common in the United States and Canada. The desire for genetic testing crosses my mind periodically, yet I wonder at the political implications for myself as an individual, as part of a family, and as a scholar. Each role holds its own responsibilities as does the knowledge and how it is interpreted in the various roles I hold. To date, I have not pursued the testing.

In my opinion, Rose's (2007) acknowledgment of controversy surrounding the genome project and recognition of a multidisciplinary approach to scholarship around human genetics needs further structure and commitment to discourse than is being applied. The legacy of eugenics and the politics associated with it are a constant reminder for collaboration across disciplines.[40] The same can be said of scholarship pertaining to authenticity of culture, trans-racialism, or perhaps even transgender.

"Definitions of ethnicity reveal as much about the workings of power, the articulation of ideologies, and the imposition of social hierarchies integral to state building, as they do about notions of cultural distinctiveness."[41] The mass exodus from the coal mines and hills of southern Appalachia to the industrial conglomerates of Detroit and Chicago illustrate the desire to escape not only the social hierarchies but also imposed ethnicity: hillbilly, redneck, white trash, poor, Melungeon. Our society's emphasis on multiculturalism imbedded in pop culture and mass media may offer a back door entrance into balancing the dichotomy of power between ascribed and chosen ethnic identities. But it is precarious: just ask Rachel Dolezal and Caitlyn Jenner.

The history of Melungeons describes a complexity indicative of the structural violence perpetuated by governments.[42] This systemic racism was orchestrated on behalf of Euro-American settlers who found persons of mixed ancestry in direct conflict with the economic concerns of whites. "Culture sits in places," according to Anglin.[43] The ethnicity or culture of Melungeons and other non-whites in southern Appalachia cannot be understood outside of the historical context of the Appalachian South. Common experiences constructed not only knowledge and behaviors but also values and traditions as an outgrowth of environmental adaptation.

Perhaps this is why so many of the co-researchers sought to *understand* more than *become*. The Melungeon identity is compounded by the binary racial classification in the United States that labels individuals as *white* or *nonwhite*. In fact, "Melungeons appear to have occupied disenfranchised political and social relationships to surrounding whites."[44] It became a matter of degree of whiteness that determined cultural values and behaviors in the Appalachian South. One wonders at the relative safety provided through anonymity on a website discussion board that affords the opportunity to explore racial identity and the power differentials associated without risking public scrutiny. These concerns must remain at the forefront of any Melungeon researcher. The dangers associated with revealing racial admixture is still very real in southern Appalachia where the very people this project hopes to empower and understand, are those at greatest risk of further oppression.

"Categories really are social constructions: they exist only because people tacitly agree to act as if they exist."[45] The current Melungeon Identity Movement is no different. While core members of the Melungeon Identity Movement embrace African ancestry as an element in their mixed-race composition, rarely do they incorporate African material, culture, or artifacts into their lives or acknowledge African origins as a primary source of their heritage. "The movement thus seems contradictory, embracing multiracial ancestry as a means of deconstructing whiteness, but excluding Africanness from meaningful participation in its ideology."[46]

I believe that the movement has the potential to disenfranchise further and erase the original cultural memory of a historical group ascribed the status of Melungeon. My fears mirror the types of racial identity issues raised by African American and various Native American groups in which "the emergence of identities is a product of academic construction" and perhaps even the consumerism prevalent in selling ethnic identities.[47]

Exciting research looked beyond racial classifications in the construction of Melungeon identity and should be revitalized.[48] The importance of kinship and association with a specific geographical locale shed light on the cultural aspects of identity rather than on one determined by physical characteristics. "Kinship talk is extremely well developed in the Appalachian repertoire and functions predominantly to place individuals both within a network of relatives and at a specific geographical locale."[49] Family relationships, according to Puckett (2001), establish rights of access and the symbolic meanings attached to kinship and geography and are again validated by life-long residents who insist that each neighborhood and ridge has its own culture.

This evidence of non-material Melungeon culture, like kinship talk, supersedes the markers classified as essentialist racism. In fact, many of the *unions*, blogs, and genealogy websites for Melungeons focus on developing and comparing family trees and specific geographic landmarks associated with the co-researchers. Individual and family narratives serve to further solidify one's identity in context.[50] These narratives remain fluid as one's identity is developed, massaged, and owned. Co-researchers often relied on place to situate their identity by indicating where they lived at a certain age, or what was happening in their life when a business or highway was constructed.

Although I acknowledge that my family's photographs are not scientific evidence, the number of photos of old family homesteads, schools, train tracks on which they walked to school, and the coal mine they passed on the way are iconic. They capture a moment in time, in context while in their personal collections they hold a special place that also tells a tale. According to some researchers, "those haunted by 'family secrets,' political persecution and the wars of previous generations can use photographs in memory work, to challenge, critically and creatively, silences and collective myths and create new stories and relations to the past."[51] Through photographs and other visual technologies co-researchers compare experiences and interpretations of family history, refining their sense of self, while garnering the power to redefine and assign meaning through today's perspective.

Every family gathering or reunion of mine is spent reminiscing over artifacts including recipes, cookbooks, pictures, and stories. We are constantly reminding one another of how they are related, who was this cousin's mother and was it through their parents or grandparents that we are connected—maternal side or paternal side. The kinship talk in my family may indeed be another piece of evidence that in scholarly research has revealed as pointing to a Melungeon ethnicity.

Understanding the historical and political contexts that defined the racial make-up of Melungeons and the subsequent cultural values that formed as a result of oppression and the (dis)appearing of a culture may help those involved in the identity movement appreciate the impact that inclusive, multi-disciplinary research will have on their own descendants. "In particular, black ancestry is not allowed to participate fully in this mapping of relations of place ... they are denied rights of access to the privileges, empowering networks, and cultural prestige that genealogical discourse grants whites."[52] The importance of place when situating race and identity and the extensive opportunities for transracial contacts in the Appalachian South makes the lack of research on white racial formation a place that could use additional attention.[53] One co-researcher suggests that there aren't any Melungeons left today, just descendants, because "there ain't a high percentage of black left in 'em."[54]

Experts suggest studying through adaptive work that includes the members as active co-researchers.[55] Trying to grant only a technical solution (DNA testing) to an adaptive process (ethnic and racial identity construction) is ineffective. Given the unique dynamics present in the Melungeon Identity Movement and the leaders that propelled the movement into the limelight, Resonant Leadership could be utilized to strengthen the movement and provide sustainability. "Emotional and social competencies represent the specific behaviors that enable a person to generate a sense of shared hope and vision with others, shared compassion and shared mindfulness—the key components of resonant leadership relationships."[56] Imperative to sustaining leadership that is resonant with (in tune with) Melungeon followers requires systems and organizations that sustain emotionally intelligent leadership through structured practices.[57] Placing emphasis on incentives and sanctions for such practices within the various Melungeon groups could empower them to conduct research and scholarship that leads to sustainable social change within the movement. Specifically, the group could, with Resonant Leadership, focus less on the racial make-up or origins of the population and more on the politics and policies that continue to oppress and marginalize people of various racial and cultural backgrounds.

Scholars working to explore and further define the markers of Melungeon identities hope to bring awareness of how current dialogues absorbing mixed race peoples into whiteness still reinforce the idea that blacks are to remain nonwhite. Such researchers facilitate and mediate discussions that bring awareness of how language and relationships construct racial classifications and how the discourse about race can change those constructs and the associated power differentials. Using a multidisciplinary approach to exploring identity construction focuses less on race and phenotype and more on the experiences that help populations recognize their cohort groups.[58] In a 1998 article Sturm discusses the racial self-definition of Cherokee Indians during the late 1980s court case over several freedmen's right to vote. While racial self-definition may be a sovereign right, the court ignored the history of "cultural and political association ... by conflating race with culture and politics."[59]

Philosophical and Theoretical Framework

Melungeon scholarship has focused on history, origin theories, and oppression/privilege narratives. The research I sought was to better understand the interaction among the internal and external perceptions of *Melungeon-ness*, the meaning attributed to *being* Melungeon, and with what knowledge or understanding did one come to that decision.[60] The portraits presented illuminate the perceptions of the co-researchers, in dialogue and relationship with me, of their accepted or rejected Melungeon-ness. Three lenses shape the view of this work: Being Melungeon, Knowing you are Melungeon, Group verification that you are Melungeon.

Being Melungeon. Using data from the 2000 Census and the 2001–2005 American Community Surveys (ACS), researchers found that Appalachian identity is alive and well, though not in the ways we might have imagined. The researchers found that Appalachian identity certainly exists but only barely so within Appalachia itself. To the extent that the question is capable of addressing the issue, Appalachian identity is created and maintained by out-migrants and their descendants. The ways of being Appalachian (or Melungeon) remain unexamined in the literature, as is that of be-longing.[61]

Researchers examined evidence of how co-researchers deal with a discrepancy between their choice of identity and the way they are categorized by others.[62] Co-researchers' reactions to this discrepancy depend on the way they are actually treated by others, if their chosen identity is respected by others.[63] In fact, bringing one's culture of origin's values and identity into current experiences and ways of being can help multiracial individuals integrate a multiplicity of identities.

How do people *know* they are Melungeon? Exploring how co-researchers know what they know. For many, knowledge is the intersection between belief and truth.[64] People attempt to make sense of or find cohesion among the various pieces of knowledge they encounter. For my co-researchers there were several paths to knowledge and several ways to construct that knowledge: lived experience, personal and family narratives, DNA or biological studies, historical documents, genealogy, and acceptance by leaders of the movement.[65]

Group verification of Melungeon identity. Social constructivism sees consensus among different subjects as the ultimate criterion to judge knowledge. Truth or reality will be accorded only to those constructions on which most people of a social group agree.[66] Through this framework co-researchers examined how their beliefs or truths are validated, supported, reinforced, or even rejected by the larger group—the collective. Without the support of the socially constructed reality, individuals' identity and sense of well-being may suffer. This is where some participants rejected a Melungeon identity to be congruent with the "group" of Melungeon researchers.

Appalachian studies have focused largely around the issues of power, culture, race, and heterogeneity.[67] Finding that definitions of ethnicity reveal as much about the workings of power and privilege as they do about notions of cultural distinctiveness further supports the need to understand how social construction theory requires the implicit and explicit cooperation of a population. It adds greatly to the understanding and illumination of Melungeon identity to look at whiteness through the lens constructed by Southern Appalachians and to examine how concepts of race are both oppressing the population and being perpetuated by them.

It is through the understanding of the systems involved that one can understand the use of ethnicity and ethnic categories. Definitions of Melungeon-ness have not included stable attributes but rather human perceptions and understandings of people bounded by the context of time, geography, and politics—and group leadership. Further, these perceptions have been used and reinforced by governments and social agencies—in language and policies—to perpetuate the classification and definition of populations to serve the needs of the state. Together, through the method of portraiture, we explore these three frameworks; this process helped shed light on how they impacted the individuals' and their families' identity, knowledge, and belonging.

Portraiture was chosen as a method of studying and exploring the narratives of co-researchers. It very much resonates with a sense of social justice and empowerment. The narratives are created together for clarity and deeper understanding of their experiences. They are also written without specific analysis empowering the reader/audience to interpret the "data" for themselves while constructing their own knowledge of the material. With its focus on narrative, its use of metaphor and symbol, portraiture intends to address wider, more eclectic audiences. The attempt is to move beyond the academy's inner circle, to speak in a language that is not coded or exclusive, and to develop texts that will seduce the readers into thinking more deeply about issues that concern them. Portraitists write to inform and inspire readers (to deepen the conversation).[68]

My research questions were born out of countless hours spent in the field—in courthouses, in genealogy research, in cemeteries and in libraries—reading every book, article, thesis, or dissertation I could find. I have attended unions and conferences and conducted interviews with every scholar I could track down who would give me the time. Ultimately, I found the print material lacking; the information I needed to make a decision about my own identity requires more. I need to talk with people who consider themselves Melungeon and see what brings them to that conclusion. I want to present what I discover to others who were also questioning and searching. Although a picture can be worth a thousand words, a portrait created in collaboration with a co-researcher is each its own volume or book.

Most members living outside the geographical confines of southern Appalachia have little to lose by claiming a Melungeon identity, unlike those usually poor rural Melungeons whose lives and constructions of identity are more likely to include experiences of political oppression. Where the stigmatization of being Melungeon is not yet fully erased in the rural South, the population of white, middle-class, educated Melungeons further explores their own experiences at the expense of the former.[69] It is imperative that risks to those with a Melungeon identity are recognized as living in the same context that marginalized them originally and not put them at further risk to assuage my own curiosity or scholar-

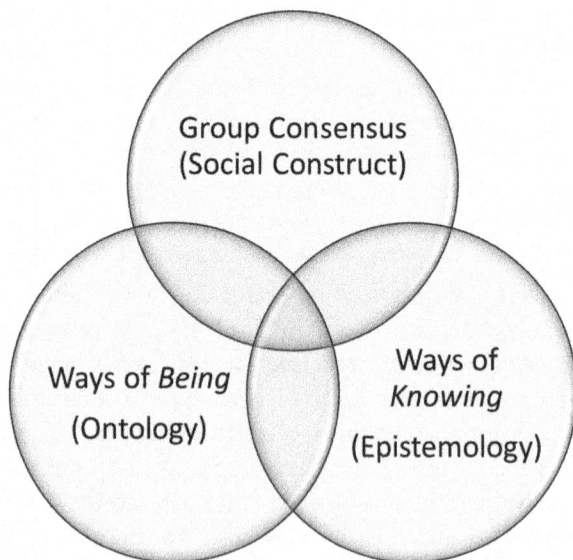

Figure 1.1: The intersection of ontology, epistemology and social construction within the context of Melungeon identity.

ship. The research project should be beneficial to the population being studied and accessible outside the realm of academia.

The scope of portraiture as a methodology presents the opportunity to examine in-depth the meaning of Melungeon identity for several co-researchers. It is my hope that this research will shed some light on the directions for future research to enhance the understanding of the presented issues. However, the nature of portraiture imposes limitations because of co-researchers who can be included due to time and resources. This study will not be able to determine generalizable predictions to the population at large or Melungeons specifically. It will offer an opportunity for readers to see and interpret for themselves the voices of co-researchers, along with their body language, tone of voice, and other non-verbal aspects of communication that are missing in traditional research projects. This type of project is also useful at understanding how other ethnicities, cultures, or social groups can explore their own identities and maintenance of them.

Ethical Considerations

An application for review by the Internal Review Board (IRB) at Antioch University was submitted and approved before beginning the research project. Co-researchers were kept fully informed of the process, collaborated in the development and creation of portraits, and approved final drafts before submission to the committee. Due to the topic and nature of the research design, anonymity was not assured. Co-researchers were given the opportunity to use a pseudonym if they desired; all chose to use their real names.

When interviewing family, boundaries were sometimes blurred and conversations about personal events mistaken for research information. One co-researcher became uncomfortable with the revelations regarding another family member and elected to have her portrait removed from the project. While the relationship was awkward and uncomfortable for a while, rapport has since been rekindled and preserved.

CHAPTER 1

Literature and Research Review

"I feel that all knowledge should be in the free-trade zone. Your knowledge, my knowledge, everybody's knowledge should be made use of. I think people who refuse to use other people's knowledge are making a big mistake. Those who refuse to share their knowledge with other people are making a great mistake, because we need it all. I don't have any problem about ideas I got from other people. If I find them useful, I'll just ease them right in and make them my own."

—Myles Horton, *We Make the Road by Walking: Conversations on Education and Social Change*

From the early writings of Will Allen Dromgoole (1891) to the middle of the twentieth century, the available literature related to Melungeons was often written for popular magazines or news sources that published articles that would be read by particular audiences in the historical context of the times. Such articles were written by dominant culture members for the dominant culture. However, to learn what it means today to be Melungeon and how a person determines inclusion or exclusion in/from the group, it is important to look at current research themes within the context of history, social construction, ways of being, ways of knowing, and identity/belonging.

I have also identified leaders within the Melungeon Identity Movement who have influenced not only the contemporary writings and understanding of Melungeons but also those who have acquired a following to theories of who belongs and what counts as evidence regarding Melungeon inclusion.[1] Through my research, I identified five themes as necessary to understanding the contexts of identity and belonging today (the leader interviews are included in the appropriate themes).

The first section of this review includes an analysis of the historical documents that shed light on the beliefs, language, and values of earlier eras. The literature illustrates the thought patterns of Appalachians who have been absorbed and integrated into systemic patterns of behavior and individual and collective identities. In the second section I present a review of social construction of knowledge, including race, ethnicity, culture, class, history, and policies that help the reader understand the influence and responsibility that communities and greater social systems bear in the oppression and discrimination that continues to occur in southern Appalachia. Using an ontological approach, the third section examines the practical application of how an individual presents self and being in a variety of roles. The fourth section takes a look at epistemological literacy that explores how we know what we know, how we learn, and how we construct our realities. The fifth theme of this literature review is identity development and belonging and includes optimal distinctiveness theory.[2] This last area of analysis will outline the development of individual and social identity, as well as the influence of belonging.

Historical Context

The morning of June 25, 2012, dawned a hazy bright morning that promised to blaze hot and humid before noon. My mother, Sylvia Ray, and I were in Johnson City on the campus of East Tennessee State University to meet with historian and radio host Wayne Winkler in his office. The office was small with an L-shaped desk and two chairs in addition to Winkler's. He was a hospitable host, inviting and warm. There were shelves of books from floor to ceiling with additional stacks on the floor, desk, and counters. Interspersed throughout the texts were video and audio recordings, labeled and catalogued. The first thing that struck me was his physical appearance. Of middle age, physically fit, and probably a good foot over my 5'2" frame, Wayne had dark skin, black hair, and bright blue eyes.

I have read and researched many books and articles that describe the appearance of Melungeons in similar fashion but found myself surprised at the distinct coloring of our host's skin and how fine his facial features were with high cheekbones such as you might find in Native American populations and coloring like my Middle Eastern colleagues. I realized how different it is to see someone in person as opposed to reading about the person in a book or article.

Winkler wrote one of the most complete, thorough, and authentic texts about Melungeons to date. Noting his own family background, Winkler researched the geopolitical contexts of the mixed race group. Although his family migrated in the 1950s during the out migration to industrial cities like Detroit, Winkler recalls holidays and summer visits to southern Appalachia and Hancock County, Tennessee. It was on one such visit that he heard the term Melungeon and inquired as to its meaning. He remembers the discreet hushes and quiet explanations that were not enough to satisfy his burgeoning curiosity.[3]

When I asked him how he knew he was Melungeon, Winkler paused a moment, then explained that his family was always considered Melungeon. He told me that his grandparents lived on Newman's Ridge (long considered the identifying geography for this group of people's identity) and that others had always considered his family Melungeon.

Winkler's 2005 book, *Walking Toward the Sunset*, outlines his discovery of his ethnic background:

> In the summer of 1968, when I was twelve years old and visiting the family farm in War Valley, I read a copy of the Hancock County *Post* with great interest. The second page had an article entitled "Melungeons" which began, "One of the most fascinating mysteries in Tennessee lore concerns the unknown origin of the Melungeons, a dark-skinned people whom some romanticists compare in appearance to Othello immortalized by Shakespeare in *Othello, the Moor of Venice.*"[4]

His interest piqued, and Winkler searched for answers to how and when he would see some of these mysterious Melungeons. As it turned out, his mother explained that his paternal grandmother, and hence his father and then himself, all had Melungeon as well as Native American ancestry. His enthusiasm was dampened by the understanding that "most whites considered the Melungeons a mix of white trash, renegade Indians, and runaway slaves."[5] It was clearly an insult, not a commitment to ethnic pride, an understanding consistent with historical texts referenced in many writings about Melungeons.

Newspaper articles and church records from the 1800s contribute to our understanding of the socially constructed and accepted meaning of Melungeon. These texts are important because they have contributed to the epistemology of Melungeon-ness. Writings cited repeatedly in Melungeon related literature have given context to the attributes associated with those so labeled and further illustrate how bits of information, often repeated, become accepted as fact. The earliest discovered text mentioning a Melungeon was recorded in church records that accused a congregation member of harboring Melungeons (Stony Creek Baptist Church Minute Books 1801–1814), and a generation later a newspaper article suggests that they are "half Negro and half Indian"; one was accused of being impudent and a scoundrel.[6]

Between 1840 and 1890 occasional mention of Melungeons, spelled in various ways, such as *Malungeon* and *Malungin*, describes the group as mysterious dark skinned people living in the area of Newman's Ridge and Black Water in Tennessee. Arguably, one of the most notable authors is Will Allen Dromgoole, whose writings reached a large audience and influenced the available knowledge about mountaineers in general and Melungeons specifically.

Dromgoole was a well-educated woman from a prominent family and born in Murfreesboro, Tennessee. Named for the son her father hoped for, Will Allen was inspired by her mother to study literature and write. She studied law with her father, but having been denied the profession due to her gender, she became a clerk in the senate, serving under Governor Robert Love Taylor. Dromgoole enjoyed traveling and was fascinated by the small group of dark skinned people with Indian features that she had come across in her job as clerk. In 1891 she traveled over 300 miles to Sneedville, Tennessee, staying with the community for several weeks. As noted by Lyday-Lee (1982), Dromgoole "had a flair for reproducing these experiences in print—vivid, colorful, and sometimes controversial portraits."[7] Her writings about Malungeons (sic) most likely cost her the clerk position because the senators claimed she had misrepresented their constituents; consequently, the mountaineers, themselves, remained angry and offended.

Dromgoole's Melungeon writings were accepted, in large part because of their wide circulation in a popular magazine, and powerfully influenced later writers. Her claims that the Melungeons were ignorant, lived in squalor, and refused to abide by the sexual norms and mores of the times have perpetuated stereotypes that have reached farther than Newman's Ridge and Sneedville, Tennessee, to include all mountaineers in Appalachia. Her writings were repeated often and are still featured prominently in most books and biographies describing the Melungeon experience.

Another contributor to the knowledge and meaning of Melungeons and other mixed race people in southern Appalachia is Walter Ashby Plecker, head of Virginia's Bureau of Vital Statistics from 1912 to 1946. Several documents authored by Plecker are in the Library of Virginia and accessible online. He was a zealous supporter of the eugenics movement, drafted Virginia's Racial Purity Act, and worked passionately to carry out the responsibilities he associated with his position. Along with a letter warning of the Virginia law and the punishment associated with knowingly registering a person of mixed race as white to clerks in several neighboring states, Plecker included a list of likely surnames that were suspect. This list has contributed to self-identity as well as social construction as noted in Pat Spurlock Elder's joy at finding her name (maiden name Spurlock) on Plecker's list.[8] While in 1999 one could experience joy at finding a Melungeon identity confirmed by a list of surnames, in 1929 finding an inscription on the back of one's birth certificate reading "*WARNING—To be attached to the backs of birth or death certificates of those believed to be incorrectly recorded as to color or race*" could limit a person's marriage partner, right to vote, right to attend school, and much more.[9]

Stereotypes have unusual life cycles and are often perpetuated in unintentional and insidious practices. Ethnography and scholarship in the 1950s was laden with description, perception, and meaning. Calvin Beale coined the phrase *tri-racial isolates* to describe Melungeons as several white-black-Indian mixture populations existing separately across the nation in islands.[10] He lists Melungeons as one of these populations and examines the geographic location(s) with which they are associated. While Beale's description of isolation has contributed to the perception of in-breeding (or Jack Goins' definition of endogamous marriages, 2012) which has found its way into the stereotyped hillbilly, some have also taken umbrage with inclusion of black, or African, admixture associated with the group's heritage. Of note, Beale published "American Tri-racial Iso-lates" in the December 1957 issue of *Eugenics Quarterly*.

Most notably, N. Brent Kennedy's memoir propelled the Melungeon identity movement into its own area of scholarship and activism.[11] An amateur historian with a Ph.D. in communications, Kennedy found him-self applying his educational prowess to research a rare genetic disease he acquired. His research led him to many theories and a passionate plea for help in uncovering the mysterious origins of the mystery people, the Melungeons. Kennedy shares photos and genealogy, along with his hypotheses.

Kennedy has been an inclusive agent, finding Melungeons wherever he goes. A charming speaker and inviting host, I had met Kennedy in Sep-tember of 2001 in his office at University of Virginia Wise, Southwest Vir-ginia. By virtue of his search for a connection between his ancestry and a rare inherited disease common to people in the Mediterranean, Kennedy was one of the first to propose a biological association with being Melun-geon. By the time Kennedy's book became a movement, people were learn-ing that they were Melungeon (or not) via Plecker's 1927 surname list, genealogy, association with a specific geographic location, census records labeling ancestors as Free People of Color, and perhaps even common experiences of being associated with a lower socio-economic class in the

Cumberland Gap area of Appalachia. Experiences included discrimination regarding whom they could marry, legal problems and challenges to land holding, disenfranchisement, or exclusion from public schools.

Most recently, Schrift's (2013) work looked more closely at how "the social construction of Melungeon identity involves a number of interrelated questions ... and on a broader level, how the articulation of Melungeon identity resonates with larger racial and cultural politics in the contemporary United States?"[12] A research quest much like my own.

Social Construction

Driving from Bristol, Virginia, to Wise led my mother and me through beautiful rocky hills, steep mountains, and acres of pasture with animals grazing at sharp angles among outcroppings of rocks. Periodically we would find small cemeteries, in a fenced-in portion in the middle of a field, high on a mountaintop, or behind an old farmhouse. We located Darlene Wilson's home about a quarter of a mile from the homestead of Wycliffe Nash, Brent Kennedy's great-great-grandfather on Pole Bridge Road, and considered Melungeon.

I was amazed by Darlene Wilson's appearance. A charming women in her late 50s, she had dark skin, flashing dark eyes, and a southern drawl that reminded me of several relatives. She beckoned us in where it was air-conditioned and plied us with sweet tea and homemade cookies. Her home once belonged to her mother and now held treasures from bygone years: photographs, flowered pillows, and knick-knacks. There were stacks of books, which she had brought down from upstairs to share with me, and she had put out the "company" china and tea towels in the bathroom. The social graces of hospitality I had grown up with were alive and well in Wilson's home: making guests feel welcome, providing food and drink, and making things attractive and decorated so guests feel special.

After we settled in, Wilson began to explain in a professorial fashion what we should know about Melungeon-ness:

> Melungeon-ness is traced in the set of performances that are manifested on platforms of eco-social change. The Melungeon is confined at the civil war to this permanent underclass that ain't never gonna get white enough. Appalachia is that place that ain't never gonna get white enough but they've got an ugly history of trying.

Wilson's way of teaching about Appalachia has three rules[13]:

> First, Appalachia is never going to get white enough but has an ugly history of trying. Second, there is nothing mysterious or hidden about Appalachian history

or their people, [they] have always been on the bleeding edge of modernity. Last, true conflict can be found between right-winged patriarchy and indigenous matri-local, matri-focal nature of everyday community life. We go to the courthouse and register things by our daddy's name. In Appalachia we don't live like that, your momma's people are just as important as your daddy's people. In Appalachia the *women* are the place keepers.[14]

Wilson went on to explain that Melungeon is just a word, a label used at various times in our history in a variety of contexts. The meaning depends on when it was used and under what circumstances. "It is a way of saying I'm none of those people you are afraid of don't kill me I'm not English, French, Spanish, African, or Indian." The latter becomes very important by the late 1780s and '90s when being Native American could cost you your life and your property. At this point Wilson brought out a fashion doll similar to a Ken doll. The figure was in poor shape with its hands and feet missing. She held the doll up to make a point and says,

The other side is "Don't kill me, I'm not an Indian." Being Melungeon becomes a way of avoiding the trap of the box—you can't put me in a box. I don't fit in the white box, I don't fit in the African box, I don't fit in the Native American box. See here? I have this Melungeon man. You know how I know he is a Melungeon man? He done gnawed his hands and feet off to get out of a trap. Found that buried in the dirt on a strip mine.

Wilson's frustration with the Melungeon Heritage Association (MHA) was evident as we discussed recently published DNA studies.[15]

I broke with them [MHA] over the first suggestion of DNA studies. The human genome project wanted the MHA to be involved, you know, as a control group. Well the whole thing just raised visions of Walter Plecker. You're not gonna get a biological definition of what a Melungeon is—there ain't no such thing. The best we can hope for is a cultural definition. There are cultural markers across all of these things if we would just open our eyes to them and quit thinking that modern science is going to come up with a definitive test that's gonna say I'm a Melungeon and you're not—the same as we have a diabetes test that says I'm diabetic and you're not. It aint' gonna be that easy, and after all—why should it be that easy? What's the goal here? What are we trying to prove?

A cultural definition of Melungeon would bring with it socially constructed meanings of behaviors, traditions, and language—in effect the construction of a new ethnicity or culture. Hill (1996) explores the possibilities of ethnogenesis and describes the interaction between vast multilingual and multicultural networks that result in the emergence of new ethnic identities and the disappearance of others.[16] Most useful is the examination of the various religions, myths, and symbols in the building of new ethnic identities, including those appropriated from European colonizers. Internal divisions among the group members often emerged as they struggled to arrive at consensus in developing strategies to cope with the dominant society and its control of access to wealth and power. The dynamic structures of new cultural identities differed greatly from pre-contact social formations. Sider's view presents an explanation and under-standing of the struggles against domination that are not directly related to class. The exploration of historical and regional contexts looks at the identity development of Indian identities in the American Southeast. These constructions of ethno-histories through processes of differentia-tion and resistance have been examined and provide further evidence of social construction of cultural identities and the meaning attributed to various behaviors.[17]

In places around the U.S., cases of identity and ethno-genesis are present in well-known groups (New Houma Indians, Creoles, Seminole Indians) and other lesser known groups, such as the Jackson Whites, Brass Ankles, Pell Mellers, and more.[18] Racial laws in Louisiana influenced the identity of New Houma Indians through marginalization and segregation in legal cases and educational segregation. The oral tradition of belonging to the Houma tribe was negated by the legal system that determined the tribe is actually a mix of Native American, African, and European. Again the politics of race influenced the identity of a people.

Dormon's (1992) article traces the ethno-history of Creoles of color, beginning with an examination of the social-historical order out of which they emerged, and argues the case that Creole marginality has been the major determinant of the Creole ethnic experience. Although it is impos-sible to pinpoint the precise timing of the ethno-genesis of the group, it was certainly in the latter decades of the eighteenth century, during which the group emerged as part of a three-caste social system in colonial Louisiana. During the eighteenth century the dominant Louisiana popu-lation—the hegemonic population in current usage—was that of the white European elites (or those descending directly from such elites): large landowners and planter/merchants, along with colonial officials, both civil and military. The increasingly large slave population, normally perceived by Europeans as African, provided the agricultural labor deemed essential to staple crop production. Within the colonial social order in Louisiana, blacks were separated from the white population by caste lines written into law and generally enforced by social as well as legal sanctions.

From the beginning and, despite legal provisions forbidding the prac-tice, whites and blacks established sexual contact, producing offspring that shared the genes of both parents and the identity of neither. Laws, such as Virginia's Racial Integrity Act of 1924, criminalized interracial marriage in the state of Virginia and influenced behaviors in much of the American South. Such laws would be enforced for over forty years until overturned in 1967 in the case of Loving v. Virginia.

Mildred Jeter Loving's self-identity as an Indian woman was refuted by the lawyers' focus on her tri-racial community of Central Point, Virginia.[19] As a legacy to the racial purity law of 1924, Loving's marriage to a white man was rejected on the premise that she was hiding or denying a heritage of color that would make their marriage illegal. It was commonly held that one could still be classified as white with up to 1/16 Native American ancestry. Plecker, and his ally Powell, "were not bound by empiricism, but by ideology. That ideology prompted them to drift far from the mainstream of eugenic orthodoxy in offering legal proposals to ensure their vision of white supremacy and social inequality among the races."[20]

Blood quantum arguments have been used for generations to determine who was removed to other lands, who was to be considered white, and more recently—who might lay claim to Cherokee national identity that qualifies its members for educational benefits and more. In fact, it was just such a hope that sent my mother first looking at the Dawes Rolls for her grandmother's name that would help verify her claim to Bureau of Indian Affairs college funding. Quinn would argue, as quoted by Garroutte in *Real Indians* (2003), that we were "illegitimately attempting to exchange [our] true racial identity for what [we could] construe as a more romantic one—and one that may also be more economically profitable in our age of affirmative action."[21]

Cherokee identity is socially and politically constructed, and that process is embedded in ideas of blood, color, and race that dominate the discussions of social belonging, particularly in the United States.[22] The relationship between racial ideologies and identity among people of multiracial heritage is understood in the context of local, regional, and national discourses and legislation that are internalized, reproduced, manipulated, and resisted.

Much as southern Appalachia's geopolitical forces influence the identity and power differentials of its inhabitants, Fraley (2009) examines the history of discrimination that has continued against people of Appalachian origin that migrated to urban areas like Detroit and Cleveland. The discrimination is identified from early instances of newspaper ads stating hillbillies need not apply and employing racial profiling in city riots, as well as in the local ordinances regarding housing. Fraley finally reflects on the implications of legal protection methods for Appalachians as an "emergent ethnic-regional identity within an established democracy."[23]

When analyzing the contribution of social groups on the construction of norms, issues of domination and control should be unpacked and examined. Adamson (1980) explores Gramsci's theory of cultural hegemony, which suggests that the prevailing cultural norms of a society, which are imposed by the ruling class, should not be seen as natural or inevitable.[24] Conversely, they should be recognized as artificial social constructs that must be investigated to discover their roots as instruments of social-class domination.

All of these examples show multiple ways by which societies and ethnicities are constructed socially from within and without. Various historical contexts, along with agreed-upon meanings for behaviors and phenotypes (both overtly and covertly), contribute to how one understands, accepts, or rejects labels, such as Melungeon.

Ontology: Perceptions of Being

For years the idea of Melungeon-ness was decided by those from the dominant culture who have had access to knowledge and resources as well as the means and credibility to spread their opinions to the masses (i.e., via popular media, legislation, etc.). However, a close look at the scripts and norms of behavior from within the group has yet to be accomplished. The dichotomies of universal and, in particular, essence and existence are intriguing in understanding an individual's perceptions of what makes each one unique or what makes that individual part of the group. For example, is a particular way of cooking or talking, living or celebrating, universal to Melungeon? Is a distinct attribute indicative of a particular individual or family?

I find it fascinating that most of the ways of being that I have found integral to my own being and that of my family members are recalled by bell hooks (2009) in her book *Belonging: A Culture of Place*. "Respect for all life, earth and community, where there is spiritual grounding and aesthetic celebration of beauty, where there is a pure enjoyment of simple pleasures" are ways of being.[25] She talks of the following: place, mountains, and home and the details associated with these: sewing, quilting, and preserving; making soap and poultices, having gardens and flowers, growing food, making do, and being a good hostess. She also mentions less tangible things, such as making sure that your word is your bond and treating others as you wish to be treated (including giving the best food/bed/plate/chair to a guest), which are signs of values, if not culture. Even use of language—not necessarily what you say, but how you say it—serves as a way of being recognized by others within a group.

Hooks uses case studies and discourse analysis to explore how elements of a series interconnect to distribute or consolidate power and privilege across discursive contexts. She makes the case that the use of the Melungeon label objectified within Appalachia reveals discourse processes through which white racial privilege is constructed and expanded, mixed-race classification excluded, and nonwhite disenfranchisement reproduced.[26]

Social groups design scripts, roles, environments, and contracts for behavior within their own groups.[27] These hidden scripts identify in-group and out-group "classes." The behavior is not limited to the poor, but also the elite who have an image to maintain and perpetuate. These behaviors often demonstrate deceit and passive aggression where the powerless exert what control they can and the elite use their energy to keep up appearances. The private musings are spoken behind the backs of one another, secretly. Much like Goffman (1990), Scott explores the social contracts within groups that demand conformity and collaboration in the use of power.[28] Many roles and disguises that have interacted throughout history are examined, along with the tensions and contradictions they reflect. He describes the ideological resistance of subordinate groups— their gossip, folktales, songs, jokes, and theater—their use of anonymity and ambiguity. In the case of Melungeons, the choice to describe one's self as Black Dutch or Black Irish to outsiders can be considered a hidden transcript wherein meaning from within the group has given them power to self-identify. While the power-elite may understand what the hidden message is, they, too, play their part in writing down the ethnic labels of the individual.

Katherine Vande Brake helps to situate the stories, myths and memories of Melungeon literacy. She further advances our understanding of the uniqueness of Melungeon features/phenotype, explores origin theories, discusses marginalization, and analyzes the impact that race and privilege has on the group labeled Melungeon, those choosing a Melungeon identity and those doing the labeling.

> I did not ... understand the power of long years of prejudice and discrimination. For people with Melungeon blood, their history has shaped their perceptions of the society around them and their expectations for the future.... By far, the most mind-altering part of my research has been getting to know Melungeon people. This has happened in a variety of ways ... there are the men and women I have interviewed. They have probably been the most influential. Their stories, insights, and answers to my questions sent me back to the books, articles, and websites

with a new perspective and hints about what to look for in those texts. They have lived the "legend" and are willing to talk about it in a focused way.[29]

More recent multicultural literature that identifies challenges within the experiences of Melungeons points to a renewed ethnic pride via the formation of the Melungeon Heritage Association (MHA). Historically, oppressed and discriminated against, the more recent formation of the MHA has restored self-esteem in Melungeon identity and endorsed a new group of people who identify as "being" Melungeon, reclaiming an old epithet and assigning it a meaning infused with pride.[30] The stories shared by co-researchers emphasized the effect of generational family and cultural values, historical trauma, and stigma on the ethnic identity development process. Similar to Vande Brake's findings, Tugman-Gabriel's co-researchers shared ways of being Melungeon that they have identified as inclusive of a cultural identity. Negative stereotypes of Appalachians persist in defining the people as uncultured, uneducated, and exploited by a missionary movement in the 1900s where the nurses and ministers further colonized the mountaineers. However, a robust culture rich in the arts has survived and thrived in the mountains as a testament to resilience and self-reliance in a rugged environment.

"Law and the arts can shape a community's identity over time, by exploring the unique parallels between the common law and the folk music of the Appalachian region of the United States—two cultural transplants from the British Isles to the early American frontier."[31] Social norms and mores of the time, along with musical traditions, influence normative attitudes and function as a communicative process. Jenkins contends that as living traditions, the common law and Appalachian folk music open small spaces for pluralistic discourse.

Ontologically, Melungeon folk have navigated the hidden transcripts with a fierce independence. The literature points to a strong connection (through the Melungeon Heritage Association) between reclaiming the meaning of being Melungeon and viewing the term with a strength-based positive psychology. The controversy that continues is the idea that there is a universal definition of what a Melungeon is and that one's lived experience is not in itself, legitimate evidence. Hence, the splintering of the movement's groups that explore alternative origin and identity theories that include: the short lived Melungeon Historical Society, and many current online communities such as Melungeons and Friends, Melungeon and Proud of it, The People Called Melungeon, Gibsons and Collins from Newman's Ridge Tennessee, and too many blogs to mention. Along with examining such a definition, this view excludes the examination of the essence of Melungeon-ness.

Epistemological Influence

Carefully, I parked my car in the barest of a clearing behind Shirley's Lexus SUV on the hillside where the old homeplace used to stand. I got out and carefully picked my way through the soggy earth and ancient blackberry brambles. We began the climb next to the creek at a steep angle as Shirley and Katie began pointing out their first home, then to where Mamaw and Papaw lived, and finally to Aunt Rose Doan's old chimney. Shirley stooped down next to a scarred place in the earth where someone had had a fire. She grabbed up an old salad plate made of china with small pink roses in the center and a scalloped edge. She handed it to me, explained that the property was "caught up in heirs," and likely belonged as much to my sister and me as it did to the occupants currently living in mobile homes at the bottom of the mountain. This acceptance by my ancestors and extended family struck a chord in my soul as one thread was connected to another. I picked a couple of bricks from the old fireplace and handed one to Schuyler, Shirley's granddaughter, and felt a continuation of family from one generation to another.

"Our ancestors and Elders ... carry the knowledge that we need for continuity and integration. Traditional knowledge weaves its way into the contemporary context for our present and future endeavors." Some of the ways we know or learn who we are is through the stories of our ancestors or Elders. The use of narratives is not confined to indigenous peoples, oral traditions "provide powerful bridges that connect our histories, our legends, our senses, our practices, our values, and, fundamentally our sustainability as peoples."[32]

Another way of knowing ourselves is through our ancestors, outlined through genealogy in a family tree. For some historians and researchers, verification of Melungeon heritage is only available through tracing one's direct ancestors back to the two men commonly accepted as the "original" Melungeons of Hancock County—Shepherd Gibson and Vardemon (Vardy) Collins.[33] It is likely that "the descendants of these early settlers were of a vastly greater number than we had previously supposed."[34] Due to stigma, discrimination, and miscegenation laws, it is believed that many Melungeon families avoided census takers and moved frequently, further challenging the contemporary genealogist and historian trying to document that Granny really was Cherokee.

As genealogy proved difficult and the focus on multicultural education and pluralism became politically correct, many third (and subsequent) generation descendants of immigrants began searching for ethnicity. They longed to understand the meanings attributed to traditions and cere-monies as well as to glean value from family stories and artifacts. Produc-tion of bio-histories based on DNA analyses became more accessible.

Current projects associated with bio-historical identities are being examined and exposed as being backward looking, a culture of remem-brance.[35] The access demonstrates complexities in how the current consumer drive for genetic history is challenged by generational and auto-biographical narratives that may contradict how bio-socialities are uncov-ered.

Hirschman and Panther-Yates (2008) were represented once again at the 16th annual Melungeon Union in August 2012 by their representa-tive Phyllis Starnes who spoke on the merits of a Melungeon DNA test. Panther-Yates is owner and principle investigator of DNA Consultants in Phoenix, Arizona. Hirschman is a professor of marketing at Rutgers Uni-versity and has published more than 200 articles in marketing, consumer behavior, sociology, and semiotics. In their present study, they suggest that Melungeons represent an amalgam of Mediterranean, Middle Eastern, North African, Sub-Saharan African, and Native American ethnic groups. They also entertain the possibility that some founders carried South Asian and/or Gypsy/Roma ancestry as well.[36]

While using a sample size of 40 individuals that have self-identified as Melungeon (most other studies have also used people who self-identify), the researchers found no universal genetic make-up consistent in all sam-ples other than European. Identifying as Native American, Panther-Yates's research appears to embody both sides of the same coin:

> From my perspective, you either are or are not an Indian, depending on whether you have an Indian Spirit.... You can become a White person, but you cannot become an Indian. You are born one. You can have the ancestry of Crazy Horse ... but be white in your actions and effectives.... You can have only a drop of Chero-kee blood and be a role model for your people."[37]

On the other side of the coin, the meaning of a DNA test for determining Native American ancestry seems to contradict his own ideology.

The impetus for research ethics is currently being analyzed and reformed due to controversies between experts and laypersons regarding the use of DNA results for identity claims. Brodwin (2005) argues that the relationship between biology and sociology demands ongoing discus-sions about power, politics, and ethical research policies.[38] Due to the work of laypersons such as Jack Goins, a well-respected and self-taught historian and genealogist, researchers call for a multidisciplinary and inclusive approach to examining identity.[39] Including non-traditional scholars in the discourse may alleviate much of the power and politics currently rampant in such discussions. The demand of robust discourse about the power differentials and possible consequences to the very people we are trying to empower and understand is imperative.

The changing relationship among population genetics, family genealogy, and identity warns about combination of information that could create new forms of "imagined genetic communities" while reinforcing older patterns of exclusion or inequality. Considering specific social and cultural contexts where genetic knowledge is embedded and the way that it interacts with other kinds of knowledge is also critical. It highlights the need to explore the processes in which people identify with certain subject-positions. The legacy of eugenics is lasting, and its lessons should not be underestimated in the age of easy access to genetic material.[40]

After my trip to the Melungeon Heritage Association's 16th Union, I met with Katherine Vande Brake at her summer home in Michigan on July 12, 2012. I had read both of her books, *How They Shine* (2006) and *Through the Back Door* (2009), and we had spoken on the phone. She was excited to see what my reaction was to the Union and to hear what all had happened at the meeting.

We met for lunch at a restaurant near Harbert, Michigan. A very direct and professional woman in her late 60s, Vande Brake was careful not to have our small talk or menu orders recorded. Gracious and generous with her research, when I did get the taping started, she got right to the point:

> What I came down to by the time I finished [my research] is that there are two questions [regarding Melungeons], who is included, and what counts as evidence. That's where the dividing line is, Jack Goins and company [say] you got to have the papers, you've got to be from a certain family, to be able to trace back through records. Brent Kennedy, and people like him, [say] some of the experiences and family stories count. There are people who have left Appalachia who are Melungeon based on some of those things; discrimination, family stories, oral history.[41]

The whole idea of shared experience came up again when Kevin Jones, the original presenter from England, talked about the first DNA study. He said, "My DNA replicates the DNA of the people from common Melungeon areas, but I am from Britain. So what is the difference? Shared experience."

It seemed that my original perception of a divide in the Melungeon identity movement was supported in Vande Brake's findings. It might also explain the dwindling participation in the MHA and more recent Unions, as researchers create their own groups and define their own research goals.

The following statement made by Vande Brake suggested that some people felt secure in their Melungeon identity, but others were hoping to verify their membership via shared experience.

> The point I wanted to make is that the people who *really* are Melungeon, people like Druanna Overbay, don't participate in any of the email lists, she just doesn't participate. She comes to the unions because she is afraid someone is going to say something and she won't know. She is very secure in her identity and she doesn't need any of the other stuff, she doesn't need to *go* to the unions, she doesn't need to *speak* at the unions [for verification of Melungeon identity]. I mean, her grandfather was Batey Collins [direct descendant from Vardemon Collins, one of the "original" Melungeons], and she knows that.

In the case of Melungeons, the conflicts and tension arise from a traditional sociological dilemma—in-group vs. out-group membership. Just who is the other, and who am I? In a society that appears to be celebrating diversity and bringing greater awareness to ethnic identity, we may be searching for group membership to verify and give meaning to family traditions and stories: a shared history that has positive connotations and meaning. With other scholars focusing on origin theories, historical context, geopolitical forces of the region, ethno-genesis, and complications of race and eugenics—I believe I found a niche for my research in how families develop an ethnic or cultural identity and what it provides for them.

However, after years of coursework on leadership theory and practice, I am also intrigued by how leaders are defined and how they exercise their leadership in such a grass-roots movement. I hear terms like *real Melungeon, DNA evidence, documentary evidence,* and *shared experience.* Certain authors' names have come up consistently as leaders in the movement; not all have educational or traditional scholarly credentials that are often associated with leaders. How these leaders use their influence can greatly impact the development of and sustainability of a cultural and collective identity. As Belton (2013) notes, "A community that without cost or sanction lets anybody in and potentially everybody out, which allows for the core of its rationale to be questioned, critiqued, attacked and supplanted, logically invites its own demise."[42] I cannot think of a more important task in an individual's life—or a leadership role with more responsibility and need for ethical consideration—than that of exploring a people's very being.

Identity Development and Belonging

It would appear that there is growing support for the idea that those claiming a Melungeon identity and having out-migrated from Appalachia may have a less stable self concept than those who still live in the area, "Such groupings are criss-crossed with internal differences that in practice constitute identities within identities."[43] Intersectional oppression is more than the sum of its individual responses; it is the collision of several instances of discrimination against several facets of an individual's identity and their accumulative affect. This stability of self-concept may influence the cognitive overlap of whether one projects personal attributes onto the group, self-anchors, self-stereotypes, or conforms to group norms.[44] Those of us who have moved away or have fewer opportunities for social verification of identity (we are physically further away from "in-group") may have a less stable self-concept and look to conform to the group in order to achieve social identity and the verification and inclusion that come with acceptance. The systems at play with optimal distinctiveness theory and social identity theory illustrate a fluid dynamic at play in determining a salient identity at any given time, place, or context.

The need for cross-discipline work in social research is apparent as scholars look at how the above desire for an ethnicity or distinctiveness may explain not only the Melungeon identity movement, but also an exploration of it via Optimal Distinctiveness Theory (ODT).[45] One can consider a continuum where, on the one end, one is part of a group, and the other end one is a unique individual with distinct attributes and firmly outside of the group. Then it becomes important to consider that each has an optimal point on that continuum where one belongs to the group but is recognized and celebrated for uniqueness. The discussion between ethnic blandness and ODT can contribute greatly to current ethnic identity discussions, specifically regarding the motivation for a specific identity. As mentioned earlier, the integration of ODT and Social Identity Theory helps researchers understand the motivation for a distinct identity as well as how that development is developed or sustained in the face of support or threat.[46] Social Identity Theory, or SIT, allows for further analysis of how one defends or adapts to social challenges or norms of an identity.

Cross-discipline exploration of identity offers an opportunity to gather a variety of theoretical positions in psychology, leadership, sociology, anthropology, and even family studies. The amalgamation of ways of viewing the data provides a more complex view of the data than examining it in only one discipline or perspective. It also helps expose co-researchers to alternative ways of viewing data that may be helpful in understanding individuals' lived experiences and practical strategies for making positive changes in their lives. As interracial marriage and families grow in social acceptance and in number, these theories may garner more attention.

In the case of Melungeons, optimal distinctiveness may rest as much on the geography of place as it does on knowledge of ethnicity and culture. In areas where Melungeon is not a known identity or population, the distinctiveness can be too great to garner respect and admiration from peers. Yet, in literature that espouses specific documentation or DNA as evidence of belonging, that belonging becomes the distinguishing factor that gives an edge over others in the group lacking such proof. For example, at meetings of the Melungeon Heritage Association, where everyone is considering a Melungeon Identity, the addition of genealogical lines to the Gibsons of Newman's Ridge may add a bit of distinction to set one apart from the homogeneity of the group. This speaks again to the importance of exploring intersectionality of roles lived by the variety of co-researchers. Dhamoon (2011) suggests a focus of analysis using a "matrix of meaning making." This analysis is not "just a focus on domination but the very interactive processes and structures in which meanings of privilege and penalty are produced, reproduced, and resisted in contingent and relational ways."[47]

The more one becomes invested in the group identity, the more salient that identity role becomes. Where some co-researchers relied on intersections of identity to enact a sense of self that was integrated and holistic, at least one presented Melungeoness as salient identity.

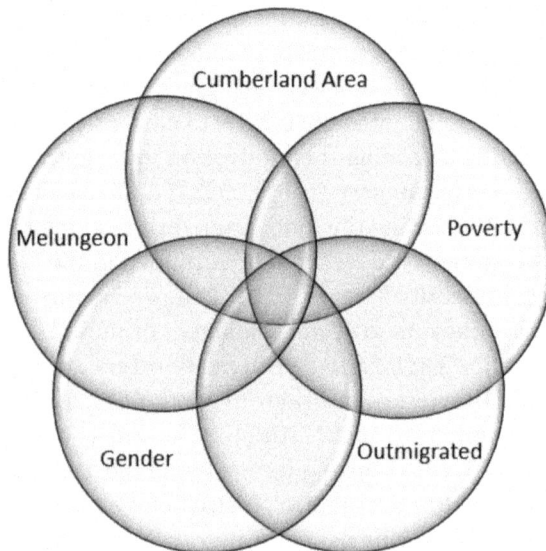

Figure 2.1: An illustration of one version of intersectionality when exploring Melungeon identities.

The intersections of geography, socioeconomic status, gender, and more work to making meaning of the experiences that are complex and understood in divergent realities for the co-researchers of this project. When viewing this framework from the context of the Melungeon Identity Movement, the lens of intersectionality helps us rise above the "conceptualizations of oppression organized around single axes of identity." As researchers note, those of us in academics who have "benefited from our cultural capital" need to hold one another accountable and "resist accumulating academic capital at the expense of others."[48] With the many and varied Melungeon groups, one could very well risk the power of a collective voice by further marginalizing and oppressing diverse voices from within the movement itself. By understanding the intersectionalities of people contemplating or confirming a Melungeon identity, effective leadership can expand and build on collective similarities to address power differentials in policy making.

Examining relationships with co-researchers and how together we navigated experiences with identity within the context of media presented a unique and complex view of group identity. Podber (2001) grapples with such issues while analyzing determinants of in-group and out-group status and the meaning ascribed to each and by each. His text is outlined to address how various media: radio, television, and internet, influence identity formation in Appalachia and for Melungeons.[49] The messiness of co-constructed research with co-researchers can be challenging, yet the empowerment and validity of analysis can prove to be very rich when doing collective biographies as pointed out by Davies and Gannon (2006).[50] Taking the time to intentionally recall events and feelings and then discuss life experiences and their meanings may also add greatly to the ontological understanding of Melungeon-ness. It also brings to mind the cautions of crisis of representation where as the primary researcher on this project I must take responsibility for telling the story, because it is ultimately my story as much as the data is co-constructed with the co-researchers. Due to the classic observations of divergent realities within family systems and co-researchers in the project, it was imperative that I carefully gained the perspective of each individual, stopping short of claiming to tell each individual's unique story.

Using literacy and social media (internet presence) to examine the Melungeon experience, Vande Brake (2011) calls *the insider mentality* a type of literacy to which one's experiences give context and meaning. She maintains that shared experiences provide an understanding of the group rather than a biological definition. Offering many paradigms for understanding the Melungeon experience and situating it within the larger Appalachian society, she uses various narratives (personal stories), historical documents (from Vardy School and Church), photographs, and countless scripts from email list discussions, blogs, and more. The search for and analysis of primary sources bring details and a richness to the research, hence the combined investigations into family specific census records, genealogy, narratives, photographs, and interpretations. The meaning attributed to documents and evidence of heritage is also carefully documented, co-constructed yet still owned by the primary researcher, acknowledging the power differential inherent with the role.[51]

Whether it is a desire to be special or distinct, to find meaning in family traditions and artifacts, or to be accepted and appreciated, belonging seems to be a universal human need.

Assessment of the Literature and Research Review

Within the realm of her historical context, with geopolitical events and places, an individual within a family system must construct a satisfying identity. Sometimes this knowledge comes through other people or events, and sometimes it is through personal experiences and perspectives. The individual accepts (or rejects) an identity and constructs roles based on this identity that function to bring about a sense of belonging to a group where, her unique attributes are recognized and appreciated, thus allowing for a degree of self-actualization.

My research co-created portraits that explore the essence of co-researchers' identities and explain how they found meaning in their lived experiences. Together we examined our discovery of heritage and ethnicity, how we have constructed our knowledge of who we are and how we have performed roles assigned to us by various social systems, or how we have resisted these roles to construct our own identities. The definitions of Melungeon identity, who espouses that identity, and whom we choose to follow or believe is explored through authentic and transformative leadership theory. We explored how various roles have collided and shifted through the years and stages of our lives and how those intersections might also define identity and meaning within our experiences, and our potential selves.

CHAPTER 2

Portraiture as Research Methodology

When considering the issue of Melungeon identity and the Melungeon Identity Movement of the late 1990s, I felt it was important for me to understand the historical and political contexts of the area. I determined the most appropriate way to understand the issues was to consider the complexity and contexts in which the geopolitical history occurred.[1] I decided qualitative research would provide the best methods to inform my understanding. As Stake noted, "the qualitative researcher emphasizes episodes of nuance, sequentiality of happenings in context, the wholeness of the individual."[2]

In this project, to illuminate the stories of several co-researchers while examining them through the lens of my own experience, I employed the qualitative research method of portraiture, a blend of phenomenology and ethnography.[3] To best capture the essence of the co-researchers' lives and lived experiences portraiture methodology combined with collective biography and multimedia seemed most appropriate. The project was informed by a combination of interviews and the co-creation of written portraits that explored and clarified my experiences and those of my co-researchers as well as our understanding of them.[4] The methodology and data collection require repeated interviews and shared experiences and provided the best opportunity for exploring ethnic, narrative, familial, and historically framed identity. These methods also allow for participants and me to clarify, process, and create the project together as co-researchers.

Social Construction

While having focused on the epistemological and ontological paradigms included in ethnic identity, one cannot ignore the influence of social construction on such an identity. These are processes whereby an individual constructs knowledge of self and others through socialization. This information can come from family and neighbors or institutional systems, such as schools, media, and public policy. History and lived experiences also inform knowledge of self and are used to construct an identity. This is especially important when viewing those who claim a Melungeon identity, have out migrated from the area, and are essentially living middle class White experiences away from the mountains. These experiences are being integrated into a way of knowing devoid of the racial implications common to Melungeons currently living in southern Appalachia. Researchers have argued against "an oversimplification of binaries toward a broader recognition of the multi-textured bricolage" of race writing.[5] Instead of viewing a person or population as either a Melungeon or not, researchers are encouraged to view their experiences in the textual complexities inherent in their life.

Such a view of race writing has become more emphasized when considering populations, such as Melungeons. It becomes imperative and, ultimately, more informative, to

> re-imagine and to think outside the category of race. What is at stake is the viability of race as a meaningful concept in ethnographic exploration and the political ramifications of deploying or erasing it from future enquiry. Decisions to pursue or resist this line of thinking will in large part rest upon the political consequence of these choices and the dilemma of whether as race writers we prefer to work through or against Identity Politic.[6]

These concerns continue to plague researchers of Melungeon identity who are now using DNA and genetic testing to prove their heritage. Since many do not share the same lived experiences as either the core group living on Newman's Ridge or those currently identified as Melungeon who live in the Cumberland Gap area, they appear to be using science to push their agenda of belonging to the group.

Williams and Thornton (1998), in their discussion of social construction, find that systems often define racial experiences as homogeneous and distinctive. Simply put, researchers have assumed that the meanings attributed to populations by the society they live in or near to define personal experience. I am discovering the meanings are much more complex. Individuals with Melungeon backgrounds and identity have a large variety of lived experiences from a plethora of influences that have made finding a universal or common Melungeon experience difficult. What a Melungeon uses to construct identity in Michigan is vastly different from the knowledge and experiences that have contributed to the construction of

Melungeon identity in Tennessee. Individual experience often differs in the social expectations of Melungeon writers and researchers.[7]

Portraiture

Seeking to provide a deeper understanding of co-researchers' lived experience, Lawrence-Lightfoot and Davis (1997) pioneered portraiture as a research technique rooted in the tradition of ethnography and phenomenology. They consider the process a blending of "literary principles, artistic resonance, and scientific rigor" that crosses several boundaries. "We navigate borders that typically separate disciplines, purposes, and audiences in the social sciences—bridging aesthetics and empiricism, appealing to intellect and emotion, seeking to inform and inspire, and joining the endeavors of documentation, interpretation, and intervention."[8]

The specific goals of portraiture are:

• Portraiture emphasizes "goodness" (p. 8). Developed in response to a pathological viewing of social science, the focus on failure distorts perceptions of strength and resiliency in populations already marginalized and oppressed. While weaknesses are not ignored, in portraiture they are presented in the context of lived experience of individuals or groups who are striving for good.

• Portraiture attempts to merge the "systematic, empirical description with aesthetic expression, blending art and science" (p. 3). It's the blending of the rigor of traditional ethnographic inquiry, phenomenological illumination, and the artistry of deep and meaningful description. It is the dialogue between the researcher and her co-researcher that creates the richness and meaning that is crucial to the authenticity (as opposed to validity) of the final portrait.

• Because the research portrait is meant to reach out to the reader, portraiture allows the researcher to "reach beyond the walls of the academy" (p. 9) to become an agent of social change. By using language and writing formats that are easily accessed by lay readers, the researcher can facilitate a connection between academic research and "public discourse and social transformation" (p. 13), empowering readers and becoming a stimulus for change.

• Portraiture allows a robust role for the researcher. "The identity, character, and history of the researcher are obviously critical to the manner of listening, selecting, interpreting, and composing the story" (p. 13). In portraiture the role of the researcher is included as an instrument of inquiry.

It is the co-construction of the final portrait that lends itself to the success and authenticity which makes the particular project successful. Co-construction also takes into account the meaning derived by the reader, who interprets the portrait again. It is the availability of alternative hypotheses or understandings through the inclusion of rich description that provides room for another voice to make meaning of the portrait.

This description of the researcher's role seemed intriguing and convincing as I would also be exploring my identity throughout the process. Because I was examining my family members' individual and collective identities, the technique was particularly fascinating as it encouraged the incorporation of all of our views. I was excited to use Portraiture as it would encourage the use of my own voice and perceptions in framing the project. Besides the crucial importance of context and the robust nature of the role of researcher, Portraiture requires the consideration of many aspects of voice.

Voice as witness. In this phase the researcher as witness observes holistically from a distance what is taking place and in what context while interacting with the stimulus or person and then documenting all that she sees, hears, and perceives. She looks for patterns and documents all that adds to the meaning or perceptions of the event or phenomenon taking place. Again, patterns, themselves, can be indicative of the researcher's subjectivity.

Voice as interpretation. In the next phase, the researcher acts as interpreter. Great care is given to provide enough description in the work that the audience can add their interpretive lens to the portrait and perhaps find an alternative hypothesis. Care is taken to gather enough information to provide *thick description*: description that will help readers understand and interpret the environment and context themselves. The provision of description that is rich in detail and robust in its fullness also allows readers to arrive at their own conclusions.

Voice as preoccupation. Following the interpretative phase, the researcher explains the theoretical framework of her work. In this project ethnography and narratives were used to support comprehension of identity development and the meaning family members have made of their lived experiences. In this phase of the project it is imperative to share with readers my/researcher's framework of understanding and what motivated me to embark on such research. This aspect of voice is the lens through which the researcher sees and records reality.

Voice as autobiography. In this phase of the process researchers share aspects of their personal stories, such as culture, family, and worldview that have shaped how they see, frame, and interpret the project. Again, the need for transparency and understanding of my various roles and the intersection of those roles required delicacy and commitment.

Voice discerning other voices or listening for voice. In the following phase the portraitist listens *for* voice, taking a more assertive stance than one who is listening *to* voice. Listening for voice requires intentionality and responsibility. In this case it also required the consistent and ongoing clarification and co-construction of the portrait. The researcher attempts to portray "texture and cadence, exploring its meaning and transporting its sound and message into the text through carefully selected quotations." Lawrence-Lightfoot calls these hesitations in speech or changes in body language and posture "mixed feelings" and suggests they are key to describing a fully nuanced portrait in all its complexity.[9] It was especially this aspect of voice that compelled me to incorporate a hypermedia method of collecting and interpreting data where the medium could help capture and portray co-researchers' voices including hesitations, spaces, stutters, or mispronunciations. The speech patterns added depth and dimension to the portrait that would have been missing if edited.

Voice in dialogue. This is the phase during which the researcher captures the "dance of dialogue," revealing the relationship between the actors and researcher, including the intimacy and trust necessary to provide effective, rich, and illuminating portraits. "The texture is very different from the portraitist's use of voice as witness, a position on the periphery of the action, a place from which she can observe patterns and see things that might not be visible to actors. It is in this framework of voice that the researcher purposefully engages in the middle of the action."[10]

Voice interaction. In this phase of voice, the researcher presents a platform for dialogue between the co-researcher and researcher's voices, allowing one to influence and interact with another. It showcases for the reader the researcher's methodology and how she and the co-researcher make meaning of the events together—both questioning, clarifying, and building relationship in the process.

The role of context. The way that context is emphasized in portraiture inspired the narratives I wanted to understand and the historical events that framed them. The issues of identity are complex, and the circumstances in we journeyed through them become especially important. Some of us were born and raised in southern Appalachia and have stayed; others left early and came back; yet others were born of Appalachian mothers in other parts of the country and still yearn for a piece of themselves they can only find in the rocky hills of Virginia, Kentucky, and Tennessee.

When presenting data, we documented not just southern Appalachia's physical geography, but also its history and culture—how the geopolitical forces of the past have structured and further influenced identity and perceptions of "other."[11]

As Lawrence-Lightfoot and Davis (1997) note:

> Sometimes we—who underscore the power and significance of context in our work—begin to overstate its shaping influence in the lives of actors, assuming that institutional structures and ecological domains are far more powerful than they are. But in developing portraits we must also observe and record the ways in which people compose their own settings—the ways they shape, disturb, and transform the environments in which they live and work.[12]

The challenge. Working through the myriad aspects of voice while including context and relationships was challenging. I found that pulling the pieces into an aesthetic whole proved the most difficult of all. Trying to set aside assumptions and biases was challenging. However, it was exciting to understand the meanings my co-researchers had attributed to their lives and to share in their discovery and construction of self.

Working with a marginalized and oppressed population, the emphasis on goodness, which is similar to the positive psychology movement, resonated with me. Looking for the strengths and resilience within a population shifts the entire paradigm from identifying what is wrong so it can be fixed to recognizing what is going well so it can be reinforced and understood. The method offers the best alternative for a project that seeks to intertwine the stories and experiences of family members in all their complexity; in fact, it may prove therapeutic to focus attention on the benefits of upbringing and the resultant resilience of spirit born of dysfunction.

Portraiture method was inspired by a combination of ethnography and phenomenology. In order to fully comprehend the principles of portraiture, it is imperative to understand these methods as well.[13] Brief descriptions of each follow.

Ethnography

Often used in anthropology, ethnography is a qualitative research method in which the researcher observes and interacts with a population in her real-life environment.[14] Natural observation allows the researcher to see behaviors in context by analyzing them through the co-researchers' lens of understanding. This "entails a representational transformation in which, instead of a choice between writing and ethnographic memoir centering on the Self or a standard monograph centering on the Other, both the Self and the Other are presented."[15]

While there is no one specific right way to conduct ethnographic practices or research methods, the depth of understanding, immersion in the field, and context within which a population is studied all make ethnography a natural foundation of portraiture. Ethnographic practice responds to the many and varied situations researchers may find in the field. Ethnography is a deliberate attempt to generate more data than the researcher is aware of at the time of collection and is, therefore, much more suited to the study of complex emerging social systems.[16] In the project undertaken, co-researchers did much personal reflection on their own words from transcripts of conversations discovering more data for analysis than any of us had originally considered.

Anthropologists often work immersed in a society, participating and living among the indigenous people to gain an understanding of their lived experience in context of their culture. One of the main advantages of ethnography is the potential to identify the unexpected behaviors one would not find otherwise. When not focusing analysis on co-researchers' lived experience, researchers can miss the minutiae of nonverbal messages, hidden transcripts, and other behaviors unique to the people they are studying.[17] Researchers do not always know the questions to ask, nor do the co-researchers necessarily identify what is worth mentioning. Using ethnography through co-researcher observation can decrease the chances of missing something; by living and working within the society, the issues to analyze become rather obvious to the researcher.

Another advantage to engaging ethnography is the ability to present a richly detailed description of co-researchers' behaviors and beliefs. This thick description is crucial to portraitists who are attempting to portray a sincere representation of an experience in time and context. Since the portrayal is not expected to be objective, an ethnographic field study can uncover useful and relevant attitudes and emotions that help develop a robust and well-documented portrait.

Traditional studies can find authenticity problematic as they assume participants are interacting as they would if no one was observing. However, when individuals are sincerely trying to understand and interpret the activities of the group, co-researchers begin to trust the researcher and feel more comfortable being open and reflective while conversing and interacting. It is precisely this relationship building that allows for, even demands, the clarification and co-construction of a portrait in the manner of portraiture.

One of the benefits of ethnographic principles in portraiture is the diminished attempt to create a product that is generalizable to another population.[18] Unlike a pure ethnographer's analysis, it is not necessary or even desirable to make a correlation between a co-researcher and a larger population. In fact, creating a portrait a la ethnography is much like a snapshot in a specific time and setting: one that will help researchers better understand a single phenomenon, in depth, at that moment. This is where phenomenology adds to the process. By illuminating the specific event, population, custom, or phenomenon, phenomenology requires that we focus on the way things seem to be from our perspective. Adding to this illumination are the perspectives of all co-researchers and the documentary evidence and family research.

Phenomenology

Phenomenology is an umbrella term that incorporates philosophy and research methods. Husserl (1970/1936) initiated the phenomenological movement as a new way of incorporating philosophy into qualitative research in the social sciences.[19] Later, Heidegger (1927/1962) modified the phenomenological ideal, moving away from a discipline in philosophy which "focuses on consciousness and essences of phenomena towards elaborating existential and hermeneutic (interpretive) dimensions."[20]

Applied to research, phenomenology is the study of phenomena: their nature and meanings. The researcher's project is, according to Husserl (1970), to "return to the *things* themselves."[21] *Things* refers to the world of lived experience. In the current project, we (the co-researchers and I) have examined how lived experience has contributed to the construction of individual and group identity. It also has shed light on the meaning attributed to these experiences by each of us.

Our lived experiences happen before we can think about or articulate them. They are pre-reflective. We exist in a day-to-day world filled with complex meanings that structure the framework of our behaviours and interactions. My mother was reflecting on meaning in the way she grew up with certain items, like coal oil lights and a wood stove. Upon reflection she ascribed meaning to this way of life and was looking to validate or verify this meaning with others who had common experiences.

In the life-world, a person's consciousness is always directed at something in or about the world. Consciousness is always consciousness of something. When we are conscious of something (an object) we are in relation to it and it means something to us. In this way, subject (us) and object are joined together in mutual co-constitution. This important phenomenological concept is called intentionality, and it is a key focus for research.[22]

When conducting research, researchers usually pay attention to the intentional relationship between co-researchers and the meanings of the experiences they are focusing on and experiencing. As phenomenologists, researchers work to identify what the co-researchers' experiences are like and what they meant to them.[23] The hard part develops in how the researcher gives voice to co-researchers' expressions, paying careful attention in representing their ideas as directly as possible.

Meanings discovered by the phenomenological researcher often emerge from the way the researcher interviews co-researchers and frames questions. Using bracketing, the researcher attempts to suspend assumptions so that she can be open to seeing new insights or perspectives about an event or phenomenon as it appears in context.[24] The purpose of bracketing is not an attempt to represent the findings as objective, but a process of putting aside one's expectations and suppositions and focusing on how the events are experienced by the person(s) being studied.[25]

The ability to view and review conversations recorded with co-researchers offers insights and opportunities to capture the unexpected and reinterpret, as a researcher, what one thought happened. Thus, using multimedia resources to capture and present data became another tool to analyse lived experience and the ways those experiences are expressed and interpreted by co-researchers as co-constructors of the project.[26]

Choosing People and Portraits

I reiterate here how important it is to me that the people I interviewed are considered co-researchers rather than participants. Each of them was very active in questioning, reflecting, clarifying, and interpreting our conversations. They were very much a part of the research "team" instead of an object of study. They are each older than eighteen years but younger than ninety. Some have accepted a Melungeon identity; others have not. I completed lengthy portraits and discussions of fourteen co-researchers of mixed genders, with some still living in the Cumberland Gap area of Appalachia and others having out-migrated.

Co-researchers who are related to me have expressed an interest in participating in this research, including my mother, daughter, sister, and three cousins with whom I was not familiar and had not met prior to this work. Other co-researchers were introduced to me by virtue of their presence in Melungeon groups or through other co-researchers. Upon learning of my research, they have expressed an interest in adding to my data in hopes of contributing to a body of literature and scholarship that may help their descendants and themselves in understanding cultural and ethnic identity markers.

Another friend, when learning of my research, expressed some knowledge and interest in her family's origins and ethnic background. She and several of her family members also elected to participate allowing for an approach that researchers suggest is less distorted than a view from one family member alone.[27]

I used unstructured, open-ended discussions. These conversations were recorded with a digital voice recorder, at times a video camera, and a still camera documented our interactions. The addition of multi-media gave all co-researchers an opportunity to view, listen, and reflect, helping to add to the richness of the data collection.

CHAPTER 3

Gibson Portraits

This chapter is broken down into several sections representing the various families who graciously allowed me to explore with them their family stories (and secrets) that influenced their understanding of a cultural and/or Melungeon identity. Aspects of family and community leadership were explored within the context of this identity. As mentioned earlier, I chose to use portraiture methodology combined with collective biography and multimedia to demonstrate the essence of the participants' lives and lived experiences. The chapter is organized by family to allow for the best context within which to understand the individuals' portraits. These individuals are co-researchers in every sense of the word: digging through records, collecting letters, photos, and stories, writing, and lastly reviewing and co-constructing the portraits for clarification and accuracy.

All participants allowed audio recording, and many of them allowed video recordings and photographs to record the setting and nuances of posture, body language, and tone of voice. As with any good story, it's best to start at the beginning. Since this started as a personal journey, I will begin with my mother's family, the Ray/Gibson unit.

This Ray family started out with Addie Gibson and George Ray in a tiny little tar paper shack just over the Tennessee line from Addie's hometown of Edgewood, Kentucky. Before long a daughter was born to the union, Sylvia Virginia Ray. The marriage dissolved as a young son was making his way into the world two years later, forcing Addie and her two children back into her parents' three-room house on a rocky mountainside in southeast Kentucky.

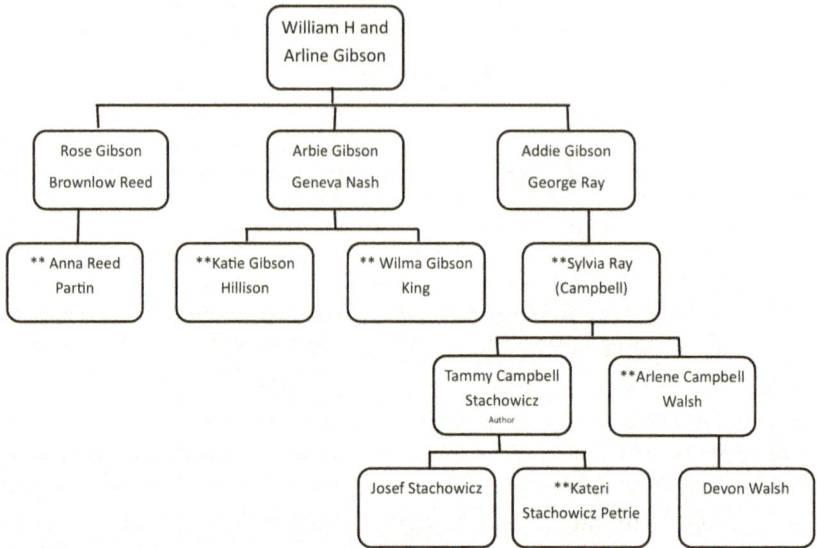

Figure 3.1: Gibson family kinship chart. Those with portraits in this book have asterisks.

Sylvia Virginia Ray

> I want to prove I have a people that I belong to. It would mean I belong some-where, I belong some place, that I *am* someone. That there is a chain of ancestors and family behind me that's where I got a lot of my characteristics and way of thinking.

My mother has been a part of my research for over fifteen years. Together we had found her biological father's family when I completed my master's program in cultural anthropology and family studies. She was integral to this project as well. I started with a pilot project that led to a documentary and presentation at the Appalachian Studies Association conference in Boone, North Carolina in 2012. The following is from that interview, along with several conversations we had for the original pilot. I will use Sylvia, her name, to avoid confusion.

I asked Sylvia if any of the answers she was looking for has anything to do with Melungeons. I was concerned that she was searching for some-thing we would never find, so her affirmative response to this question was reassuring. "Yes," she said, pausing, "you know I was real happy when we went to see Brent Kennedy in 2001, and he had said that I definitely had the characteristics of a Melungeon," she said. "He pointed out the shovel teeth, the gap in my teeth, my skin color and eyes, the way they are, that these were typical Melungeon things. When he pointed out that Devon, my grandson, as a toddler definitely looked Melungeon—the color of his skin and the folds of his eyes. I was pleased to know I was something. I couldn't brag that I was Polish, German, or Irish," she said. "I had no background."

We were sitting on the front porch of a house rented in Bristol, Virginia. Sylvia had done her hair and make-up in anticipation of the videotaped interview. Her white hair, baby fine and down to her shoulders, had been set in curlers that morning. A table and chairs sat in the corner of the large porch, and a swing hung on the far end. On the table was spread a map of the Cumberland Gap area where we were plotting out the residences of various family members throughout hundreds of years of census records. We had come in late the night before, slept in, and were enjoying a late morning and coffee and biscuits on the porch. For the interview we moved to the two rocking chairs that sat up close to the railing by the front door so that the camera could capture the conversation. I ask her to begin by describing her childhood.

"Well," Sylvia starts to explain her early years. "I feel like I was born and raised the first part of my life like most people in the 1800s—and I was born during WWII! There was electricity, there was cars, there were things out there I had no idea existed. That was the way I was raised," she said, "with a wood stove, kerosene or coal oil lights. I remember making toast on the pot belly stove by waiting until it got red hot, then taking light bread and sticking it to the side of the stove," she says laughing. "When it was done it would fall to the floor and I would brush it off and slap it back on the other side. That's how I made toast." I had heard this story several times and laughed in amazement every single time. I can only imagine the number of burned fingers a small child would endure while learning this procedure.

"I never felt poor, but evidently we were. I always thought Papaw was some big important person," she relayed. "The few times I remember going into town people would be walking up to him and waving from the street saying, 'Hi, Uncle Bill, howdy, Uncle Bill.' Some of my relatives were in basic county and state government jobs. I have a copy of a sign for my great-grandfather when he ran for magistrate," she said. "I had the feeling that people around us thought we were a hierarchy of the area. So I never felt poor—even though there were times I was downright hungry. It is an enigma I don't understand."

Hoping to glean some additional tidbits that I had overlooked up until now, I ask her about her grandmother. "She said she was Indian?" I asked. "Yes," Sylvia answered, "Cherokee. But she told the census taker that she was Black Irish," she said pausing and reflecting, "and I couldn't understand that 'cause I looked at her and she didn't look black to me," she says giggling. "You have to understand this is through the eyes of a child, a toddler." Sylvia was left by her mother for several years to live with her maternal grandparents after divorcing her husband. She went to Detroit to escape the life she had known in the mountains. I believe my mother is looking not just for an identity, but a connection to the only family she knew as a child. She had been ripped away from Kentucky to be reunited with a mother she no longer knew. Answers to questions about a culture and heritage will be easier to find than those regarding her mother's decisions.

"I'm curious and question who I am, what I am, why was I raised the way I was raised," she says. "Selfishly I want to know more about why I'm the way I am." The interview goes in spurts and starts as new questions and memories come to mind. She thinks and reflects intently; in one moment her eyes tear up and the next she laughs at different memories. She is wearing a white cotton t-shirt with flowers and butterflies (she loves butterflies), along with a pair of short red pants. I can't remember if she has shoes on, but since she so rarely does, I am assuming she is barefoot. Her hands looked aged and vascular, and she grips the arms of the chair tightly as she rocks.

"They had quite an extravagant home until the mountain slide," Sylvia continues, referring to her grandparents' first home. "With the stories I

Sylvia Ray, 70 years old.

was told about that, and what I can remember, it was extremely nice for the area and time. My grandfather had bought up four or five coalmines with the idea he would pass them along to his children. My dad tried it out," she says referring to her biological father, "and he didn't particularly like it, so that was given back to my grandfather. I think maybe Uncle Arb worked in the coalmines. Uncle Cecil worked at a gas station that he and Grandpa owned. My uncle that lived next door, Brown Reed, worked in the coalmines too. I can remember him getting up and going down to the road to catch the truck to take him

Sylvia Ray, about 2 years old.

down to the mine at like 5:00–6:00 in the morning and he would work all day. The truck wouldn't bring him home until twilight."

When Addie Gibson divorced George Ray, Sylvia's baby brother, Billie Jo, wasn't yet born. "Mom said she caught Daddy in a motel room with another lady and that she went in and beat the tar out of both the lady and Daddy and then tore the hell out of the motel room," Sylvia remembers. "Mom moved back to the shack with Grandma, it had three rooms, two bedrooms and a kitchen. The rooms were big, and Mom moved her bedroom furniture into Grandpa's bedroom and I think all three of us slept in one bed." Sylvia recalls the day her mom left, leaving her with her grandparents. "Well, Rose, Momma's sister, came down with the kids, Emily, Rhada, Anna, and Wayne, and her kids were running wild. Mom was very particular about how her stuff was treated. The kids got up and was jumping up and down on Mom's bed, she had a dresser with a round mirror, a chest of drawers and bed that all went into grandpa's room with his stuff. Anyway, these kids were jumping up and down on the bed and mom and Rose got into it. I mean a real sister fight," Sylvia says, "and

Grandpa told Mom she had to leave. So, she packed a little brown suitcase, wrapped Billie in a receiving blanket, and I watched her go. My grandmother had lace curtains at her windows. I pulled back the curtains watching mom going down the hill and I hollered 'take me too, take me, don't leave me.' Mom didn't turn around and look—I think she was probably crying, and she wouldn't do it. When she didn't turn around I kept screaming, 'I'll hate you, I'll hate you for the rest of my life.' I kept screaming and throwing a tantrum then I saw Mom get on the bus."

Addie had gotten a ticket to Detroit to live with Brownlow Reed's sisters, Glissie and Dorie, and their husbands. "One of the gals was either married to or living with a Mexican. And Mom, from what I understand, was a little wild and didn't have someone to watch Billie. That irritated her and somehow he ended up getting back down there with me at Mamaw's."

I asked how the Reed aunts, Glissie and Dorie, end up in Detroit. "I don't know," Sylvia said, "but they were already up there and that's where mom went when she left. They lived in Noetown with their mother, Artie Thomas Reed. She lived in a beautiful home with a picket fence and lots of flowers. I'm told that she looked a lot like my grandma Lizzie Ray, which makes sense since they were sisters," she says. "The story goes that Mom met Daddy in a bar, Vern Robinson, and they lived together from the time I was four until I came up there. She had given power of attorney to my grandfather for my brother and I in case we got sick. So Daddy told her he was not going to raise a kid without a marriage, Mom objected but finally she agreed to it and that's when they got me.

"I don't think she planned on getting me that time. Grandma said to her standing out on that front porch, 'Well, Ad, which kid you taking?' She looked down at me and said, 'I guess I'll take Sylvia 'cause she's big enough to help.' I always felt bad that she didn't want me 'cause she loved me, she only wanted me to help. My kids meant so much to me I couldn't have given them up for a second. I understand Mom saying she would take me, but why did she have to add that it's because I could help? In the back of my mind, I wonder if she knew I was being molested and that's why she said she'd take me. I don't understand why she only took one of us."

Sylvia's grandfather, W.H. Gibson, was known as Uncle Bill to most of the county and the other grandchildren. When we searched court records in Pineville, Kentucky, we discovered that at one time or another W.H. Gibson had owned hundreds of deeds in and around Middlesboro. Apparently he would buy deeds when people had no money and hold them until they could buy them back from him, making him a profit. "Grandpa must have been a fairly intelligent man," Sylvia recounts. "He had this huge roll top desk and ledgers. He would read the Bible, and newspapers. I don't know if Grandma went to school at all, I think she could read and write some, but being from Virginia and Indian I doubt she went to school. I thought Rhada got the Bible, but maybe Opal's got it."

Sylvia doesn't remember her mother coming to visit but two times: the first when she was about four or five. She drove up with Vern Robinson, her new love. Driving a big car that was very low to the ground, her mother and Vern had to park the car at the bottom of the mountain and walk up to the little house. Since most of Sylvia's relatives didn't own any car at that time, the shiny new vehicle meant that somebody important had come to the mountain. The couple walked arm in arm up the lane, both of them dressed pretty fancy for the area. "I ran to my grandma and told her I thought the king and queen was coming and Grandma just cracked up," Sylvia recalled. "She thought that was so funny. When she looked from the porch she said, 'Law's sake, girl, that's your mother.'" It was the first time Sylvia met the man who would become her stepfather. He was sitting on a chair, in front of her grandmother's bed, holding out a gift for her. "He kept saying he had something for me but I didn't want to go to him. He kept saying, 'I've got something for you, c'mon I'll give it to you but you have to come and get it.' It was in a box and it was a brand new doll— I had never had any toy before," she recalls. "It had pretty blond hair and a beautiful lacy dress."

The second time she remembers her mother being there she recalls her stepdad becoming a larger part of her life. "I remember when Daddy came he took me to the zoo and the Thanksgiving parade and he set me on his shoulders so I could see," Sylvia remembers. He paid attention to her, loved her, and cared for her. "Some of the best lessons of my life I learned from Daddy. Mom didn't empathize or sympathize with kids. But, she helped out each one of my cousins, each one of them lived with us at one time. I was pushed out each time one came and there was a little resentment there. I was never as good as those girls."

Sylvia's early childhood had good times, too. She remembers swinging on the grapevines and playing in the creek. "I wonder if it was my family or the times," she said. "I remember using my imagination and learning things by discovering them, the best way to learn. We'd play in the creek catching crawdads, us girls would all play together and Billie and Wayne would play together. What one wouldn't think up the other one would," she says with a grin, her eyes twinkling. "We took an old ladder out of the old homestead and put it between two chairs and sat on the rungs pretending it was a bus. We all took turns driving the bus and I always thought the faster you turned the wheel the faster the bus went," she said laughing.

Her mood turned more somber as we shared stories we had heard from the cousins about how dirty her grandmother's house was. Her grandmother was very ill much of the time, and Sylvia suspects that the hemorrhaging and being saddled with two additional children contributed to a lack of cleanliness. "I only remember one bath," she said. "Once the kids at school were making fun of me for being so filthy, I took Fels Naptha soap, went down to the creek, and washed my dress on me. Then I took it off and washed my body and my hair. Evidently, I didn't get all the soap out of my hair cause it didn't look any better and the kids were still teasing me."

She shared other stories about her great-aunt doing cartwheels without underwear on or standing with the aunts and her grandmother while they would hold their dresses out and "just pee where they were standing," according to Sylvia's memories. Although they had an outhouse, they used the whole outdoors. From what the cousins shared, Sylvia's mother, Addie, felt so bad for them that she would get them things or send packages: boxes of clothes, underwear, and new bras, to the little family community. She would shop at St. Vincent de Paul for the things to send. "Anna said that Mom taught her to sew and that's the only thing that's got her through her whole life," added Sylvia.

"Now where Wayne's living there used to be a one-room log cabin and Aunt Rose Doan and her husband lived there. He always wore a white dress shirt, dress pants, and a hat. His name was John. Aunt Rose used to like to take me on her lap and slap my leg 'til it was red. She had the biggest hands, she never had children, and I remember her being a nice-looking older woman. She'd slap my thigh then she'd say, 'What are you crying for? I'm just showing you Scotland's map,' Sylvia says shaking her head.

"Now Grandpa's other sister was Lillian and she was fairly dark, a poor little thing, I don't think she ever got enough to eat. No one ever helped her out. I can remember Lil coming up, she usually wore men's shoes, and she would come to the back door and Mamaw would sneak her some food if Grandpa wasn't looking," Sylvia remembers. "Now her daughter Suz was a big woman and had very black features. I think that's why she wasn't allowed in Grandpa's home, though there has to be more of a story to that. I can remember Grandpa coming in and yelling at Grandma for letting that woman in his house," she says, nodding her head and rocking. "She was married to Arthur Rains and we used to torment her saying 'Lil killed Arthur, Lil killed Arthur.' Suzy, they called her Suz, was married 4–5 times like Momma. The last man she married, they started a little grocery store just a little way up the road from Wayne's. It was a two-story house and the store was in the bottom. Anyway, Suzy had Buddy and Grandma. That's all she had. Like Momma, Suzy left down there as fast as she could get out."

"Mom hated Indians," Sylvia said, trying to explain her confusion between knowing her grandmother was Native American and her mother had a prejudice against them. "Daddy had a construction job in Milwaukee when

Sylvia Ray, high school photograph.

I was a senior in high school. One of the men workers, he was a mucker—his family was going with us. They had a small trailer they were pulling behind ours in a little caravan. The man was white, blonde-headed and blue-eyed, and the woman was very much an Indian. When Mom found out she was going with us, she had holy fits." Sylvia continues to rock as she remembers.

"Because my mother tried to wipe out the South from my life, out of me, I've always wondered what was so bad," Sylvia laments. "I long to be proud of who I was and where I came from. From the time I left I was told it was bad, awful, you did not ever want to admit you were from down there. You learned to speak right, to do things right. So to find out that I don't have to wipe out the first years of my life that made me *me*, that I can be proud of them, I'm all for it."

But when asked if she is Melungeon, Sylvia indicates she might be. "I thought there was a possibility, but I still don't know what I think a Melungeon is," she says. What would she need to know she is? "I'm beginning to think I'll never know because I don't know," she says, and I can't help but laugh. "I guess ancestry. If there was proof that my ancestors and family back generations had different races in their background. It would probably take DNA, I guess. Census records were changed and not all of it was truthful, I sort of question that. I don't know what kind of document,though, birth certificates maybe, but there are parts of my family that never had a birth certificate. I never had one until 1954 when I was eleven years old," she says. "Daddy thought it would be a good idea if we had them so Mom applied for all three of us: her, me, and Billie. They were gotten from Bell County, sent to us in the mail. Mine said 'as told by the mother.'"

"Family is so important, there is nothing without family," Sylvia remarks as we discuss where all this research might take us, what it explains about the past or means for the future. Together we note the many things that were different from my childhood and other children's in the '60s. "I realized I wasn't like most women," she said. "I did things that they just didn't do. Things like garden and canning, sewing and home-made dinners. Taking pride in my laundry, making sure my house was clean, it was those kinds of things, what made me *me* what made me a woman, a wife, a mother. The baking was different, the cooking, that was so important to me. It was the best way I knew how to make sure that you got all the vegetables and nutrients that your bodies needed to grow healthy," she explains. "So when I did a meal it was not unusual to have two vegetables, a starch on the table, bread, a meat or protein. My grandmother taught me that. Because when I was a child and company came I was told to help set the table. So the way I put the silverware on the table the way I set things like where to put plates and glasses and cups, I learned that from her. You have to have butter on the table, pickles, and condiments. It was never a complete one pot meal," she explains, "never."

"The first time I heard about Melungeon, you're the first one that told me about it," Sylvia remarks, "was about ten or fifteen years ago. After I heard about it, I did some research, and learned it is a tri-racial isolate, meaning red, black, and white races mixed together. The isolate part was true because I didn't know any kind of world outside of that mountain. People think that isolate means inbreeding, I guess. I've heard that people think that about the whole South but especially the Appalachian part. But back then, where I came from it wasn't unusual for first cousins to marry first cousins," she explains, "it was normal."

We revisit the changes from our first visit with Brent Kennedy and the one in 2012 with Wayne Winkler. "I was taken with the idea that I belonged to a group that there were other people like me. Then when we saw Wayne he seemed to claim to be Melungeon, was real proud of it, but still yet he pointed out that these might not be characteristics of Melungeons," she says referring to the traits Kennedy has pointed out eleven years ago. "So I am back to step one trying to figure out if I am or not. I don't know."

We saw Winkler the next day at the Melungeon Heritage Association Melungeon Union at Big Stone Gap in Virginia. He was the featured speaker among many. Sylvia had been so excited to come down to learn more about her family, about Melungeons, and about her daughter's strange research methods. We talked and laughed, sharing memories on the way to and from the rental house and meeting. Both of us were disappointed in the lack of attendance and the exclusiveness of the group. Much of the talk revolved around DNA and readings by authors marketing their most recent Melungeon or Appalachian books. One speaker gave tips and advice on doing genealogy while past speakers sat in the audience basking in their expertise and recognition.

"It will be a question mark in my life," Sylvia remarks about her heritage and ethnicity. "Does it matter now at my age?" she asks. "Yeah, it still matters," she says, emphatically nodding her head affirmatively. "A lot of my questioning and wanting to know comes from moving to Michigan and having my whole Southern identity as a bad thing, something to be ashamed of. My mother tried to erase in me any traces of Kentucky."

"I think most people are looking for the same thing that I am," Sylvia says on the ride home. "Where did I come from, what am I accountable for, how did I get here, and who did I start from?" She watches out the window of the car as the mountains, churches, and farms race past, her aged eyes taking in the curves and drop-offs of the mountain road. We count a little white church about every mile and remark about the significance of so many, and Sylvia, my mother, counts her blessings.

Arlene Campbell Walsh

Once there was a young bride fixing her first Easter dinner. As she prepared the ham she sliced off the end before putting it into the pan. Her new groom asked her why she did this. She explained it was the way her family had always cooked their hams. When his mother-in-law comes in to help, he asks her. She explains that her mother taught her to do it like that and so she always had. Finally, when the grandmother-in-law comes in and takes her place at the table, he asks the elderly woman about the custom of cutting of the end of the ham. "Well, my dear," she says with a smile, "my pan was only so big."

"I have done enough reading and listening to know well enough that I am Melungeon. It just blows my mind that you've been doing all this research and you still don't know if you are," said my sister Arlene Walsh. "I don't think you are going to find your name on a list that proves it to you." I had taken her and my mother and daughter with me on many of the trips to the Cumberland Gap area to do research for years. The quest began as a personal one, searching for answers as to why I felt a connection to a place and people where I had never lived.

Her green eyes flash and her hands wave animatedly as she gets into the topic at hand. "I just don't get it, why would you care if you didn't have some piece of paper or some document that says, 'Tammy is a Melungeon'?" she asks laughing. While she was never really into the genealogy of the family, she has listened with both joy and sorrow, to the stories and tidbits I have been able to uncover: one relative fishing with a bow and arrow, another having his wife and several children killed by Indians, and yet another about starting the first black church in Charles City County, Virginia. The genealogical documents from census records, birth and death certificates, or marriages licenses mean little to her, and she is irate to think that someone might request to see them to accept us as Melungeon. "If it walks like a duck, quacks like a duck, and looks like a duck—it's a duck," she says emphatically.

From left, Arlene (Campbell) Walsh, Kateri Stachowicz and Sylvia Ray at Kateri's high school graduation in 2012.

"Talking to everyone down [in Middlesboro, Kentucky] about Gibsons made me believe I was at least a small part Melungeon, add that to the [geographical] area and it just adds up," she explains. "For me, I just want to know, I have nothing to gain or lose from it. It won't change anything if I am 80 percent sure or 99 percent sure. I still have the same ancestors," she says. We laugh again at the hilarious recollections from the various family members. "The family stories were *very* interesting and went a long way to telling me who I am," she said, still laughing.

We had grown up with so many stories of Saponi and Cherokee grandmothers, tar paper shacks, poverty, and family loyalty that it helped put into perspective the complexities of the community in which our mother was raised. There was always pride in self-reliance, or maybe there was shame in not being able to take care of her family, especially for the women. It explains those planting huge gardens, snapping beans for hours, canning and freezing, and butchering our own meat. Our mother breastfed her babies in the 1960s, when it wasn't fashionable to do so, and sewed many of our clothes. Our hats and scarves were crocheted and our names embroidered across the bands, "God, I hated those hats," Arlene said shaking her head.

"Remember what the canning room would look like in fall?" she asked. All of the jars would be lined up neatly in rows on the shelves in a dark, cool little room in the basement, the ruby colored beets and glistening gold peaches, the green beans, tomatoes, and applesauce. "It was gorgeous, I wish I had a picture of how that looked. Remember sneaking in there with a spoon to get into the peaches?" We fall into a pattern of "remember whens" as Mom rocks in a chair nearby. I sit on one couch, Arlene on the other in her small living room, as the clock strikes 1:00 a.m. Mom is half asleep but afraid she'll miss something if she goes to bed, so slowly she rocks with her leg bent up under her. Arlene lights another cigarette and glances at her son sleeping next to her on the couch. He's a big boy, fourteen years old, and he was also loath to miss any of the conversation that grown-ups were having about ancestors he'd never met.

A small ten-gallon aquarium sits on the kitchen counter with a bulb on it for heat. The light casts a glow over the room as the tiny tadpoles busily attack food disks on the bottom. The coffee pot sits right next to the glass box, and every time one of us refills our cup, we spend a few moments studying them. We are each lost in our own thoughts for those few moments, hoping to be the first to spot the beginnings of a leg as the tadpoles make metamorphosis to frogs. A lone fishing lure sits on the ledge, marking the wall between the kitchen and the basement stairs. I am reminded of the tackle box full of lures that she gave me for Christmas the year before and how she and I and my brother, Jimmy, would sneak away to go fishing. Night-time "bull heading" was the most fun and allowed us a sense of freedom and rebelliousness.

"Who decides who's a Melungeon and who ain't," she asks as she blows smoke up toward the ceiling and sits back down, arranging the blanket back over her legs, "and why do they get to decide?" The whole idea of what makes research credible and the idea of some scholar writing a book or article and using that power to define someone's identity makes her blood boil. "It's not like it gets you anything, does it?"

Arlene had been married to my brother-in-law Kip Walsh for thirteen years. Prior to that she had had a long-term relationship with a man named Jerry, whose family, coincidently, happened to be from Bell County, Kentucky. She became very close to his mother and grandparents and spent a good deal of time every summer in my mother's old stomping grounds. In fact, she was shocked one day when my mom took her to see the remains of her old school. As they pulled in, mom asked her if she knew where she was. "I thought, shit," said Arlene, "how did she know that Jerry and I went 'parking' here?"

"Every year when I was dating Jerry we would drive to Pineville to visit his family. It seemed like as soon as the car started heading up an incline, the people changed." Arlene claims that is where she fit in, "I liked that side—the mountain people—better." The first time she met them she felt like family and that it had nothing to do with whether she was Jerry's girlfriend or not. "You didn't have to be someone you weren't. I don't know that the people on the flat land was judging me, but I felt like they were. I never felt like I was being judged up the mountain. I wasn't any less to them if I smoked or didn't smoke, they didn't look down on me by what I wore or drove either. It has been that way with everyone I met up in the hills; Katie, Wilma, and Joe. I never felt judged, just accepted."

After Mom gave up and went to bed, we talked a bit more about being rejected or discriminated against. I wondered if being oppressed was part of a Melungeon definition and if, maybe, we were not Melungeon—but that Mom definitely was. However, considering the impact on the family when Mom had been treated poorly, we decided we fit that definition too. "You know Mom never fit in, especially when she first moved up to Detroit with Mamaw. They all made fun of her, at school and in the trailer park, about the way she talked and the words she would say."

"I think now we wear our experience with poverty as a badge of honor," Arlene states. "It shows our ancestors as survivors, they were strong people, resilient, resourceful. This is what I take from it—it's a community more than a race. The minute you go up the mountains it's different, they all work together like when the housewives would get together and talk about how to get the Kool-Aid stains out of the kids shirts, and sharing how and when to plant what. People outside that community don't have the same obstacles to overcome—it just so happens that the people in them hills are tri-racials—the people that weren't accepted in town." She continues about what is important to constructing her identity. "I think it has to do with the geographical location more than the bloodlines. They overcame the environment of the mountains and a society that picks and chooses what is okay to be. I just can't get past the idea that someone could say that you're not good enough to be a Melungeon because you don't have this documentation, when the neighbors on both sides of you are Melungeon and going through the same stuff. How can they say you aren't also experiencing it?"

I do not know how to answer her so I just nod and swipe a cigarette from her pack for myself. Now that Mom is in bed and Devon is sleeping, I'll sneak a smoke as we sit and talk into the wee hours of the morning. The coffee flows, the ashtrays are emptied, and still we debate what being Melungeon means and what it will take for me to know I'm Melungeon. Her husband is a truck driver and won't be back yet for a couple more days. The breeze blows the curtains, and we sit in companionable silence for a few moments.

Finally, Arlene turns to me and we go back to discussing what a Melungeon is. "I can't differentiate between hillbilly and Melungeon, and I don't mean that in a derogatory way. Saying that's gonna bite my ass," she says laughing loudly, "and I'd never say that in front of Jerry's family or anyone else down there. In my mind hillbilly isn't a bad word, I mean, how can you plant a garden on the side of a mountain? They did. How do you raise five kids with an outside toilet?" She doesn't want to forget her roots and the gratification of knowing where her own self-reliance and ingenuity have come from. It's the hills that she equates with a rugged determination and gracious hospitality with which she wants to be identified. "So is Melungeon just a different word for hillbilly or is it a 'secret society'—and if that's what it is, a secret society, don't find anything to prove I am part of it." She stops for a moment to consider what she has just said and continues by describing her pride in Mom for teaching us which fork or spoon went where and how to set the table, where to place the glass—right at the tip of the knife. I see her struggle to articulate what it all means. I practice blowing smoke rings while she refills our coffee. "There was only two kinds of people," she begins, "and I don't," she pauses,"

"I'd rather be from that lower class. Yes, I enjoy the hot tub and air conditioning. But, I'd rather be known as the have-nots as the haves. Because it makes you the kind of people I can't stand."

Devon stirs slightly on the couch, and Arlene pulls the blanket over his lanky legs. We smile and relax a bit as we remember how warm and welcoming everyone we met has been. They have invited us in, treated us like family, fed and entertained us. "But the people on the websites and that write them books, I'd never fit in with them," she says. "And I don't want them speaking for *me*. I feel like they are judging me—do we have documentation saying that we are—and do we have proof that we are?" she says, referring to being Melungeon.

"I guess it really doesn't matter that you have proof that I am related to the Melungeon Gibsons, because that isn't going to change who I am, who my mother is and who my ancestors are," she says as we both light another cigarette. And the part that interests me—it is *very* interesting, is about people having the same experiences in that community. That's what interests me—what my family and ancestors have gone through, it is all about stuff that builds character, and why you cut off the bottom of the ham or why ... it is about the challenges and hardships they endured that gives me admiration for those people. I think it is the altruism of it all—giving selflessly to see someone enjoy just a few minutes 'cause you took the time to make them feel special."

"Ultimately, it comes down to who you *want* to be," she explains. "I don't want anyone to walk away from my house feeling unwelcome—you've said yourself I'd let Charles Manson in if he wanted a cup of coffee. The idea that you can have nothing and still be happy, take care of your family, and still welcome someone into your house as if they are part of your family and have them feel that way and truly believe they are welcome, that's who I am, who I want to be, how I want to be remembered. I don't need some piece of paper or documentation telling me that's what I am."

Kateri Virginia Irene

Now there is something else, there is something exciting, there's not just the boring ol' Whitehall girl I thought I was my whole life.

Kateri is my daughter. She started going with me on field studies when she was seven years old and has been a great traveling companion and researcher her entire life. I remember her buckled in the front seat, map on her lap, and eyes on the road signs helping me navigate through two-lane mountain highways by the time she was ten. By the time she was twelve she could determine bathroom breaks and meals by figuring one minute for every highway mile we had yet to go. She was my first GPS.

From the time she was in sixth grade, Kateri participated in Michigan's state level competition for the National History Day organization. She had made it to Nationals in eighth grade, earning the top prize for Black History for her documentary on the Civil Rights Movement. Her background with technology and research, using primary documents and inter-

Kateri (Stachowicz) Petrie in 2017.

views, laid a foundation that would influence my own research while creating a bond between the two of us that transcended many traditional mother-daughter relationships.

One of my trips for research took us to Middlesboro, Kentucky, to locate and introduce us to newly discovered family members in 2012. I also wanted to have a first-hand experience and feel for the area, the cemeteries, the courthouse, and my reception as a family member and researcher. I brought Kateri with me, and we researched together. She would take pictures, remember the recorder, and help me dig through records and traipse through graveyards. Always a good sport, she even took up a stick to warn away snakes while we looked for my great-grandmother's headstone.

"It's kind of cool to meet Katie and her sister," said Kateri with one hand on the steering wheel and one on the straw she was chewing on. "It was really interesting. Kind of validated all the stories we have heard. It made it so someone else lived that way, besides Grandma," she acknowledged. Having lived in Michigan her entire life, so far removed from the era of my mother's childhood, Kateri didn't know anyone else with similar accounts. "I probably will share these stories with my children. It is interesting, a part of our family and our history." Not thrilled with me for bringing out the recorder, Kateri continued to twist and chomp on the plastic McDonald's straw. She had just turned eighteen and would graduate from high school in June. Trying an old tactic, I asked her what were the top three things that intrigued her about her grandmother's first cousins and what they had to say. "That they lived without indoor plumbing or electricity," she started, "that they would even after being with all of that at the home, that they would go back to living that way. And lastly, that they would make their own potions and remedies from plants and things they found in the mountains." We laughed together, crossing the bridge into Cincinnati. Turning the radio up full blast, we sing at the top of our lungs, bobbing our heads and grinning.

A few weeks later Kateri agrees to allow me to video tape an interview for my documentary. I give her time to do her hair and make-up while I pose her in front of the fireplace in the dining room. My mother's high school graduation photo is on the mantel, but I don't discover that until I start editing. We both detest the formality of the interview process and just keep running the tape while we laugh and joke and try to get to the meat of the research. It will be the interspersed crystals of clarity that will prove priceless. I ask her if she considers herself Melungeon and she begins shaking her head before I finish the words. "I have thought I was a little Southern because Grandma grew up that way and we took her ways, like

Kateri Stachowicz helping with research.

canning and stuff like that." Kateri continues saying, "I really honestly have no idea, because I'm one of those people who wants facts, I want to know even—it doesn't have to be DNA, I want you to tell me what the characteristics are, then I will decide if I have 'em." We reflect on our conversations with Darlene Wilson and the comments she made about who is a Melungeon. "Do you have evidence in your family of being oppressed, marginalized, in the workplace or in the community? If you share that history, then you might be a Melungeon. If you can't find Granny on the census, you might be a Melungeon," she says. Kateri and I discuss Darlene's comments, "History would say I am Melungeon," says Kateri, "but you and me did not grow up in southern Appalachia, so we wouldn't be one. Grandma grew up there so she would be, but we would not," she reasons. "Are we looked down upon now? Have we been discriminated against?" She asks. When I shake my head she replies, "Then you and me would not be Melungeon according to those characteristics."

I ask my daughter from whom she needs to hear the answer: the documentation or family stories? "I just don't know and that's the thing. Grandma Sylvia would probably say we're Melungeon," Kateri laments, "she'd probably say it. I guess that's the hard part, 'cause it sounds like everyone down there is trying to find out what it is and the groups are different in what they believe it is and who they say can claim it. They are not compromising and each is saying the other is wrong."

Kateri has always had a penchant for rules; she feels most comfortable with issues that have clear solutions—black or white—yes or no. She will make a great accountant someday as long as her employer or client doesn't hope for creative accounting!

"So you need evidence," I ask her. "All of my life, you have stressed having historians, okay, bad examples, because they didn't live there," she says, "you've always stressed the importance of having extremely educated people who have dedicated large parts of their lives to researching this one topic. You stressed over and over that those are the credible sources," she says, making air quotes. "So, I am in between. I wouldn't want someone not very educated to tell me this is what a Melungeon is—I'd wonder do you have the resources to go back hundreds of years to find out stuff? But then, I don't want someone extremely educated making all the decisions because they weren't there, they don't know, they didn't live it," she insists. Kateri is not conscious of the camera for a few moments and is looking directly at me. "To me the people who are still living like that, that are full Melungeon let's say, they are the ones that should come up with a definition to decide who's a Melungeon."

So what does this all mean? "I think probably it is cool to say I am Southern, or I do have Melungeon people in my ancestry," Kateri says, twisting her hair. "Personally it's because you want to tell people that there is something else to you other than just here in Whitehall. Now there *is* something else, there is something exciting, there's not just the boring ol' Whitehall girl I thought I was my whole life."

The Gibson family consisted of Sylvia Ray's first cousins by her Uncle Cecil Gibson and Aunt Rose Gibson. Cecil had married Geneva Nash and had seven children in quick succession. Rose Gibson married Brownlow Reed and also had several children. With most of the cousins still living in the Cumberland Gap area of east Tennessee, southeast Kentucky, and western Virginia, these kin grew up playing with one another and still held annual family reunions.

Katie Hillison and Wilma King were two of seven siblings born to Arbie Gibson and Geneva Nash in the Middlesboro area of Kentucky. Arbie Gibson was my grandmother, Addie Gibson's, brother, making us second cousins. We had never met until this project.

Katie Hillison

My first interactions with Katie were via Facebook. I was doing genealogy and searching for relatives who might have a Melungeon connection. I had copied some pictures of people I didn't know from my grandmother's photo album and posted them online. Katie recognized them as her sister and herself in front of the girls' dormitory at Henderson Settlement in Frakes, Kentucky. We began a conversation in the summer of 2012 as I was beginning a pilot study and documentary on Melungeons. For several months our conversations consisted of chats on the social media website. I introduced myself on a private chat and immediately got a reply. I told her what I was researching, and she replied, "We have Melungeon on both sides of the family.... Gibson and Nash both are Melungeon surnames."

I was very excited to have connected and hopeful that I might learn more about my own family. I asked her if she remembered the word *Melungeon* being used when she was a child. "Not Melungeon, just 'dark skinned people,'" she replied. "I remember Daddy saying he was taken to visit at a family reunion and there were black children there. He asked why they were there and was told they were his kin. I have Indian and dark skinned people on my mother's side too," she explained. "Melungeon

Katie (Gibson) Hillison and granddaughter.

wasn't always black, they were just dark skinned." She had only just met me and seemed genuinely pleased to connect, adding smiley faces and hearts and calling me family.

We chatted a few times, and I arranged to go to Kentucky and Tennessee for research. Katie and her sister were in the process of moving to Corbin, Kentucky. I was traveling with my daughter, and we had carved out a chunk of time to stop and visit. The home was a newer ranch-style with a manicured lawn and flowers. I had a little bit of a problem with directions so Katie was standing on the porch with the phone, talking me through the maze of Corbin. She had short blond hair that was highlighted and cut into a fashionable style. She was wearing shorts in the August heat. Coming up to the car, she gave me a strong hug, wrapping her arms around me like we had known each other all of our lives. Her blue eyes lit up, she smiled broadly and invited me into the house, still holding her phone.

In we went to the living room where we all sat down and began to get acquainted. I tried to explain how I was able to use family stories and genealogy in my schoolwork and research. I talked about Melungeons and family members with dark skin. Katie was forthcoming and seemed eager to connect stories with people, figuring out who belonged to which narrative and how we all fit into the family puzzle. She laughed easily and sincerely. We talked for a little over an hour, and I promised to return with my mom, whom they hadn't seen in close to sixty years. We would plan on more time to visit other family members and take a drive to the old home place.

Over the course of the next few months Katie and I shared messages and phone calls, pictures and thoughts, about a Melungeon identity. I shared with her my first attempt at putting together a short video about my mother's search for identity, and I waited eagerly for her opinion. I shared the video with her online and waited and waited. I finally sent a message asking if she had a chance to watch it. "I ended up taking it off YouTube after a week since I was afraid that it would end up in the wrong hands, and some family members would be upset!" I explained. This was her reply:

> Tammy, I did watch the video ... you did a great job interviewing your Mom.... I'm glad you did take it off though because some people might get a little bent out of shape over the Melungeon side of it.... I don't know why ... to me it didn't mean having African American in the family it meant people with a darker skin color, not black, but darker toned ... but for some reason ... even now ... they want to hide it. I just wish there was a way that wasn't so expensive to verify if you are or not [speaking of DNA]...we may never know for sure ... but it doesn't hurt to speculate.

I thanked Katie and asked her if I should apologize to anyone or even stop doing the research. While she assured me that I owed no one any apologies, it was clear that the idea of being Melungeon and the possibility of having any black ancestors was still quite painful for many family members. Noting how tenuous the relationship was, how new and unproven, I proceeded cautiously. I was surprised at how important this relationship was becoming to me. I wanted to belong; I wanted to be accepted into the family I'd just discovered. This feeling would continue to grow throughout the project, helping me understand that studying a population was much different from telling the life story of individual people. Their experiences were like small gems in my hands that required careful protection. They trusted me, and I wouldn't let them down.

> Call anytime Tammy ... if I'm working ... just leave me a message and I will try to get back to you. Some takes offense at being labeled Melungeon.... I don't find it

offensive at all.... You are what you are ... no changing your ancestors.... LOL... My family has it on both sides.... I even think the Nash's and Gibson's have to be related also ... we have way too many family names in common. I find it fascinating ... mostly because I can remember Daddy talking about having dark skinned relatives... it didn't bother him ... just sort of shocked him....

Cousins

The next time I saw Katie I had my sister and mother with me, and we had agreed to meet at a steak house in Corbin, Kentucky. I had been visiting at Wilma's house with her and her husband Joe, so we left from there, taking Wilma with us. Katie met us there. We were shown to a long table to accommodate all of us. Joe had stayed home, which left three generations of women to gather and discuss family stories. The restaurant was buffet style, and we filled our plates and started talking. I left the recorder going as the music played in the background and snippets of conversation floated around us. As often happens when women get together, the talk touched on husbands, children, and miscellaneous pieces of life.

"They had their own language, both Grandma Gibson and Grandma Nash did," said Wilma. "Yeah," said Katie, "they'd call a dresser a vanity." "They'd be saying 'get away from that vanity.'" "And a porch was a veranda." "Get down from that veranda," two of the sisters said at once. "Yeah. And a couch was a settee." "Remember Mamaw asking you if you got your bloomers on?" "They'd call panties bloomers and bras were braziers," Wilma added. Then Mom chimed in, "Yep and remember what Mamaw would call underpants? She'd call 'em step-ins." "Yep," responded Katie, "she would call them step-ins." "And, when a girl would have her period they'd say the health come up on her, or the sickness did," added Wilma. The laughter was contagious, and it was hard to keep up with who was saying what. There was absolutely no way to control the conversation or steer it into any specific direction.

Eventually the chatter turned to the old home place and the family cemetery. "What did I tell you about going up there—don't go up there by yourself, I promise you I wouldn't," added Wilma. She described renegade people living up there growing pot and having stills. We knew there were snakes at the cemetery because of a young man who directed us to the hard to find plots. He had told us to take a stick in front of us to startle any snakes and get them to leave before we inadvertently stepped on them. "Are you serious?" I asked him. "As a heart attack," he assured me, showing me how to tap the ground and sweep with the stick.

"They say there's some money buried up there," suggested Katie. Their great-grandfather had purchased the land and added to the original plot. His siblings and children lived in small houses up and down a dirt lane that wound itself around the mountain in what used to be Edgewood, on the west side of Middlesboro, Kentucky. "Daddy told me there was a gold mine up there, a silver mine up there, and a copper mine up there," said Wilma. "Well, yes, Uncle Goode buried money up there, I know about where he had his moonshine still up there. I know about where it's at and we could look up there." A hike with metal detectors sounded exciting to all of us as the chatter ensued about money buried in mason jars with zinc lids. The cousins recalled finding jars sitting on a log with a dollar bill underneath them. My mother admitted to taking the dollar bill from under the jar and going shopping as a small child. We all laughed boisterously, amazed at the confession.

The cousins discussed various relatives who served time for counterfeiting silver dollars. "Daddy talked about it all the time," added Wilma. "They counterfeited those silver dollars, and John Doan and I believe Goode Gibson went to prison for it, and someone else I don't recall. Daddy used to talk about it all the time." The women all nodded in agreement. We all agreed that a trip to "treasure hunt" was in order.

The women began sharing stories about their husbands, and eventually everyone added to the conversation: things that bothered us, crazy notions they took, and how we all navigated the rough patches. "The women in this family are survivors," said Wilma. They each added to the tale of absent fathers, husbands that didn't help raise their children, and lack of financial support to keep the family together. Except for Wilma and me, all of the other women had been single mothers at one point in their lives. "It's hard for us to ask for any help. It's hard to ask for food," said Katie. Their struggle included fighting with the public schools to get their children (and themselves before) the help they needed with academics. My sister Arlene and Wilma talked about children with dyslexia. The common theme of transposing numbers and letters, even now, is yet another challenge to overcome.

We talked briefly about a Melungeon identity or Native American ancestry. Wilma expressed a real desire to know about her background, to find a clear identity that she could have for her own. "I want to know," she said. "Whether it is Melungeon or Indian, I want to know. Wouldn't you like to know?" she asked. "Mary Etta registered the Gibson blood line with the Cherokee Nation," said Katie referring to yet another cousin's wife who had been working on the family genealogy for years. "She put in for her family and I saw her name in there where she registered the Gibson name as Cherokee and her descendants from her husband's part of the family. They did get it. Charlie Gibson is on it."

Beans and Cornbread

Katie had promised me an authentic old-fashioned Southern dinner and was making good on her promise. She was vegetarian, very careful with their meal choices. I knew this was a gift for me, and I was anticipating it with great relish. I sat at the bar high table, asking questions and watching her in action. I ended up being a distraction, causing one whole pan of burned homemade cornbread. The burnt cornbread led to a hysterical conversation about cooking and baking. The sibling teasing reminded me of conversations with my sister, and I enjoyed the easy banter. We all laughed.

I asked how we would ever know what our identity was, whether it was Indian, Melungeon, or even Portuguese. "There wasn't any true documentation," Katie explains, "because they were ashamed of their dark skin." Katie notes that is why they went into the backwoods of Kentucky, Tennessee, and Virginia. "They hid it, they'd tell the census records they were white. Then they would marry lighter skinned, so their kids would be light. A lot of people up Stinking Creek are Melungeons, it's a place like you're going back in time. They don't have electricity, they have outhouses, and they are real tight knit, they don't like outsiders. They live up in the mountains where no one wanted to go because it was too rough to live. They even had their own language up there." She continues to explain that the difference between mountain people and Melungeons was the dark skin. "Some were African American but some of them are mixed with Indian or Spanish people. They were ashamed of it because they weren't white. They were treated like black people, caught as runaway slaves and stuff like that. A lot of white girls would have a baby by a man with darker skin and since they weren't accepted anymore they'd go live with the darker people. They are ashamed, they don't want to be associated with Melungeons—it is a shame thing."

Katie had done quite a bit of reading about Melungeons before we had met. I thought back to our first communication and realized she had been researching this area for some time, and that she knew she had Melungeon on both sides of her family before I ever said a thing. "That's how I know it is something people don't want to be associated with. It isn't just African Americans, it was a foreign race of people or Indians, just people with darker skin. Like some Indians are just so dark they are almost like a black person—their skin was darker. Around here I don't recall ever seeing a black person period, they didn't associate with white people unless they were the help. Here you will find, not like up north, people still, especially in this area here—they still have the KKK, the Klan, and race things in Barbourville. It still goes on. They'll come in and hold a meeting there."

She continues, obviously disturbed by the local sentiment against people of color. She shakes her head, still stirring the beans and remaking the cornbread mix. The potatoes had already been peeled and sliced and were frying in an electric skillet. "I don't understand where poor white trash come from either," she said, "just 'cause you're poor doesn't mean you're trash. I just don't get that at all, just because people's house isn't up to someone else's standard. Poor white trash, TRASH," she says again with disgust, "I just don't get it. Just 'cause they're poor." Katie scurries between the pans, stirring and checking the oven to be sure the next batch of cornbread doesn't burn. She is so open and sincere that it is easy to see the empathy in her facial expressions as she discusses the treatment of people in this community.

"I admire you for this; it's stuff people don't want to delve into," she says brightening, looking at me with a smile. "I don't know how you're going to present this stuff though. You have to process it in your mind. They don't want to be found, some thinks you should leave it alone. They hid it when the census takers came around, said they was white. They felt better 'cause they put it down and thought that was it, from then on no one would know the difference. They'd be white."

"Now some people say, 'Yes, I am [Melungeon].' There is no way to prove it. Unless you get that DNA done. Then you can see what amount of Indian blood you have in you," she explains. I ask her what if she got the test done and the blood work said there wasn't any Native American in her. "That would be hard," she replied, "because we've always been told, even look at Grandma, you could tell." She thinks on this a moment. I wonder aloud, "Aren't our personal stories from our ancestors more important than DNA?" She chuckles a bit, "I'd like to think so."

I explained some information I had received from another interviewee that said Melungeons couldn't go downtown and get food so they had to raise their own. Immediately she jumps on the statement. "Did you hear that part? They couldn't go to town," she says emphatically, "they weren't allowed in the stores, they couldn't use the bathroom in town, they would have to go way around out of town to use the bathroom just because they were darker skin. I recall all the black people moving into their own community, they were not allowed to ride the school buses, they had their own colored school, their own colored church, they stayed in their own community. There were some they called yellow skinned, there was white, and really black, black people—not brown," she explained.

Referring to the family stories, the only thing she ever heard about ethnic people was the story about the reunion that her father went to as a child where he saw black children being referred to as kin. "That's the only thing I ever heard about dark skinned people except for Indian and they've always been proud of that far as I can remember," said Katie. "I'd be proud to be called Cherokee," she added. "It is all so controversial."

Dinner was done, and we were just waiting for Katie's sister to come home from her job. Katie went to her room and brought back a stack of books written by Johnnie Sue Bridges who describes growing up in Middlesboro and then heading to Detroit like so many other families. Johnnie Sue had taken the books home to sign them with a personal note and Bible verse. She offered to let me borrow them and send them back down to her through the mail when I had finished. Katie told me that there were stories about other relatives within the book. "She mentions Opal [a first cousin on the Gibson side]. She would swing on grapevines, we all did. She was a real pretty girl. I told Johnnie Sue that was my people you're talking about," she replied, telling me about another story referencing her mother's sister.

Speaking of her mother, she wanted to explain another tale about hiding under her maternal grandmother's house during a storm. "Mommy was trying to hide us from the law," she told me. "Daddy got full custody of us and Mommy didn't want to let go," Katie explained. So she hid us under Grandma Nash's house. It was storming, raining real bad, with thunder and lightning. We had a blanket to lay on and one to put over us," she describes, "and me and Katie was both wanting to be in the middle. Then our big sister got in the middle and told us 'there, you're both in the middle,' and somehow that quieted us down."

But her father couldn't care for all of those children appropriately, so William H. Gibson, his father, stepped in, insisting that the kids go to Henderson Settlement, a home and school for kids in the area who needed caring for. They stayed at the settlement for five years. "I had just turned 12 when we got there," said Katie. "It was my first ever birthday cake and ice cream. We never celebrated birthdays, hardly ever even had a Christmas tree. And we sure never had no three meals a day, we didn't know what to make of all that food. We had breakfast, we had lunch, we had supper, and we had a snack," she exclaimed. Katie, Wilma, Goldie, Sue, their older sister, along with their brother Buddy, all went to the settlement. The youngest, a baby named Joyce Ann, stayed with her mother. They all remember the settlement with fondness and gratitude, even if there were some heartbreaking moments. While the siblings recognize the shortcomings of their parents, there is also a great deal of love and loyalty. They express a considerable amount of empathy and protection for their parents' memories as well.

"I was just a little thing and I could remember when each of my brothers died," said Wilma. "We were having a terrible storm, awful. It was raining and had been for a long time and there was floods. I don't know where Daddy was. Bobby Wayne had that spina bifida and I remember Mommy carried him off that porch and stepped down two steps and then down into the water. She had to wade in the water and some man with a hat came to get her. He was standing there, and he said, 'C'mon we got to get out of here.' She went down there covered in a homemade quilt, I remember thinking how is he gonna breathe under there? She took him to Middlesboro hospital and the ambulance driver that took them to Knoxville said she was screaming at them, 'My baby's dying, someone help me.' And they said there wasn't anything they could do, so they went to Knoxville and that driver told Sis all about that. I just remember he told Sis about Mommy saying 'He's dying, he's dying, someone help me.' And that water was so deep.

"That Christmas before he died, the Salvation Army brought us a box of toys, they were used. We never had a Christmas tree or gift until the settlement, didn't even know what Christmas was. But, that year they brought us two dolls, and me and Katie got a doll and we got names out of the reader from school and named them Peter and Jane. After Bobby Wayne died, we buried the dolls in shoe boxes in the back yard down there in Middlesboro behind the grocery—now this is the way two little girls cope with the death of their brother, knowing he wasn't never coming home. I was 5 or 6 years old. And Mommy wasn't never the same."

"I had just left my husband," Katie told me, "and me and the girls went over and lived in Barbourville. Someone called me and said, 'You better go see about your dad, he's walking up and down the middle of the road and he's not looking too good.'" Together, Katie and Wilma "kidnapped" their father. He was lying in a bunk very ill with pneumonia when the girls got him in the back of Wilma's truck. "He just was so sick, could hardly breathe. I said Daddy, you're not gonna make it if you don't do something," Wilma says, "I'll tell you what, you let me know when you have to throw up and we'll pull over." "You can live with me," Katie told him. "He was so dirty I was ashamed to take him to the hospital like that. I said 'Daddy, you can come home with me right now, but I'm not taking you back to this filth.' He thought about it a minute and said, 'I'll go with you.' I said 'now Daddy, I'm not gonna bring you back,'" she says seriously. "I took him to the house and put him in the bath, even though he was sick, and got him some clothes. They told me when I brought him if he had not come in that day he wouldn't have made it. I had to burn the clothes he was wearing." Her face is flushed with the memory as she stands in the kitchen, a spoon in her hand.

"Mommy sold Joyce Ann," said Katie, continuing to reminisce. "Yeah, Mommy sold her for $500 to a lady over in Frakes. Johnnie Sue loves this story," exclaims Katie. I grabbed a plate over by the fried potatoes and started loading up as she recounted the story. I put a serving of potatoes on my plate, then got a piece of cornbread. Over by the beans there was a stack of bowls, and I filled one up with crumbled cornbread, putting the beans over the top. A pan full of greens rounded out the meal, and I headed to the table.

I try to convince Katie to let me get a picture of her cooking. She is a paradox of sweet kindness and blunt honesty. She seems to be the voice of reason within the family, practical and hardworking; she is also the one most likely to worry about protecting the feelings of others. She won't let me get her picture, holding her hand up and turning her head. The rest of us laugh in acknowledgment. Katie wins, and I don't get a picture.

"Mommy would tell us, he wasn't our daddy," Katie said resignedly. "We'd be saying something and Mommy would say, 'What are you worried for? He isn't *your* daddy!' She said it to all of us as we got older."

Geneva, their mother, had said she didn't quite know to whom Katie belonged. "So really, ain't none of us could be kin." Then we all hooted with laughter. Katie continued, "That's what Buddy was getting at about doing the DNA, he said, 'You really want to go there?'"

Wilma King

"I would want to know," said Wilma about being Melungeon. "I'd really want to know, whether it was Melungeon or Indian, I want to know." Joe, Wilma's husband, had told her there wasn't any Cherokee in her background. He'd tell her to go look in the mirror to she was too light skinned with blonde hair. "I've had trouble with my identity. I want to know where I come from. I would love to get the blood test about Melungeon or Cherokee. I want to tell Joe, 'You never seen my grandmothers and great-grandmothers,'" Wilma says. "They were Indian."

I had driven up to Wilma and Joe's on one visit by myself. Mom and Arlene were staying in the hotel room after an exhausting cold and windy day, traipsing through cemeteries. Arlene and I had done some grave rubbings with charcoal on the backs of a desktop calendar. I was excited to show Wilma and see if she remembered any of the names or could explain any connections to the graves I had found. *M*A*S*H* was playing on the television in the background while Joe was sitting at the table smoking. I laid out the papers on the kitchen island and began to describe where all I had been. One of the graves had three links of chain on the headstone, and we had looked up the meaning and found it had something to do with being a Mason. "These are very important," said Wilma, examining the papers. It was hard to make out the writing on some of them, and we discussed the possibility of changing the resolution on the pictures I had taken to see if that helped.

I had been stumped about the above ground crypts and was hoping either Wilma or Joe would know why so many Gibsons were buried that way. There was one couple, J.N. and Elizabeth Gibson, who were buried in Virginia around the turn of the century in those same kinds of crypts. I wondered who they were, and Wilma had no idea. "Keep in mind though,

Wilma (Gibson) King.

over in Tennessee and Virginia there were a LOT of Gibsons," said Joe. We talked a bit more about genealogy, what we could find in historical documents, and what it might tell us about our background and ethnicity. We were laughing about so many things we might never know that I admitted to one of my more comical research mistakes: a two day search for a cluster of women with the last name Lnu. Finally, I googled the name to find out what background there was and discovered it stood for Last Name Unknown. We laughed hard then, almost crying over the silly mistake that had cost hours of research time.

"I wanted to show you these pictures of when we first went to Henderson Settlement," said Wilma, sliding a newsletter over for me to see. In the *Kentucky Missions* newsletter, dated March 15, 1963, was an article featuring before and after pictures of all six Gibson children under a headline that read, "Henderson Settlement Six Million Dollars Richer." The article starts by saying, "We have recently taken into our care six wonderful children—the Gibson children. We figure that each one of them is worth no less than a million dollars. Therefore we count that we are six million dollars richer, at least, than the last time we went to press." It was a wonderful interpretation of events in the Gibson family and the Henderson Settlement community. Licensed by the state of Kentucky as a child-care institution with a public school on the grounds, the settlement was home to the Gibson children for five years.

"I remember them putting us in the showers, it was oh so bad, they disinfected us thinking we had bugs or something," described Wilma, "you know, like when they did that to prisoners. There was a bathroom out in the back and it had a shower, they took us back there and made us take off all our clothes and put new ones on after we took a shower. They washed us, we was all scrubbed down, washed our hair and scrubbed us with stinky stuff. That was traumatic," she described. The first day at the settlement seemed to her as one necessary evil to an otherwise good opportunity.

"Other than that they was so good to us. Sometimes Katie thought they was mean to us. They had chores for us, some of us had to work the kitchen, or the dining room, I loved to work in the kitchen til they stopped all the girls from working in there. I loved to help the cook, she was the sweetest woman you would ever meet. I loved cooking, helped bake cakes for the girls for their birthdays. I made my clothes, even the eighth grade graduation dress," she says with pride. Wilma continues, describing those first days when the caregivers allowed Buddy, their little brother, to stay with the girls in the girls' dormitory until they all settled into a routine. "Eventually, they took Buddy to the boys' dorm. He was little, the bigger boys liked to have killed him, they treated him awful. They took him out one time and rubbed poison ivy all over him, in his eyes, all over his poor little back, and more," she says with sympathy. She looks back to me, blue eyes clear and sincere. Her short blond hair is curled and styled, and her skin seems to glow. She wanted to see her brother—and she begged them to let her see her him. That's when she "seen him lookin' all broke out. He had those little puss sacks oozing all over him, his eyes swollen shut ... he never did anything to those big boys. He had such a hard time, got picked on all the time."

Wilma describes how she ended up going from her mother's house to her father's custody and, ultimately, to Henderson Settlement. "Grandpa Gibson hated Mommy, hated her with a passion," she explained. "It was so bad with Grandma and Grandpa Gibson, we knowed him as Uncle Bill. Mommy was beautiful, but Grandma Gibson hated every one of them Nash girls—I don't know why, and I don't even know how they knew each other since they didn't live near one another," Wilma says calmly, explaining the relationship between her mother and aunts with her paternal grandparents. "They looked like Indians—Goldie Thompson was a sister to my grandmother Doshie. Grandma Gibson and Grandma Nash did both look like an Indian, too. Grandma Nash's hair went all the way down her back," she said, "they was Holiness and didn't believe in cutting their hair. She would plait it and then wrap it around their head and sometimes put a wrap or scarf around their head to keep it up." Wilma describes her Grandma Nash teaching her to plait hair by letting the little girl brush and practice on her grandma's hair.

"The one house we had that had the dirt floors, our grandparents lived in that before we did," she continued describing her early years. "Mommy told Daddy when he came home to get out and go get a job— that his kids was starving to death and he needed to get some money and help raise them kids. He worked, picking up scrap metal and junk. He just never seemed to make much money." Geneva would get commodities, such as flour meal, powdered milk, eggs, pinto beans, and lard that she would try to stretch to feed seven growing children. To the girls it seemed Geneva would prefer that Arbie stay gone and send a check home while she continued to collect commodities and run around.

We continued to look at other pictures and papers that she had collected to show me, Wilma describing people and places as we went through them. "Luke Mason," she said, "lived down on the beltline there in Middlesboro and took a lot of them pictures." This was another name I was quite familiar with as my Grandmother, Addie Gibson, had maintained a decades-long love affair with him. She had even brought him to our childhood home in Michigan to visit while separated from the man I knew as my pawpaw. I described how I knew Luke Mason, and Wilma revealed her own knowledge of infidelities and broken families. "You know Daddy and Grandpa was like that," she said. "They all was messing around. You wouldn't know just how many children Grandpa had there around Middlesboro." We laughed as we wondered if it wasn't a good thing that my family had left Middlesboro, since "at least we will know we aren't marrying our brother," we giggled.

We laughed about Joe's childhood stories until our sides hurt. Pranks, such as pouring water on the road to make ice so the school bus couldn't get up the mountain; calling the radio station, pretending to be the principal's son and calling off school; or even grabbing a still they found for the scrap metal. He talked about meeting up with the sheriff, with the still in the trunk, and telling him that they hadn't heard of any moonshine still around the area. Joe described Melungeons as a kind of Indian and knew a lot of them from Tennessee. "Sharps Chapel is a good neighborhood," remarked Joe, "we used to do a lot of fishing down there on Norris Lake. Instead of going down through Tazewell—we went down through the Powell Valley." He'd hold his cigarette with his thumb and middle finger, blowing the smoke up to the ceiling while we talked. His face, weathered and tan from years working construction and flea markets, Joe laughed easily and took joy in picking at his wife. Wilma described his morning ritual to annoy her making bubble noises with his mouth popping and clicking first thing in the morning. "It just annoys me to no end," she says. "I know it," grins Joe, "why do you think I do it?"

Joe and Wilma took me on a tour of the house, describing the years of work, patience, and faith it took to complete. "Took us ten years all together," Joe explained, "two summers to clean up the land. I came home one day with six windows and Wilma said, 'What are you gonna do with them?' I told her I was gonna build me a house and put 'em in." Joe laughs at the recollection, and his laugh is so contagious we all start in. "We didn't even have property then. I took her up there and to see if we can see what property was available and see if I can buy it. We drove around, it took us about two hours—I told her 'I think I'll buy it,' she said 'I hope you see more than I can see!'" The house is beautiful, decorated with antiques and mementos found over the years or collected from family and friends. Wilma has a craft area where projects lay in various stages of completion. Around every corner is a new discovery: a display of antique toys and games or an assortment of glassware.

We discuss my plans to meet Wilma the next morning with the metal detectors to scour the mountain, and I tell her I hope she can join us. I promise to give a call when I get up since we are leaving early, and she agrees to let me know when she is back from a medical appointment for Joe. I turn off the recorder as I gather my things, and I am still laughing, amazed at some of Joe's antics. I reach out to hug them both before leaving and think of one more question. I asked if it bothers them the way Southerners are portrayed in some of the reality shows now on television, stuff like the Turtleman, *Swamp People*, and *Here Comes Honey Boo Boo*. "No, I don't get mad about them," said Wilma. "But, when they have a tornado come through and they dig up some woman with curlers and no teeth and a diaper wrapped around her head saying 'We didn't know it was a'coming till we heard it like a train—whooo, whooo.' I wonder just where do they dig up these people?"

Treasure Hunt

On the way back to the hotel, I stopped at the Walmart right across from where I was staying. Katie had suggested I needed hiking boots, or at least rubber boots, and I wanted some other supplies for the hike: a small garden spade, some bug spray, and a hat. I found a pair of high rubber boots, gathered my other items, and checked out. Prepared for the following day, I fell into a fitful sleep. Anticipating the treasures we might find, I tossed and turned, also worrying about the likelihood of running across snakes. The next day promised to be hot, in the 90s, with high humidity. We had decided to get up early before the heat set in and drive out to the home place. I had purchased three metal detectors so that all of us would have the opportunity to discover a treasure. I met them at the designated parking lot, and we transferred my purchases to the back of Katie's van alongside another metal detector, an ax, and a shovel. We stopped to get the batteries that I had forgotten the night before and then headed up the mountain.

Our first stop was a little spot where the Gibsons had their house. The chimney was still standing, and I grabbed a couple of fallen bricks as souvenirs. I also picked up the small broken pieces of a glass light fixture. In my mind's eye I thought of how I might add them to a mosaic of other mementos we found. Quickly we noted that the vegetation had grown quite a bit since last fall, covering paths and landmarks. The wild rose bushes reached out and snagged our arms and our pants, combing through my hair, leaving thorns and leaves. Right away the detector buzzed and we didn't dig far before finding a rolled up piece of fencing wire. I dropped it in my bag, and kept going. The machines kept buzzing as we found nails, pop cans, an oil filter, and more small pieces of plastic coated wire used in electronics.

My next treasure was a corroded hinge, with pieces of rust and mud flaking off, that still opened and closed. In the bag it went as we kept on trying to find where the old still was. We were really looking for money or counterfeited coins and any other evidence of the mines. We loaded everything back into the van, deciding to drive up the mining road as close as we could get to where the still had been. There was no way we would make it up the side of that mountain through the briars, shrubs, and kudzu vines. We decided it would be easier to drive up than try to find our way down from our present angle.

We were all excited, but hot, draining bottles of water as we hiked. What a sight we must have been. I was in the worst shape by far, huffing and puffing up the steep, rocky, muddy road. We left all but one detector in the van, taking one shovel and the bag with water in it. Twice we were sure we had the right spot; the second time we wound through a tiny path we could still make out. A small stream wound itself in front of us, and the ground all around us got a little boggy. Here and there the detector would buzz, and we'd stop to dig for a bit, finding pieces of long buried trash. Our hearts never ceased to jump with the familiar buzz and fall just a bit when the metal was uncovered. As we turned a corner in the path, a little clearing came into view on the other side of a row of trees. On the edge of that little clearing, I could just make out a tiny shack that looked inhabited before Katie quickly turned us around with urges to be quiet and "get the hell out of here." I slogged through the hillside as quickly as my chubby legs and rubber boots would let me, trying to stifle a giggle. By the time we got to the dirt road, we were all laughing out loud, figuring we had just escaped being noticed. The adrenalin of the moment hit us as we ran to the van, hopped inside, and headed back to where we had started.

The novelty of the hunt was wearing off. Katie and I dug for a bit more, trying to unearth what was most likely a car part. The detector emitted a strong buzz near a hole (where the barn would have been) that was 1.5 feet in diameter by 1 foot deep. The metal object we had found was large, and the earth was not about to let it go. Eventually we gave up, marked the spot to come back to in the fall, and filled in the hole.

I glanced in my bag to inventory my treasures: pieces of glass, a brick, a hinge, a wire, and a plate, which I had found on top of the ground near the path. Sitting in the van, heading back to my car, I completed the inventory: pieces of history, members of family, answers to stories, and questions still begging to be answered. We finished the morning by going to the Cumberland Gap Park to see an old iron furnace. We also visited a bicycle museum and took pictures next to an old grist mill where the water wheel was still spinning. We grinned at one another, finding pleasure in the tinkling of water over the rocks and the way the sunlight sparkled on the moss growing on the damp rocks inside the oven. Katie showed me how to suck the nectar of a honeysuckle flower.

Katie continues to reminisce about her mother. "The best thing about her I remember is she loved to sing hymns and she had a decent voice. She sang on the radio station with her sisters when she was younger," she says. "I think ALL the experiences you go through in life makes you the person you are at the end of your life," says Katie, much like Wilma says, "everything from being at Henderson Settlement to being stuck under the floor, it all makes us who we are.

"Life was really hard back then and there wasn't many happy times. But my Dad took the time to do a little dance when he came in from work," Katie says, describing how her father would get the kids to laughing with his rendition of an authentic mountain jig. "Even though it was hard back-breaking work, he would try to find humor and a laugh where he could. He was a hard worker and worked his whole life, he just never made a lot of money and sometimes he was out of a job for a while but never for long. He was delivering meals to people when he was in his late 60s and 70s and still digging graves to make extra money. He took us to parks (a lot of times without my mom) and on visits to family. People always spoke highly of him. He wanted to keep in touch with everybody he could, used to take us to visit people all the time," said Katie. "And if he could have remembered where the people were located in Tennessee he would have taken us to visit our dark people," she said laughing. "He had a remarkable sense of humor."

Anna Reed Partin

> We're second cousins, cause me and Sylvia's first cousins—so we are double kin, that's why we feel like sisters.

Anna Reed's mother and my mother's mother were sisters—and my mother Sylvia's paternal grandmother and Anna's paternal grandmother were sisters, making them "double kin."

"Now did you know your Grandma Addie?" Anna asked me. I explained that I had known my Grandmother Addie all my life, until she passed away when I was twenty years old. "She wanted us to call her 'Ann,' and she only ate ever' other day," she said laughing. "She'd say 'It ain't my day to eat!'" Anna laughed easily. Her silver hair and brown eyes looked so familiar to me, it was almost like looking at myself in twenty years. Laugh lines framed her eyes and mouth, and her eyes twinkled in that way all Gibsons seem to—with small, tilted eyes, that are expressive, revealing every thought and feeling. Anna is tall, probably about 5'7" and seventy years old. She

Anna (Reed) Partin and author Tammy Stachowicz, 2013.

is wearing jeans and the same red and black paisley shirt she had on the day before when I had stopped with Katie. She offered me a rolling desk chair in the large sewing room where she works. The antiquated industrial sewing machines and sergers were sitting on tables with spools and bobbins of thread in a variety of colors lining the walls. A curtain was stretched between two poles to make a dressing room for customers coming for alterations.

"I keep busy," Anna exclaimed as a loud buzzer went off announcing the arrival of a client. The petite woman in her 60s came in with an armful of clothes to be altered. Stepping aside to draw the curtain, Anna laughed and kept up a stream of conversation between me and the woman changing her clothes. "Your grandma used to hang out a lot with Cecil's girl, Anna Pearl," she said. I told her an experience I had had in Florida with my grandmother, Anna Pearl, and her daughter. Grandma had a beauty shop in one end of her house trailer with a ramp leading up to the door. The ramp ran perpendicular to the house, creating a small yard under massive pine trees. Lawn chairs were arranged along with a green canvas hammock where my mother, siblings, and I sweltered in the July heat. Anna Pearl and her daughter Sherry were sitting in the air-conditioned trailer while we were ordered to stay outside during the heat of the day. "How come that?" Anna asked. "I have no idea," I laughed, recalling the discomfort of a small child of seven or eight, baking in the Florida sun. The woman stepped out, revealing the lopsided look of a shorter leg that became obvious with the mid-calf length pants. Anna knelt down with a handful of pins, evening out the leg length, while asking the woman to look in the mirror to okay her work.

"She's doing family stories for her school work," Anna tells the client. "Oh, don't let us tell you any bad stories," she says, laughter echoing in the room. The buzzer went off again, announcing someone else at the locked back door. "I'm popular," Anna exclaims, "I'm a sew-er!" "You're a seamstress," says the woman behind the curtain. "Oh, is that what I is," Anna asks giggling. "I had someone do some work on the family background," she added, "I think I've still got it." The woman steps out from behind the curtain again. "Well," says Anna, "which one do you wish for?" she asks, gesturing to the length of the capris. She turns to me saying, "You don't know the amount of people in this world that have one leg shorter than the other." The buzzer goes off again, and Anna's husband comes through the door. "This is Tammy, Jack—Sylvia's daughter.

"We've got problems down at that home—the heat pump went out," he mumbles around the wad of chew in his mouth. "I been working on the house for Janice to move back near home. Lord have mercy—the way we got everything piled up I don't know—I 'xpect RB will know," he says, referring to a heating and cooling firm he has called out. "Gotta move a tractor up out of that holler yet, too." He sits on the chair across from me, chattering away. I see that his finger is stiff and swollen, mangled a bit, and covered in a purple inky color. "See that," he says, "smashed it in the tailgate o' the truck, can't move it. I got that gentian violet on there, it will damn sure heal everything. When one of them girls would fall down and scape their knee, Papaw'd put that on there and the kids would all ask her about it at school. But it would heal overnight." The finger looked broken to me, and I wondered if he hadn't ought to go see a doctor about it. "Ain't never been one to go to the doctor and ain't gonna start now," he says grinning, blue eyes peeking from under a ball cap sheepishly. I mention that maybe he should think about retiring then. "Ain't gonna retire til my toes are turned up," he grins again, the soft Southern drawl tempered with the mumbling. "Don't believe in retirement…. I can't just sit around, hell, I gotta be up and out doing something." He motions for me to come with him out to the barn; he has something to show me. As we head out the door, Anna yells, "You be good to her," and I grin at the admonishment.

By the time Jack and I are back in the shop, Anna is busy with yet another woman, pinning and measuring. She calls everyone "honey" and is genuinely good-natured and happy. She is the proverbial sweet person that we all, at one time, have wished to be like. "Honey," she says to the new woman, "me and her mother were double first cousins. Our mother married a brother—like brother and brother—or something like 'at, I get it all mixed up. Her kids must be grown—she comes back and she wants to hear about the stories," she says chattering away. "Now me and her mother is just like sisters, Grandpa raised her 'til she was about eleven years old and we was real close."

After the clients have gone, Anna and I sit and drink bottled water she has in a small refrigerator in the shop. She goes into the house for something she wants to show me and returns with an envelope full of Ancestry.com charts and family trees. She had paid someone $20 for the small bit of research she held in her hands. Some of the papers were yellowed a bit, stapled into groups, and Anna tried to keep them in the same order, putting them back in the pile as Jack and I looked at them and gave them back. Jack began describing all kinds of Gibson relatives from the area as he picked up on names in the paperwork. He recalled several of Addie's daddy's brothers: Henry, Sherman, and Matt. "Then there was a Bill Sherman, Aunt Rose and Mamaw said he was William F. Gibson's bastard," he laughed, explaining the wayward ways of the Gibson men. "Now, Henry," he said, "he had some horses over there," gesturing up the mountain, "and did loggin' and he had a woman up there who was a secretary and Aunt Jeannie up there in the house." He kept his head down laughing, the tobacco still in his mouth, obviously tickled with the revelations.

"You'll put the pieces together," said Anna. "I can't—I don't even have a computer. I'll be seventy, God darn it—can you believe I've been with that sucker over fifty years?" she asks. The couple exchanges glances as Anna takes a seat back at her machine. The night before she had spoken to a gathering about losing weight and was proud of her presentation. Sitting there, she lifts her shirt and shows her underwear up above the waist of her jeans. She says, "since I lost my weight my panties come up under my thing." Jack says, "you's posed to hide your thing." "Well, I know," she answers, "but since I lost my weight my panties comes right up under my titties." Raucous laughter follows as well as other talk about panties and bras and great-aunts living their whole lives without such inconveniences.

Jack is leaning against the table where Anna puts notes and garments that require altering. "Now don't lean against that suit, honey, 'cause I'll have to pay for that if I done anything wrong to that suit." The familiar buzzer signals another customer as Jack opens the door in anticipation. "Tell me you love me, honey," the customer says to him, bringing the now recognizable handful of capri pants to be taken in and shortened. "I love you, honey," he replies, leaving and closing the door behind him. Anna explains who I am to the woman with the oft-repeated phrase, "we're second cousins, cause me and Sylvia's first cousins—so we are double kin, that's why we feel like sisters." Our conversations are interrupted time and again as Anna conducts business. I observe her treatment of every person, excited to see them, pleased that her work is recognized, and glad for the opportunities. She treats them all special, like they are long-lost sisters and brothers and that sewing is as natural as breathing and walking.

I longed for more information about my mother's family and knew she may very well hold the answer to several questions. She had never heard anyone talk bad about George Ray, my mom's biological father. But she did have an idea of why the couple broke up. "She was in love with Luke Mason," she said as if it was common knowledge. "Addie said they could heat a cover off a bed. She had left Vern to be with Luke at least once."

Anna was going back and forth behind the curtain and back out again, pinning and writing measurements on little post-it notes. They discuss how the presentation Anna did on the weight loss went. "It went pretty well, I guess," Anna says as the women discuss taking in the pants the client is wearing. "I know, honey," Anna soothes, "Look here what I can do with these pants." She grabs the waist of her jeans with both hands and yanks them down to her knees, demonstrating that she can pull them off without unbuttoning or unzipping them. They laugh as she stands there in her underwear, jeans around her ankles. The talk turns to weekend plans, family, and church.

"See why I love sewing? I meet lots of nice people and make me some friends," Anna exclaims. "Aw, I don't have time to clean house," she giggles. Conversations are all interspersed with customer comments and the language of sewing: pins and needles, types of fabric, double and single seams, and how to make garments more flattering. "I cut my finger with scissors this morning. I got to make sure I don't get no blood on anything," Anna says. "You want to know how to get blood out? If it is your blood you just spit on it and rub it around and it'll come out—if it is your blood. Now don't go sucking on no one else's blood, you'll get them diseases."

We sat back with our waters to swap stories after the shop cleared out. "Now Ad and Emily was real close," she said of her older sister and my grandmother. "They lived pretty close in Michigan, Ad went first then Emily went." She got to thinking about it, "She had to go with somebody, 'cause back then she didn't drive ... she didn't have a car. I bet anything she went up north with Luke Mason. Cecil [Addie's brother] went up to Michigan, and he had married a Mason, Luke's sister. That's how he came to be in the picture. I bet Mary Etta would be able to tell you." Mary Etta was Cecil's daughter-in-law and the family historian. I had been in touch with her on and off for years while working on genealogy.

"Now, I don't know how old your mother was when she left, but I used to play all the time with her when she lived with Gran'maw and Papaw," Anna explained. "We used to live next door to the grandparents. All us kids used to call her 'Granny Grunt' teasing her and it made her so mad she would chase them kids with the broom," she said, laughing once again. I laughed along with her, learning where a familiar phrase had come from. Grandma Addie would tell us kids she was our Granny Grunt. I'm not sure why that tickled me, but it did. One more piece of the puzzle was put in place.

"Now, Papaw was cruel," she went on, "used to make the kids mind. He'd hit them with a strap or switch, and sometimes make 'em stand on one leg," she said, then added, "Now Mommy [Rose Reed] thought her Daddy was *it*. She really loved him, thought a lot of him." Then she turned her attention to her grandmother, "Mamaw was humble and good-hearted. She would tell you stories about ghosts, to scare you of the dark so you wouldn't go out in the night," she said reminiscing. "I remember her mostly being sick most of the time—Papaw would buy her special foods to try to get her strength up. She had the awfullest nose bleeds. We don't know what she died of, she died at home."

"Mamaw had a black preacher at her funeral, and he stayed down with Mr. Owens," she told me, describing the family's death rituals. I had heard the oddity of my great-grandmother having both a black and white preacher at her funeral. "The preacher and Mr. Owens were good friends of Papaw. Mr. Owens was white, I wished I remembered the preacher's name. They brought Papaw and Mamaw both to the house and then you sat up all night with 'em," she explained.

I looked around the shop with its concrete floors and clutter of strings and threads and couldn't help notice a symbolism in the utilitarian space, coupled with the clutter of life brightened with colorful threads and jars of buttons. What a great analogy for Anna's life, I thought. Nothing fancy, surrounded by happy busyness—colorful and useful—a bit aged and, yet, sturdy. This was Anna.

"I believe Mamaw Arline was almost a full-blooded Indian," she said when I asked her about the dark skin noted in pictures. "I think the Thomases also had so much Indian in them, too—they was on both sides of the family. But I never heard about the word Melungeon—no, never," she said. The Thomas sisters were the great-grandmothers that made my mother and Anna double cousins, Lizzie and Artie. "Yeah, double kin," she said again.

I asked Anna about her childhood. She and her husband built their house almost fifty years ago, not two miles from the old home place. "When we was growing up, we got almost confined up on that mountain," she said. "We didn't get to go play with those kids in the camp, you know, they called it a camp. That's what made it so hard when we got grown. We didn't get to be around people, we didn't get to play with the neighbors' kids." Anna described their house when they were growing up, a house my mother referred to as a tarpaper shack. "There was no water in the house, no toilets, just outside toilets, no rugs on the floors, newspaper for wall paper," she says. "That's how we's brought up—but the whole neighborhood was poor, that's how we was all brought up. When ya got growned, that's why it was so hard. You could only play with the kids at school, not at the house or in the camps. You stayed home, you took your good clothes off, got the wood and coal and carried water. You didn't associate with the kids 'cept at school—or at church."

I wondered what denomination the family had belonged to and asked what church her parents attended. "I never knowed my Mommy, Mamaw, or Papaw to go to church," she said. "But they believed, you know. We'd go to church, us kids. I think why we'd go on Sunday night was 'cause that was Mommy and Daddy's times together," she said laughing.

Brownlow Reed, Anna's father, worked in the coalmines: Capito, Garmeada, or wherever he could get a job. "One time when I was sixteen years old he got a job in Fort Wayne, Indiana, cause he couldn't get no job in the mines," she explained. "He didn't stay up there long—I'd say about six months." Life was hard in the mountains; there were few jobs outside of timber and coal, both of which were hard on the body and on the women at home. Family life revolved around coal camps and company stores.

Groceries and dry goods were purchased with scrip coins that didn't go too far and often left families more indebted to the mine owners. "All the kids was poor like that, some of 'em might have had better clothes," she said. "We got clothes sometimes from Ad who would come down and bring clothes in for the kids. It's 'cause of her I learned how to sew. Because of that, at twelve years old I could sew them clothes up real good, make 'em fit us," she says with obvious pride. "I've been sewing ever since."

"We kept our food in the creek, or you killed your own chickens right on the spot and ate them right then," she explained. "You canned, you picked berries, it had to been living like the Indians." I asked her about bathing, especially in the winter months. "Honey, three of yas would bathe, one after the other, in the same darned water—it's funny now, but back then it was the way of life. We didn't know no better.

"Now Arbie was the workingest man I'd knowned," said Anna of her uncle. "I think Papaw was the one had those kids put in the home," she said, referring to Katie and Wilma going to Henderson Settlement with their other siblings. "Well, at least they got to play with other kids and be around people," she said, her Southern accent inflecting between an exclamation and a question at the end of her sentences. "How'd your momma make it up there in Michigan?" she asked, " 'cause she was from the hills. How did she make it?" The question seemed to require no answer but rather an acknowledgment that leaving the mountains required courage and strength.

"Once when I was sixteen, I went back to Michigan with Ad and I didn't know nothin'. I didn't never see an indoor toilet," she says laughing, describing her first experience at a public restroom. "We went into that commode and I could tell other people was a-peeing, but I didn't know what to do. I didn't even know how to flush, Sylvia had to come in and flush for me," she shakes her head laughing loudly at the recollection. She has her forearms on her legs, leaning forward, shaking her head and laughing, "and me almost sixteen years old."

"Ad would come in and just spend a few days and she'd be back off again," Anna said. "I guess she left here 'cause she wanted a better life than what she had, and I suppose she got it."

CHAPTER 4

Johnson Portraits

Angela Johnson Blankenship

> You have that desire to belong, to know who you are, to know about your family, and to know if they're truthful—we have a desire to know—tell me the story about the day I was born. We just want to know—it's the not knowing (that's hard).

Angela, "Angie" or simply "Ang," and I have been close friends for over twenty years. She is forty-five years old and employed as a hairdresser, but a couple of years ago she returned to school to pursue a degree in social work. Her large dark eyes, normally heavily lined, are expressive and manage to be both laughing and mournful at the same time. She is capable of saying volumes, without ever uttering a word, by using facial expressions and body language. She doesn't hold back, and you never have to wonder where you stand with her. Her brother describes her as being loyal, generous, and straight to the point. While her language style is free-flowing, it is also littered with colorful metaphors. She laughs easily and doesn't mince words. I recall a conversation we had many years ago when I had asked her to stop saying "fuck" in front of my children. She replied, "Okay, as soon as you stop saying 'Goddamn' in front of mine."

Angela, her first husband, and their children had moved two doors down from me not long after my husband and I bought our first house. She loves to visit and talk, but small talk is not her forte. She prefers to discuss "real" matters and explore how others think about a variety of subjects, including politics, current events, and salvation. She is a self-professed "bleeding heart" who thinks this country should focus more on correcting social injustices. She became my sister and my rock. We fought like true siblings and leaned on one another like family. We loaned and borrowed from each other until it was hard to tell where one household stopped and the other started.

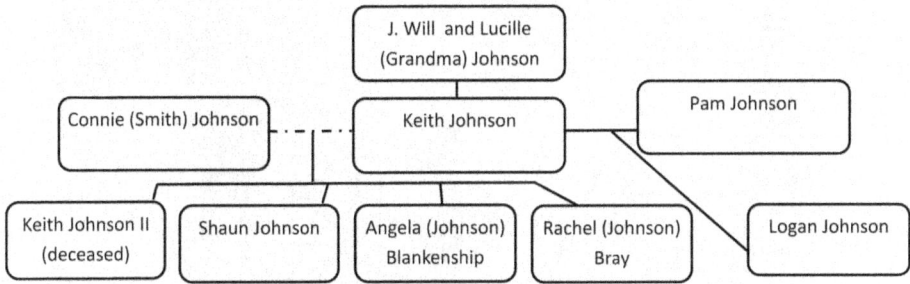

Figure 3.2: Johnson family kinship chart.

It was fourteen years ago that she moved from Michigan to Virginia. Although we stayed in touch throughout my master's degree, we never really discussed my research on Melungeons until recently. It was then we discussed her family's origins in Union County, Tennessee and examined the possible explanations for her darker skin and exotic looks. I marvel that we hadn't connected any dots before now. The more we talked the more I became convinced that a Melungeon heritage might be in her ancestry as well. Together we began to do some genealogy and construct a family tree, finding documentation and photographs that told a clearer story of her parents' and grandparents' lives.

As a little girl, Angela had noticed the difference in her father's coloring. As children often do, she voiced her observations and received staunch denials that confused her at the time but left a strong memory of the event. "One of my earliest memories of my dad actually becoming upset with me about anything was when I was probably seven or eight years old and I had been collecting baseball cards. I don't know who the player was or what team, but he was a black man on the card—and I said, 'Daddy, you look like him!' And my father was NOT pleased with me. I said, 'But Daddy, he's got the same gap in his teeth and his lips look the same, and look at his nose.' And my dad was pissed." Her first recollection of an ethnic connection between her family and those of color left a profound impact.

Angela is familiar with the story of how her paternal grandparents met. At twelve years old, Grandma had just lost her father in a quarry accident when she met J. Will Johnson. As the oldest child in the family she was expected to do a man's share of the work, from plowing rocky mountain soil with one bottom plow and horse to hauling water, planting and harvesting a garden, and preserving food. J. Will, named for J. Will

Angela (Johnson) Blankenship at Grandma Johnson's house.

Taylor, a relative, politician, and family friend, was sixteen years old when he came to help the grieving family. It was rumored that he had told friends that he was going to marry her if he could "ever get a pair of shoes on her." Eventually they married, not long before he headed to serve in the Navy during World War II.

"I get asked all the time if my dad's Mexican or related to Saddam—I don't know what he is," she laughs heartily. Her father, Keith Johnson (also featured in this project), was born in East Tennessee in 1945. He lived there until he was about seven years old. "Grandpa had lost his arm coming home from the war—that story is sketchy. The best I can tell, he was horsing around coming home from the war in a boxcar. He reached for his hat or got pushed and fell off and the train ran over his arm. He couldn't get any pension because he had already been discharged from the Navy." So they headed north. Like so many other families during that time, they were hopeful one or both of them could find a factory job.

The Johnson family, which included J. Will; Grandma; their two sons, Ted and Keith; and their daughter, Sharron, left their beloved mountains and farm of Tennessee to live in the city and flat lands of central Indiana. While there were visits back home to Tennessee, there was little family surrounding and supporting the Johnson family in Indiana. Family stories were slim, and almost all were provided by Grandma, who was secretive and private. There were subjects that were off limits and others that were alluded to, but never really explained. "We don't have a large extended family that I know of—so we don't know much about the family. However, there have always been family secrets," explained Angela on one of the many phone calls we had to discuss the research. She was very excited with every new discovery that framed the identity she longed for. She also admits to having a "mini identity crisis" with every new piece of evidence that appeared, wondering what the truth is.

Like many of us, Angela admits to not having a real interest in her background until now. Fortunately, her grandmother is still around and able to fill in some of the blanks, but knowing what questions to ask is also challenging. "I don't know what's there to find. Dad doesn't know a lot of it—and I wonder what was covered up, what was changed to protect other family members.

"I get stopped all the time and people ask where I'm from and I tell them Kokomo, Indiana, and they laugh because they're expecting I'm Italian, I'm Greek, I'm Jewish, I'm something [besides white]—and I'm like, well, I'm sort of like a mixed breed," she says. Angela's physical appearance was nothing out of the ordinary for me, and I don't believe I ever gave it a second thought. She is petite, and her dark hair is short with highlights and worn in a fashionable style. She wears jeans and chic tops with large earrings and necklaces. She will visit all morning without "getting ready," lingering over her morning coffee until well after noon if she has no immediate plans. We discussed the Melungeon population and common family narratives, and I began to question her further. The more we talked the more intrigued she was about the possibilities of a Melungeon ancestry, and we did some sleuthing in genealogical research on Ancestry.com. Many of the common tales and documentation began to emerge. One such tale we discovered involved a great-great-great-grandma who had been listed as white on every census but had been buried as a "negra." A family story explains that when Norris Dam was built in Union County Tennessee, they had to relocate several cemeteries. A great-great-grandmother's casket (the granddaughter of the woman buried "negra") was opened so that the body could be reburied in a newer one. It seems they had buried her in an underground spring. Her face and hands were preserved; her dress was intact down to every tiny button. A family member who was summoned to oversee the process remarked, "She looks just like the old Indian she was."

Angela had known this story. She had heard it many times as a child. We could, however, find no references in census records or otherwise that lists her as Indian. This was, Angela suggested, when a trip to Kokomo to visit her ninety-three-year-old grandmother might be in order. I traveled from Michigan and Angela from Virginia, and we met in Indiana to see what old records and photos Grandma Johnson could dig up. We called ahead so Grandma could put her guard dog in his cage, and I made it to the front door of the nearly one hundred-year-old, two-story house. I had been there once in 1994 on what I remember as a very steamy July visit, and Grandma recognized me. After she hugged and kissed the granddaughter she hadn't seen in almost a year, she welcomed us in. The front porch had been enclosed since my long ago visit, and a large Christmas cactus, probably six feet in diameter, took up about a third of the space. On through the living room we walked on our way to the kitchen. Angela had mentioned the tendency of her family to visit around the table, and she grinned as she was proven right.

The living room was rather dark with a fireplace on one wall, antiques and knick-knacks decorating the space, and a baby grand piano settled into the windows near the fireplace. The plaster walls had seen better days. The wallpaper and carpet had been removed almost a decade earlier in preparation for redecorating; however, no patching or painting had been started since. Against the wall opposite the fireplace, sat a rather large and re-finished Hoosier type cabinet. Angela motioned with her hand to keep walking and follow her. On to the small eating area of the kitchen we went where three places were cleared. Each place was marked with a pink and white flowered cloth place mat. A built-in china cupboard housed a collection of blue and white Currier & Ives dishes. Stacks of papers, boxes, and ninety years of living were pushed to the walls for a path. The walls had the plaster removed so the insulation, studs, and slat boards were visible; however, decorative plates, a clock, and other mementos were tacked to the studs aesthetically. The ruffled country style curtains at the large window, combined with the exposed bare boards, made the room feel cabin-like. On the table sat a beautiful porcelain lamp that gave off a warm yellow glow that added to the cozy atmosphere of the room. The middle of the table was cluttered with medicine bottles, vitamins, and other miscellaneous items—a few notebooks were stacked to the side, and the newspaper's crossword puzzle was open and partially completed.

We were seated at the table when Grandma brought out dishes of freshly made rhubarb sauce, still warm, and served us in her special china. It was absolutely delicious, and it was evident that upon expecting company she had gone to great pains to welcome and serve us while we visited. As we talked about my family and hers, Grandma used a pencil to make little marks on a piece of paper every time she made a point. "There was Sabra," slash on the paper, "Louvetta," another slash on the paper, and so on. Angela tells me then that the piano in the living room had belonged to Aunt Louvetta and had been acquired after her death. I walked to my bag and retrieved my audio recorder, put it on the table, and asked if she minded if I recorded our conversation. "I do," she said. I must have paused a moment because she said again, "I do mind. I'm a private person and I don't want to be recorded." Calmly I assured her I understood and put the recorder back into the bag. She explained what she could, patiently, while we finished our rhubarb and then led us to the dining room where she had stacks of photos, history books, genealogy charts, and more.

Angela mouthed "I'm sorry," when we took our dishes to the kitchen. She looked apologetically at my bag of cameras and recorders and shot a look of annoyance in her Grandma's direction. The dining room was maintained much like the living room, years of accumulation lined the walls, shelves, and every available space. An extra table was set up to handle even more papers. The *History of Union County* was on the table, and I greedily began to thumb through the pages she had marked. "Now who are your people?" she asked. "From Union County, that would be the Rays and the Willifords," I told her. She began also thumbing through the books looking for my people. Every so often she would come across one of her relatives or her late husband's relatives and show me the clipping, photo, or essay. Cautiously, I asked if I could scan any of the genealogy charts and articles from the books. "Hmm, yes," she said slowly, then lifted her eyes from the paper she was looking at and pointed a finger in my direction. "But if you scan and publish any of my photographs or the ones I sent to Angie, I will sue your butt."

"Oh, NO, Grandma," Angela exclaimed in shock. "She wouldn't do that. She is just doing research for school. It's about *me*—my family, and hers." Again, Angela glanced in my direction and shot me an apologetic look and, again, I silently reassured her it was okay. The information was invaluable, and as we continued into the evening, Grandma relaxed and started handing me even more things to scan. Eventually we dragged ourselves away with assurances that we would be back to go through more papers and ask more questions. As we headed across town for dinner, she apologized for her grandmother's behavior. "I told her you were coming and why," she exclaimed. "I just don't know why she has to be like that." We discussed some of the explanations that Kennedy and Kennedy (1994) had suggested in their first book, *Melungeons: Resurrection of a Proud People.* They had described photos with relatives' identifying features torn off or whole collections of photos burned. She was not sure of her grandmother's motives in denying the publication of photos but seemed to accept and ponder my possible explanations. As upset as she was for herself, she was more concerned for my research.

We met Angela's sister, Rachel, and her family at a local chain restaurant. Before placing our order, I noticed a bit of a commotion on the other side of the table. Rachel was visibly upset, and Angela was getting frustrated and raising her voice. Rising from the table, Angela took her four-year-old nephew to the restroom. Rachel was wiping away tears and trying to explain that she didn't understand why Ang would repeat something so hurtful and why Grandma would have said it in the first place. Evidently, while we were at Grandma Johnson's house she had mentioned that Rachel's son annoyed her. I hadn't heard it, nor could I comfort Rachel and explain away the hurt by describing the context or intent. Angela and I discussed the conversation later in the privacy of my car on the way back to Rachel's house. I asked why she would repeat something so hurtful. Angie explained that Rachel needed to know whom she could trust and whom she couldn't. She said that Grandma always seemed to pit one kid against the other and probably always would. "Grandma, hell everybody, is always talking shit about my kids," she explained, "what makes Rachel think she wouldn't say anything about hers? Anyway, you can't protect yourself against other people if you don't know what they're doing behind your back."

From left, Rachel (Johnson) Bray, Lucille (Blackmon) Johnson and Angela (Johnson) Blankenship in 2015.

They dynamics of the family relationships would not be ignored. The hurts and tragedies of the previous decades would influence everything and enter into every conversation I had with all parties in this family—except Grandma Johnson. In 1989, Angela's oldest brother Keith was confronting his cousin Travis who was living in Grandma's house. Travis was the oldest son of Ted Johnson, Angela's uncle and Grandma's favored child (according to some family members) who had recently died of cancer. Keith had been upset by the way Travis had treated Uncle Ted while he was on his deathbed. In the ensuing encounter, Travis shot and killed Keith, leaving an agonizing rift in the family that is still being played out in all interactions. A court case followed where Travis was acquitted of all charges. His attorney was thought, at the time, to be paid for (at least in part) by Grandma Johnson although she has denied doing so. Several years of exclusion resulted, and now the relationship between Grandma and her remaining son and his family remains strained at times.

The background also explains why there were no pictures of Ted's family shared at Grandma's table. The fragile truce was declared between the family and matriarch by agreeing not to discuss Travis or his brother David when Angela's family is present. However, the mistrust was evident in the encounter at the restaurant. Grandma Johnson had betrayed the very value of survival in Angela's family—loyalty. Just as she chose to side with Travis when Keith II was killed, she was siding with Angie over Rachel, regarding their children. Even though Keith's family has agreed to maintain a relationship and in spite of loving her, Grandma's sense of loyalty will not be completely trusted. In future discussions I would learn just how important this value of loyalty was to Angela's family. Ironically, this value was probably passed along by Grandma Johnson herself.

Angela's sense of loyalty is strong, and she is quick to defend her Grandma. She tells me, "I love my Grandma very much and I have no doubt she loves me. Has she made mistakes? Fuck yes, she has made terrible ones! But who among us hasn't or won't?" She adds that she has deep respect for her grandma's strength in the face of hardship. "There were times in our lives that had it not been for Grandma, we might not have had food in our bellies or shoes on our feet," she says sincerely. "She has worked her ass off and would never allow any member of her family to go hungry." On her grandma's ninety-third birthday she paid tribute to Grandma on her Facebook status. It read: "My grandma is ninety-three and she can still kick YOUR ass!" Angela says she has been called "Little [Grandma]" on occasion by both her Grandma and her Dad. "That ain't ALL bad," she proudly tells me.

The economic struggles Keith Sr. faced as a construction worker with long layoffs between jobs was compounded by his challenges with alcoholism. There was a time when Angela's family lived with her grandparents because their house was uninhabitable and it took months to get enough money for the repairs. Later they would put a trailer house on the acreage that her grandparents owned and plan to build a home. These circumstances led to Angela spending much of her formative years in the care and company of her grandfather. While Grandma gained employment at the local Delco Electronics plant, J. Will had been employed in a television repair shop downtown and had started his own repair shop on the side in his garage. By the time Angela was born, he was able to work strictly in his own shop. She would spend many hours there, and he would refer to her as his "assistant" to customers. He would hold tools with the stump of his arm and use his good arm to manipulate the fragile glass tubes for the television sets. When the inevitable cuts and injuries would occur, he would call for his "nurse," Angela, to help him with Band-Aids and ointment. She describes her "Scramps" as a good-looking, handsome man who was loving and calm. He would talk slowly, choosing his words carefully and often starting his conversations with a long drawn out, "Well...."

Angela tells of her Scramps (the nickname given to him by the grandchildren) squatting over the heat register in the very room we sat in with Grandma Johnson. He would hold his cup of coffee and try to warm his thin frame over the blowing heat. The large register was in front of the built-in china cupboard, set into the blue and white tiles that she would use in a kind of "hop scotch" as she skipped past him, waiting for him to grab for her. He would only let go when she "hugged his neck," a game she describes nostalgically. She recalls him standing or squatting but rarely sitting in a chair unless he was eating a meal at the table or on the front porch where she would sit on his lap, afraid she was hurting him. She describes caressing the vascular dark-skinned arm as they would sit there in silence. It was Scramps's great-grandmother, Mary Hughes Arms, who was buried as a "negra" in 1924.

The time of her burial is imperative in understanding the context of how this woman who had been listed as white in every census had come to be labeled as black upon her death. The Racial Purity Act of 1924 had gained ardent support in the office of Virginia Clerk of Registers. While Mary Hughes Arms had lived in Tennessee, Plecker had written letters to the counties in neighboring states, explaining the legal consequences of disobeying the act. Knowingly indicating white race on a document when the clerk knew the individual had any other racial admixture could result in a fine and possible jail time. The family narratives indicate that Arms was actually a Cherokee Indian, yet Angela, her father, and her siblings would like stronger evidence than Grandma's say-so.

"What difference would it make?" I wondered. I asked Angela what it would mean to find such evidence and what kind of evidence would she need? She explained that it would increase her desire to learn more about that ethnicity and that it would possibly explain some things. "There is a reason I get so dark, a reason for why I look the way I do—a sense of knowing who you are." She uses an intriguing analogy to illustrate her feelings. "You know if someone makes you a cookie, you taste it and you try to figure out what all went into it. You know? I taste a little bit of this and maybe that ...and then you find out it has none of the elements in it that you thought it did. Then when you see the recipe you say, oh, is that what that was? I thought I was tasting ginger but that was really nutmeg. I think people have a desire to know who they are and where they come from, to know what their roots are, what all went into making them who they are."

"I would hope to find out that I *was* something. Not that I had no value as a human, but that I have an identifiable ancestry that is a part of who I am and how I react and behave." She continues by expressing an understanding that perhaps Irish people have a temper, or Native Americans are more in tuned to the earth. "I have nothing to say I'm like this because of a heritage. I fight because my father was an alcoholic. I fight because I had to." Moving constantly with her father's jobs and ability to find work along with not having a lifestyle that most of her friends had, Angela felt she never quite "fit in." She searches as much for a sense of belonging as an identity. It seems much of her life has been spent struggling financially, being hungry, not having her own family home. The communities she lived in were not made up of families similar to hers. Fathers had jobs, mothers drove kids to events, and families went school clothes shopping. Angela became the caregiver for her siblings and her parents.

Angela's mother never learned to drive and suffers from anxiety, resulting in hours spent waiting for a father to be sober enough to remember to get her from school or walking miles to get home. It meant parents that couldn't be there for her as they were suffering with their own maladies and survival. By the time Angela was sixteen, she was married with a baby on the way. Her parents moved once again. Not only leaving her to have her first child without family nearby for support, they also took Rachel back to Indiana with them. It was a loss she would remember and feel keenly for years. By the time Angie was twenty-three, she had three kids, a husband, a mortgage, and a desire to create the all American family for her children.

As I sit at Rachel's kitchen table, the chaos of a bustling family is evident. Dogs scratch at the slid-ing door to come in, kids laugh and clamor for "Aunt Gigi's" attention, and the coffee maker hisses with the completion of another cup of coffee. Everyone seems to be talking at once, laughing at inside jokes, while the refrigerator opens and closes and sippy cups are filled. Voices get louder, trying to be heard over the din, and the recorder blinks its little red light, capturing it all. Logan, Angela's younger brother, and his wife Samantha stop by with their daughter to hear about our discoveries and to add to the conversation. Angela asks about the cost of DNA testing as the siblings discuss how they will really know anything. When

Angela (Johnson) Blankenship in 2015.

she does do research she feels, she has no place to start, nothing to delve into to declare, "This is who I am."

We discuss the $99 offer at Ancestry.com and how that could help connect to others on the site to possibly better define what lines are related to her family. She ponders this for a while as she considers what kind of evidence she would need to feel she was or was not Melungeon. "I would need DNA or documentation possibly—and that would depend on what kind of documentation it was. Because if it came from the mountains–I don't know—because those things were all altered." She continues by adding a story about a friend who found out later in life that her grandmother was black. Her parents had left the area and didn't maintain any connection with that part of the family. When she found out, she thought, "Oh, that explains it." The family loyalty comes up again though as she worries about the future implications of genetic testing.

"If I was to get genetic testing right now, I would be fine, okay—but you don't know what the climate is going to be in fifty years. If it is documented would I be able to hide if things changed? Especially if we have proof—you don't know what is ever to say we won't ever face that again. I think that is why our grandparents think the way they do—my ninety-three-year-old grandma is still preparing for the next depression. When you are really down there and people have worked so hard to out run that stigma, you don't want to go back. What if they find out I'm black, or Portuguese, or Middle Eastern—what will happen? I can see where people would worry about that and not want to know—I can see how my grandma wouldn't want to know. She found out that there were slaveholders in her family and she is very disturbed by that—she had prided herself in her family never being like that. She would never tell me that—she told my aunt who told my dad who told me. She is afraid of the backlash—like—what if the black neighbors found out that her family owned slaves? Is it realistic today? Who knows? Maybe in some areas it is!"

It is at this juncture that she turns to her own physical characteristics. She didn't realize how much different she looked until her oldest son, Christopher, was asked by a classmate if his mom was part black. Angela came from the era of sun-tanning and sporting a deep bronze glow during the summer, so at first she didn't think much about it. However, she recalls considering the comment while standing in line at a department store and noticing that her skin was darker than the African-American woman in front of her. "I remember thinking, 'Well, I guess I can see how kids would ask that.'" Still, even with the explanations of a Cherokee grandma, that reasoning never came to mind when examining her looks.

"Now my Grandma Smith, Mom's mom, said she was 'Black Dutch,' whatever that is," she laughs. "She also said they were from the Netherlands." She describes her maternal grandmother as being a beautiful woman with dark hair, dark skin, brown eyes, a bit on the "eccentric" side. "She swore we were Black Dutch." The stories from that side included her grandmother's grandmother who was not allowed to speak to the children. Her grandmother would tell of combing her long hair—reaching almost to her feet—but they wouldn't speak. Her parents didn't want her to learn the "old" language. They wanted their children to assimilate into the American culture speaking only English.

"My mother's mother was also very dark skinned, and I look the most like her. Here's another part of it, I don't know much about that part of the family—far as we know they only came from Indiana. My great-grandfather lived in the black neighborhood, not like it is today, but go back to the '70s—where the blacks and whites were in very different areas. He was the only light skinned person in the black neighborhood. My grandmother would take me with her twice a day to help him with groceries, make meals, and stuff. I grew up as a small child playing in the streets with the black kids. Before I started school and during the summers I would go with her and play there. I never went inside the black family homes, but we would all play together in the yards and in the street—no one really knew why he lived there. What made him choose that?"

Finding out what the ethnicity or heritage is on her mom's side might also explain her dark coloring and certain traits. In her mind she thinks that a Melungeon or Black Dutch ancestry might explain why her great-grandfather lived where he did or why the family loves music and dancing. Angela laughs energetically, and, still chuckling, says that is why she has a taste for Southern foods. "It would be cool to be able to say I have that culture and that's why I'm so comfortable with it. There might be something born in you that helps you relate to that—not that you're a closed person if you don't, but it could explain choices, decisions, thoughts.... I think it would be a cool thing. Many of my [African-American] friends will say 'You ain't all white'—that I have a 'tan' soul. Maybe that's why—it's in the genes!"

During the course of our joint research on genealogy, Angie expresses a frustration that no one in her family has been able to verify family stories of J. Will's father being a Tennessee state representative. His name was Bishop Johnson. "I haven't been able to find anything—it is so sketchy I have to wonder if there is organized crime in there. Maybe moonshine, I hope! I think that's part of it, you don't want to be average and normal and—wouldn't it be great to find out you're related to Bonnie and Clyde?" She busts out laughing, "wouldn't it be cool to find out that my grandfather had a big moonshine still somewhere? It would be something—instead of—ah, I don't know."

Angela notes that she learned in school about America being a great melting pot, but we still have Greek festivals and Black History Month. "We still have the celebrations of culture and ethnicities and customs, but there are so many of us that don't know what we identify with," she says. "You go back to whether it is environment, or biogenetics—is it chemical? If I'm a hot-tempered person is it an environment? Is it nature or nurture? You know, it might help if you knew this ethnic group was more prone to a certain disease—that would it be good to know."

After our visit we continue to call and chat online. Angela renews the research on her own, discovering possible links with the diseases listed in many Melungeon websites. The ailments sound familiar to her family's symptoms and stories through the years. Grandma Johnson was asked if her ancestors were Mediterranean during a medical work-up back when her Keith was a child. Angela's own gastrointestinal problems and oral ulcers could also find plausible explanations within the Melungeon diseases, as well as her brother's breathing problems. Some of our other discoveries include that her mother's family had immigrated much more recently than anyone had considered, and many of her mother's ancestors were from Switzerland, a country that no one remembers being mentioned.

Angela has been trying to process whether she could be of Melungeon decent and if she is, what it would mean to her. The following is an instant message she sent to me:

Ok.... Now I was reading all of your other stuff. Arlene's sort of hit me.... You know when we were talking about whether Melungeon was a shared culture or race/genetics? Well, her interview made me be able to put it into words, I think.... It seems that Arlene thinks of it more as a shared culture.
Here is what I've been trying to put into words...
So, for instance, Let's say we knew for a fact that I was Anglo-Saxon—completely 100% white—but my parents were raised in a native African village. They ate the same foods, worshiped the same way, were immersed in African culture ... then they moved away and had me.... I would not BE African. I may still feel a "kinship" with the native African people if I met them as an adult because of shared culture my parents raised me in. I don't think that would make me African—no matter how badly I may want to be. So, if Melungeon is a term we have assigned to a biological mix of particular races then I would have to say I would need biological proof. If Melungeon is just another word we are using to describe "Hillbilly"—which I always thought of as a culture—then I would most definitely be Melungeon. What I DO know is that I come from a long line of Hillbillies!! I have never thought of the term "Hillbilly" as a negative term. I've always

thought its definition was: Hardworking people who had lived hard lives. They will welcome you into their home and offer whatever they have, even if what they have is barely enough for themselves. They are loyal people who do not trust easily. Once a person EARNS trust, it is given freely. Once you break that trust, you better guard yourself as though your life depends on it, because it DOES!

Connie Smith Johnson

Mom was always compassionate. And a little goofy. She looked for the good in everyone. Only my mother could get a prank heavy breather phone call and talk to him for an hour. She, true to her blonde roots, got off the phone and looked at us and said, "Maybe he just didn't have enough toys when he was little." I was maybe seven or eight. We all busted out laughing. Every time my brothers got in trouble they would yell, "I didn't have enough toys when I was little!!! It's not my fault!!"—Angela Johnson Blankenship

Angela led the way, once again, as we walked through yet another door of a family member taking this journey with us. All so eager to share and learn, Connie, her mother, was no exception. As soon as we walked through the door of a modern single level apartment, Connie wanted to know if we were hungry and began to tell us what she could fix if we were. The kitchen and living room were an open floor plan that had vaulted ceilings. Connie provides daycare for Rachel's children, so the living room had toys haphazardly lining most of the walls. The end of the kitchen counter was somewhat of a catch-all and held things waiting to be put in their proper place. Red and white curtains with apples on them were hung at the kitchen windows. There was a little "secretary" in the corner that held a few photographs of her children. The ceramic tile and wood laminate floors were scattered with throw rugs. In spite of the airy openness of the space, it still felt cozy and comfortable.

Connie (Smith) Johnson, 2013.

Connie had brought out photos and her mother's Bible in anticipation of our visit. There was one small photo album, but the Bible was crammed full of clippings, photos, and other family mementos in a disorderly fashion. Two stacks of pictures and documents, wedding invitations, and birth announcements sat on the kitchen table. Connie sat on a walker that she used as a chair. I was later informed that her newly acquired preference for her walker instead of a chair irritates Angie and Rachel. She had recently had her hair cut and colored and was running her fingers through it, fluffing the bangs and back. Her eyes are hazel and she has the same dark circles under her eyes that Rachel has.

I had met Connie many years ago when she lived with Angie in Michigan so I was prepared for her habit of saying aloud random thoughts that popped into her head. It was amusing to watch Angie try to redirect her mother's thoughts and give meaning to some of the more fragmented bits of conversation. With a snicker and eye-roll Angie describes conversations with her mother as, "ADD at its finest!"

"I spent a lot of time with my grandparents," Connie said. She lived with them and her mother who cared for her parents and her children. "I don't know where my brothers were at," she thought, "But when Mom was working at Delco she was still nursing me so she would run home on her lunch hour, nurse me, then go back to work." Eventually her mother left the factory to stay home and care for her mother as she died. "Then after Grandma died, I stayed with Grandpa," she explained. Angela filled in a few details, recalling a summer night when she was about ten years old and she had found her mother lying on her bed sobbing. "She was crying so hard, I went in to ask what was wrong," Angie said. "She said she just missed her Grandma so much. They were that close."

"Didn't you have a nervous breakdown?" Angela asked her mother. "No, I never went to the round house," Connie said. "I had ulcers and was throwing up. After I ate this watermelon I got real sick throwing up, felt like food poisoning. I was throwing up for almost a month," she said, "went from two hundred down to one hundred and fifteen pounds. They said I had a peptic ulcer, and of course it affected me mentally, and your dad didn't help, he was drinking and running around. I started going to church and they prayed over me and I got healed. I continued to eat small portions, and I tried not to get too upset. They gave me nerve pills and I flushed them down the toilet. Keith thought I was bipolar or had a chemical imbalance 'cause I would get up in the middle of the night to clean and do dishes and stuff when we lived in Gateway. There was two little babies a year and a day apart," she explained. "I couldn't let 'em play outside and clean inside cause I couldn't keep an eye on them out there." "Mom had a very strong faith when I was little," explained Angela. "She spoke in tongues. She prayed over us when we were ill. Hell, we were dragged to church every stinking time the doors were open."

Connie was still a large woman, tall and stocky. "I remember feeling so sorry for her," she said, gesturing towards Angela. "When she was a little girl, she would just rock. Then I thought about killing myself 'cause I had these two mean boys and this little girl and I couldn't even drive around the block without throwing up. I felt like I was falling," Connie described, "I had such depression that I felt like I had a black cloud following me. I was lonely, scared, I had horrible stomachaches –I mentally disconnected from your dad then," she says looking at Ang.

Her anxiety had really limited Connie's participation in many activities. It has kept her from learning to drive, which has made her rely on public transportation, her family, and cabs. "That's why I had to take a cab today and go myself," she explains, referring to her trip to a store earlier that day. "I used to couldn't go into a crowd by myself. I have to work myself into it. I wanted to take my time," she says, "I wanted to prove to myself that I could do it." She isn't the only one she remembers as having these concerns. "My dad didn't want to go in stores either. I don't remember him ever going in a store, something about crowds he didn't like," she says. "He didn't go to my wedding, didn't go to any school functions, or nothing. He went hunting, fishing, out to drink beer, play the guitar." She describes another side of her father, "He took care of my grandma and aunt, went to church," she said, "and when he was younger he sang in the choir, used to sing real well. Mom said she had to buy all his clothes and everything."

I asked what her father did for a living. "Well, every job he ever got he quit," she said. "He came home one time, Mom was home from Delco and asked what he was doing home so early—he said he quit, was going fishing," she said laughing. "One time he was a librarian. He did odd jobs, like painting. All he wanted to do was hunt and fish and play guitar. When we was living with him he would fish and hunt to feed us," Connie explained, "I think his sister paid a lot of the bills." After caring for his mom and sister, and watching them die, Connie's father moved in with her brother. Eventually having a stroke, he went to live in the nursing home until he died. "He had leakage in his heart, he drank, ate greasy foods, used to dip his bread in grease and eat it," she described. "That wasn't good for him," she said.

"My eyelashes was dark all my life," Connie said, random thoughts coming to mind and being spoken aloud, "and you know now I'm losing my eyelashes. That happens when you get older." She describes the various jobs her mother worked after quitting Delco. "She worked in nursing homes and her last job when she had a heart attack she was a nurses' aid at the hospital. See how big my mom's hands were?" she asks showing me a picture. "My mother's parents, my grandma and grandpa, worked to put in a garden and canned. She crocheted doilies and bedspreads, rag rugs—they were farm people in clay city. Grandpa was a janitor."

"I wonder if there was some Romanian in your mother's side," Angie said examining the picture. Connie and Angela started laughing about the antics of Grandma Smith. They lapsed into a conversation of "remember whens," explaining bits and pieces of her life. "Her and Glen, her second husband, went all the way to California by car and went to Disneyland and visited his brother. Then they came all the way back home dropped their suitcases and Mom said, 'C'mon Glen let's go for a ride.'" Angela shakes her head, and Connie laughs some more. "Oh and your dad, was talking about taking Mom and going over bumps and she'd say 'Do that again!' She was like a big kid."

"She got tap shoes for her and Angie and they was dancing all over the place," Connie said. "Yeah," said Angela, "Grandma came in and said, 'Got us some tap shoes, Angie, put 'em on.' And Dad said 'Goddammit Evelyn, what are you doing?' 'We're dancing,'" she said. Ang stood up and started mimicking the dancing and tapping around the kitchen. Connie and Angela were both laughing, remembering how Grandma Smith would annoy Keith. "He would say, 'Ah hell Evelyn, why don't you get a semi-truck full of candy, back it up to the house and shovel it in them kids,'" Connie laughed.

"Grandma was babysitting us one night and she was brushing our hair dry," said Angela "and I said 'Grandma what's it like to smoke?' And she said, 'Well, here you go, kid, try it.' I was only eight or nine years old! She would have Sanka parties—take a TV tray out in the front yard and bring Archway sugar cookies. And we'd sit there and drink our Sanka and eat cookies. She was really eccentric," Ang says proudly. "Whenever I got my hair cut she'd tell Felicia [Connie's childhood friend who was a hair-dresser] to cut hers like mine. She'd dress like Rachel and me, big sweaters, leggings, Eastland shoes and bomber jacket. And she never woke up before eleven." Connie and Angela flip through pictures, finding one, taken by Grandma Smith's sister, of her wearing a blouse that snapped at the crotch, pantyhose, and heels. They laugh as they look at her posing in the strange outfit.

They show me another picture and explain that Grandma Smith had shaved off her eyebrows when she was younger. "She would take pictures and put lipstick and eye brows ON THE PICTURE!" they exclaim. "Just look!" We all looked at Evelyn Smith's photo that hung on Connie's wall for years. Her eyes gaze out of the portrait, seeming to look directly at you. Her shoulder length hair reveals the natural curl, and you can see the mischief in her smile. She must be about twenty-five years old in the photo, a younger version of Angela. "So you think she looks like a gypsy from Romania?" Connie asks her. "Well then, maybe they weren't Black Dutch." We look back at Evelyn's face: her tawny skin is evident and her looks are exotic.

Connie didn't fall too far from the proverbial tree. She is still a bit silly, and maybe somewhat naïve, yet she has suffered many tragedies in her life: she has no father in her life, was raised by grandparents, had her best friend die of leukemia at age nineteen, had her husband cheat on her and have another child, and suffer the loss of her murdered son. If not for these tragedies, I would say she is innocent. Somehow, her naivety is endearing. She still sees the good in people. She loves to laugh and be silly. A disciplinarian she is not.

"One time Dad took off his belt to beat Keith's ass for something he said to Mom," recalled Ang. "Mom grabbed Dad's belt and said, 'Oh no, you don't! I'm beating his ass this time!' She dragged Keith into the bedroom and slammed the door. We all stood there wide-eyed with open mouths. Apparently, once they got in the bedroom, she whispered to Keith, 'I'm gonna hit the bed and you need to scream like I'm killing you so your Dad doesn't beat your ass!' Before she let him come back out, she made him rub his eyes and throw water on his face so he looked like he was crying." We all laughed, wondering how anyone would have believed that Connie had actually whipped her son.

> Mom played UNO with us and we would cheat until she had the entire deck in her hand. She would laugh so hard she couldn't breathe. She was the mom that you could tell anything to. And she never judged ... and she loved us just the same. Keith adored mom. He called her "Mommy Honey." I remember mom telling Keith she wanted to lose weight he said, "Mommy Honey, even cows get fat on grass" and he grinned his crooked grin at her. Keith would've died for Mom. And he would've forgiven her for anything. She changed when Keithy died [Angela Johnson Blankenship, 2013].

We had been there for a while when Logan stopped by with his family. Connie welcomed him with a hug and exclaimed over how big his one-year-old daughter was getting. An explanation is helpful here to round-out a more complete portrait of Connie Johnson. Logan is the offspring of Connie's ex-husband and his mistress, now his wife.

Keith Johnson

I can hear my Daddy's voice, and see the expression on his face. Even with his faults, I was a daddy's girl. I thought my "Daddy Boy" [the nickname I gave him when I was younger than three] was a big, tough, construction worker. I thought my Daddy Boy hung the moon. When Mom went into the hospital to have Rachel, we lived at Grandma and Grandpa Johnson's and Dad let me sleep on his arm and it was so hot we slept with our heads at the foot of the bed near the window to catch a breeze. He danced with me on his feet. We lay on the balcony and looked at stars. You see, this is the REAL climate of Pop. He talks rough, gruff, and uses a lot of improper grammar—even though he knows better and is quite well-read— but he is really just a big softie. He is a deep thinker and a very smart man. When Olivia was born [Rachel's daughter] they had her over at the "workstation" cleaning her, weighing her, and they gave her a Vitamin K shot. Pop's face screwed up and turned red ... and his heart broke as soon as his little granddaughter began to cry.

Keith Johnson with wife Pam Johnson at home in Kokomo, Indiana, circa 2013.

He looked at me and said, "Sis, it ain't right. We bring this tiny, innocent baby into the world and the first thing we do is cause her pain." And there is just something so hard about seeing my Daddy Boy cry that I just have to cry along. So there we both were, red-faced and crying, in the delivery room [Blankenship, 2013, on the "essence of Pop"].

(Note: Keith Johnson had married Connie Smith and had four children: Keith II, Shawn, Angela, and Rachel. Later he had Logan, with second wife Pamela Moore. Keith II was killed by Travis Johnson, Keith's nephew from his late brother Ted Johnson and brother to David Johnson. His mother is Grandma Johnson, who is referred to in several portraits.)

Keith sat on the love seat in the living room of his son's house. His soft brown eyes peeked from under a billed cap, observing everything, taking it all in. His tan face was etched with years of working and playing outdoors—as evidence of a life often fought for and hard won. He is much slimmer than I remember last seeing him due to acquiring diabetes. He still looked strong and vivacious, packing a few extra pounds on his 5'7" frame. His daughter-in-law had just served us dinner, and we were now sitting in the living room to record an interview. Keith's wife, Pam, was a photographer, and I recruited her to help with the video recording and camera duties! While Keith sat in one corner of the loveseat, Logan, his son, took his place in the other.

The walls in the living area had been painted a deep, rich red color with a fireplace at one end of the room near where we were sitting. On either side of the brick fireplace were built-in oak bookshelves filled with hard covered books by Edward Koontz and Dan Brown, among others. One whole shelf was dedicated to children's classics, like Mother Goose and Dr. Seuss. A door opened to the back porch, a covered patio, and molded concrete steps. Opposite the door was a large oak library desk with more books. The house was cozy, with small tidy rooms that were warm and inviting.

Logan was eager to begin the interview and started by asking his father, Keith, if Grandma was ever comforting or acted as his shoulder to cry on. "Did she ever hold you when you were sick?" "Nah, not really," said Keith. "She just doesn't seem to be too loving, you know? I remember hugging on her one time, and I didn't know what I did wrong, but she tried to slap the piss out of me. I'd already pissed her off about something and didn't know it. I was just a little kid and she tried to slap the piss out of me," he swings his arm as if knocking a wayward cat off a kitchen table, " BAM!" He was quiet for a moment. I can see him visibly shake off the memory, tuck it away on a shelf in the back of his mind. He grins, rolls his eyes, and in a split instant seems angry. He takes a swallow of his beer, the first one he's had in months, he tells me.

"Mom was always embarrassing me. One day I wanted to buy a girl a necklace and she said you better be careful who you go buying things for." He couldn't have been in more than third or fourth grade, he explains. He purchased a small trinket for a blooming love, and his mother unwittingly, yet effectively, squelched his joy, humiliating him in the process. The hurt is still there, under the surface, and labeled as anger. "She was just stupid, just stupid—she was just such an embarrassment to me. She would be putting on airs, trying to act better than everyone. When Mom went back to Tennessee, she'd be dressed to the nines."

Then softly, in a gravelly smoker's voice, he explains that his mother "lost her daddy at twelve years old, and that's a hell of an impact on a young person's life. He was laid out in the house, cleaned *in* the house, you know?" He takes another pull on his beer, looks down, and seems to hang his head for a moment. I sense a guilty feeling for saying anything against his mom. "Then she had to be the 'man' of the house." His loyalty is evident when anyone else says something that may show Grandma in a negative light. "But she's good in lots and lots of ways," Keith will say in an effort to hush whomever may speak poorly of her. "She's my *mother*."

We talked more about his childhood and move from Tennessee to Indiana. "I never really felt like I left Tennessee because every year we'd go back down there for weeks. Stayed with Granny Blackmon. I could run across the roads going back and forth switchbacks to go down the mountain and get there before a car would."

He tells about his dad saying that he didn't realize the kids were so sad to leave Tennessee. "I told him, 'Dad, if I'd thought you would have turned that car around I would have really turned on the tears,'" says Keith laughing. "I remember being in Tennessee and running the woods," he says with a look of nostalgia in his eyes. "I seriously still do miss Tennessee—that little farm, that's why I got it. It's just my little piece of Tennessee.

"I had a couple of teachers who were really good to me and I remember them—and I had one that was a bitch to me. You could just tell that someone don't like ya—you get to feeling it. I set a plate to sailing with some cake in it and it hit her in the head and that really pissed her off." We laughed again, Logan, Pam and Samantha joining in. "It was at a Christmas party—but she hated me before that happened, I mean hell, Christmas was halfway through the year. There was this one wonderful teacher, Mrs. Croon, a frail little woman. She was a harelip, seriously she was, but she was so good to me, such a sweet thing—a good woman. One day a teacher had it in for me and she told me to come into her class. She said they'd have to go through her to get me. She is the one who told me later that the principal hated poor people, he was a drunk, but he also just hated poor people."

Looking like an aging Hell's Angel, Keith Johnson easily moves between hard-core badass and crusty burned marshmallow. As I was getting up from the sofa, I start pulling out some documents I had previously found that pertained to Keith's family: a genealogy chart and maps of New Loyston that show where his family had owned land before the building of Norris Dam. I also show him a photo of his grandfather as a Tennessee state representative in the 61st Congress, and explain that I have copies for his mom, too.

As we examined the maps, I began to explain to Logan, aged twenty-six, what the map represented. Keith chimed in to explain to his son that the Tennessee Valley Authority (TVA) came into the area to build a hydro-electric dam on the Clinch River. The land claimed by the government included a great deal of overworked farmland that was located in Union County, Tennessee, near Sharps Chapel and New Loyston that belonged to ancestors of Keith's mother *and* father. "They practically stole that land, according to mom," he said. "I guess that's when Kipay's dad's kids from the Oklahoma wife, she was the Indian, came back to claim their share of the money. I heard they didn't give 'em much more'n twenty-five dollars an acre."

"Kipay" was Keith's grandfather. Evidently the grandchildren started calling him that, and it stuck. His name was Bishop L. Johnson, and he had been a Representative for the State of Tennessee during the famous 61st Congress. Shaking his head, Keith said he had heard that Kipay was all for women's rights. I was able to tell him that I learned not only was Kipay for women's rights, but also the term he served was instrumental in women's suffrage. "In 1920, Tennessee was the deciding state in ratifying the 19th Amendment, ensuring women nationwide the right to vote," I tell him. "Well, I'll be damned," said Keith. "I remember Mom taking us up to the state house and showing us his picture on the wall, but I never could find nothing on him. Began to wonder, you know?"

We shared many stories during this evening: stories about his son's murder and my own brother's death. He told me of his love of reading, that Jesse Stuart was his and his son, Keithy's, favorite author. At one time he'd even thought of becoming a writer. We shared a couple of drinks and tons of laughs. Every so often someone would step out on the porch for a smoke break or stop to refill a tumbler with wine. There is a long pause on the audio where we all walk out back into the cool night air where I bum a cigarette and practice blowing smoke rings. Logan shows me the baby bunnies in the corner of their raised garden bed while Pam and Samantha sit on the concrete steps. Grandma Johnson, Keith's mother, lives just kitty corner across the street from Logan and Samantha. We can see the light on at her house and hear the dog in the yard. As we head inside, Keith begins to tell me about his move back to Kokomo from Arkansas.

"We was broke, and Mom said Delco's hiring so I went to take the test," he started, "well, I found out later I fucked up the test 'cause it had all that algebra on it and stuff. I thought they was going to ask me about what I was doing, you know? If you've got a compressor with a motor so big, and a pulley so big, and a piston so big, I can tell you how much per cubic feet it's gonna pull, but I can't tell you about an isosceles triangle." We all laugh loudly, commiserating with him sympathetically. "So I was broke and got up here in the winter time in a Volkswagen. Been driving back and forth to Indianapolis in a car with no brakes, doing construction, welding you know? So I quit, especially after waiting constantly for my pay.

"One time, before I moved to Arkansas, I got into it with the doctor. I took Angela in and he said he had to get lab tests, and I said, 'Do you got to do the lab tests?' And he said, 'Are you trying to tell me how to do my job?' I said 'No, I'm telling you you're too goddamned expensive.' He said, 'How about you find another doctor?' and I said, 'How about I bounce you off these fucking walls?' Well, that didn't go over too well," he laughs.

"So, six years later I'm back in Indiana and I got real bad sick and was going to go to the doctor, and he wouldn't take me. I was sitting in the ER, and I am hurting all over, and I'm waitin' and waitin.' I go looking for the doctor and I find him in a room reading a book, and he says 'I'm trying to find out what's wrong with you.' I said 'I got to go,' and he says 'You need to be in the hospital,' and I said 'I ain't got no money,' and he says, 'If you die you don't have to pay'—honest to God—he says that."

He describes being sick for weeks, running fevers and sweating all night, hurting and weak all day. However, he continued to meet at the Union Hall and grab jobs when he could. His father had passed away by then, and Keith's family had moved in with his mother. "Then mom throws me and Connie out of the house, and Rachel too. Shawn finds me an apartment in the bottom of this house in town. The people that lived upstairs was real heavy," he says in the low gravely tone of his, "and every time they walked across their floor my front door would open." We all laughed wildly. "I couldn't keep that damned door closed and it wouldn't lock. Found out later I probably had Lyme disease from all the ticks and critters in Arkansas."

On we talked into the night. Keith talked about his girls, how worried he was about the men they had chosen to marry. He was afraid that Rachel's first husband was planning to murder her. Keith describes the way their house was being built with an obviously large stairwell with no railing that he "just knew that crazy son of a bitch was gonna push her down."

At one point he was worried enough to go to her house to check on her. "I feared for her—went over to the house and tried to kick their door in once. I tried to knock and they wouldn't let me in, so I tried to kick the damn door in. I told him, 'You son of bitch, you hurt my daughter and I'll fuck you up to the point of killing you.' I told Steve [Angela's first husband] the same thing."

With great pride and a mischievous glint in his eyes, he tells me a story about Steve pushing Angie to her breaking point. He grins as he describes the scene: Steve standing on the front porch, taunting his wife and daring her to hit him. They lived across the alley from each other, and Keith could see Steve bent down talking into the house at Angela. "He was saying, 'Go ahead, c'mon—go ahead and hit me,' and she hauled off and busted him right in the mouth," he puts his head down again, shaking side to side. "He wasn't expecting that!" He took a drink of his second beer, shaking his head, still laughing.

"Angie thinks about being a prison advocate. Did you hear about her raising hell when Shawn got MRSA? She called up to the prison about his medicine and told them 'This is a federal penitentiary, heads WILL roll.'" There is no apology, no outward show of shame or explanation for Shawn's incarceration. He tells the story as a matter of fact, more proud of Angela making things right and fighting for her brother than anything else. In fact, he teases her about her youngest son, William, who has earned a coveted spot in the governor's school, a special high school for gifted and talented students. "Did I tell you what I told Angie about Will?" he asks. "I told her I was disappointed, he's never been in jail, never stole a car, hasn't got a girl knocked up yet—and at his age, fifteen!" He grins and chuckles, then admits with pride, "He's a pretty good kid. For a smart kid, he isn't a damn dumbass."

Regretfully, noticing the time and that Logan had been up working since very early, we called it a night. I promised to stop by Keith's house in the morning before heading back to Michigan. Rachel had assured me a place to sleep at her house, and I had promised to stop at the local bakery, Dirty Dan's, for a donut run. The bakery opens at 1:00 a.m., and the line begins long before that, especially on Friday and Saturday nights. It was well past 2:00 a.m., and the line was quite long. At 3:30, I made it to Rachel's to find her sleeping on the couch, trying to wait up for me. Gently I woke her up to let her know I was there, and then I climbed into the twin bed with Pottery Barn children's bedding in two-year-old Olivia's room. Still in my clothes, I fell into an exhausted and sound sleep with Olivia sleeping peacefully in the crib against the far wall.

The next morning, Keith met me out by the garage of his home. A tarp covers a truck wrecked a few years back by his son, Logan, and the yard is overgrown with perennials and shrubs collected for years from friends and loved ones. We walk through an archway covered with vines on a path leading to the back door. He begins to apologize for the condition of the house, explaining that the dog tore up some of the linoleum in the kitchen. "I told Angie, my house is a wreck and Tammy's coming down—and she told me 'I've seen her house at her worst and she's seen my house at her worst, she's held my hair out of my face while I puked—she won't care about your house.'" We laughed as I recalled my house and Angie's during those years we lived close to one another. "I don't care," I told him. "I came to see YOU, not the house!"

I laughed and pulled out a chair at the kitchen table that was tucked next to the window between the stove and refrigerator. The room was tiny and cluttered with antique kitchen gadgets, old collectible bottles on a shelf above the door, and open pantry shelves. The walls were artfully crafted from old barn boards taken from the family farm. The cupboards were also made from the old barn wood, giving a homey cozy feel to the room. An old stovetop percolator was on the stove with hot coffee that he poured into a cup for me. "What cup did you give her?" asked Pam. I told them, "It doesn't matter what cup I got since you put boiling coffee in it!" We all giggled like reunited high-schoolers.

"I still haven't got my check from those bastards," Keith explained as we were talking about his last job driving a truck. He had problems with the truck breaking down and the company not supporting his efforts to complete the job and get home. "They're gonna send me that check—they won't want to, but they'll send it," he said. "Or I will call the DOT and tell how insistent this company was about pushing times and cheating the log book. So they might not pay me, but they'll pay."

Pam was scurrying around finding pictures and paperwork that she had collected on the Johnson family. She brought out a plastic box full of photos and began going through them and showing me the ones of Keith as a younger man and places where he had worked. At various times, he had worked on turbines, driving, welding, and constructing. Often he would work out of town for weeks at a time. "There are some squirrels out there," he said, describing experiences of staying in cheap hotels and splitting costs with partners. He had left the door propped open on several occasions so that his driving partner at the time could come in after drinking. "One time some woman came in wanting to know if I wanted to buy a set of Hitler's dentures. I said 'No, they won't fit me!'" he chuckles. This seemed to prompt some other stories from his days on the road.

"Hey, did I ever tell you about when I saw flying saucers?" he asked. "Nothing ever happened to me because of it." He laughs, "It was in the day time on the way to work. We was headed to work about 6:30 in the morning and I see these three shiny things in the sky, three orbs, we sat there for about ten minutes watching them. They were probably over that place in New Mexico, you know? Then first one went to the right, *wsht*, out of sight. Then another one went to the left out of sight, *wsht*, then the last one was gone. But they never had no adverse effects on me—no implants or anything," he laughs. "Shawn's ex-wife's mother said they took her and implanted in her—well, you know what—I can't prove they didn't," Keith says in all seriousness. "Hey Pam, I was really handsome wasn't I? My hair was a little bit too short though," he says, changing the subject.

"There were these pictures I wanted to show you of me wrestling a bear down in Texas," Keith says while glancing through a stack of pictures. Discarding them all and not finding the one, he starts into the story. I knew it held some significance since Angela had already asked me if her dad had shown me the photo yet. "I told the guy I don't want to go first," said Keith. "I said, 'What do I do?' and he said, 'just grab him.' And that bear whooped me—someone had said, 'Which one's the bear?'" I am certainly surprised about the bear wrestling, and several questions come to mind that I ask him about. "Yes, he had a muzzle on him and was declawed," he answered. "You know how they got him off ya? With a two-liter bottle of Pepsi. I thought if that bear got sick of Pepsi, well, I'd be in trouble." I still wasn't sure about the significance of the event and its importance to Keith, but it did seem appropriate to include the story in this portrait.

We started talking about the Johnson and Blackmon ancestors and what he knew about them. "My granddaddy, Kipay, would sign a note for anyone who wanted him to, and if they didn't pay it he was stuck with it."

Keith did the now familiar head shake and started laughing, "He also pulled teeth for people. He had a pair of pliers he'd pull 'em with, then give 'em a glass of salt water and send them on their way." He describes a grandfather who was well-accepted in his community, a caregiver who helped anyone who asked. "I guess I look like Kipay," he says.

"Granny Bunch's daughter, Louvetta, played piano, she played 'Music Box Dancer' for the kids," says Keith, recounting a story I had also heard from Angela. "Mom said that Alice, Kipay's mother, studied to be a concert pianist. Mom played, too, and Dad played piano, too, before he lost his arm. I could never play a damn note," he says laughing. "Did Mom tell you about her family that had slaves and let them go when they went to Texas? After about four years, a black man knocked on their door and were recognized by the man's hands and ended up staying with Mom's family for years and working together. They had 'em somewhere, so anyway—I can't remember all the details but they had owned a few [slaves] and set them free and they followed 'em to Texas and they probably all ended up sharecropping together, or maybe worked for 'em [the family]."

Talk turned to more personal matters. "We used to call him Freddie Fender and he would be down to the bar singing into his pool stick," said Pam about Keith. "We'd been going out about six months, and I told his friend to go get Keith and we'll go get some chicken and beer. Well, he said 'no, I can't do that,' then he looked at me and said, 'You really don't know do ya?' 'Know what?' 'That he can't come 'cause he is married with kids.' No, I didn't know, I mean I knew he had kids, but I didn't know he was still married. When I saw him that night at the bar, I said 'We need to talk,' he said, 'About what?' I said, 'About this here,'" she says, gesturing to her ring finger. "And he said it ain't no big deal. Well, I knew people like that, so I didn't think much of it at the time."

Keith said, "Me and Connie kind of grew separate—did Angie ever tell you how we came to be divorced? I had been to work and I came back in town and stuck my head in the door and Angie was there with Connie and Angie said, 'Dad, we're divorcing you.' I said 'Okay,'" he grins, "and slipped back out." I get the feeling he has a sense of pride in his daughter for standing up for her mother, even if it was against him.

Pam goes on with the story, "Logan was about three at the time, and we were all living in the duplex." "You and Logan AND Keith?" I ask. "Yep, we got into it that one time—that was going to be the end—I wasn't playing this game no more—he was having his cake and eating it too," she says raising her arm and waving her hand, "so see ya later, bye!"

"If she hadn't of divorced me, I would have kept going on like I did.

Just like my great-granddad—my mom's granddad—Eula's daddy had been gone. He liked to play the banjo, drink, and run. Story goes he brought home some watermelon and she wouldn't let the kids eat the melon so they gave it to the pigs and the pigs died, they figured he tried to kill 'em. He went back to his ramblin' ways—then he went on into Kentucky and had a family up in Kentucky. My grandma hunted him up and went to see him when he was an old man." I asked why. "Same reason you want to know who shot your brother—closure I guess, maybe some answers," Keith replied.

We were back into the Melungeon identity again: what it might mean and how it could be associated with his family. I explained that his mother doesn't seem to be upset about being Indian, but I get the impression she wouldn't be too pleased to find out she was part black. "You'd have the right impression," he said plainly. "And I wouldn't like blacks no better if I was one. I haven't got much use for black people, in fact, most black people."

"Hell, I used to belong to the NAACP," says Keith. "Like I said, I don't care if I'm part black, but I'd rather be Indian—'cause they're the most downtrodden people on this earth." I pondered on this a moment and asked "Why?" "'Cause I always hated the establishment and that just gives me an excuse to hate 'em more. They were doing genocide, trying to just kill all the Indians that ever lived. They wanted to eliminate every Indian that ever was." He describes how he was busy raising his family and working when the American Indian Movement began at Wounded Knee during the '70s. He would have liked to have been right there with them and feels a real connection.

Keith shares candidly with me his thoughts about his struggle with alcohol. "I mean, we've been dysfunctional since 12 B.C.," Keith says laughing again and shaking his head. "I used to drink a LOT—I said I was a functional alcoholic—I did my job, and maybe tried a little harder cause my head was screwed up. That dysfunction is what makes people what they are. I knew guys whose parents were drunks and they would never take a drink, my dad never drank when we were growing up—until he was dying—I never saw my dad drink and my mother never drank, never, never, never. But I drank like a damn fish, me and my brother, we'd tear it up..." he says, his voice trailing off.

"I worried about Logan but I never knew what he was doing, drinking and wrecking cars. The tarp on the truck?" he asks, "Well, he was supposed to be going in the Army and gets drunk and sideswipes a car. So if he gets popped with that truck, there goes the army, so I put that son of a bitch in the garage for six months." Logan never did go into the service, but Keith covered for him when he could. At this, I once again contemplated the family's loyalty and desire to protect one another.

The coffee is poured again, all around, with tidbits of conversation floating chaotically like confetti sprinkled at a party. He tells me how Connie's father could cook carp that tasted great and how his late brother was stingy with tools. He asks me how I eat my beans and cornbread and teases that I am too far removed from my heritage if I eat them in a bowl. "You put your beans, cornbread, and fried potatoes on a plate to eat 'em," he explains. "My dad would pour his hot coffee in a saucer and drink it out from that," he continues.

We begin to wrap up the conversation and I asked Pam for a picture of "Pops," Keith. I see the lined face as I look at the photograph, yet no smile. "He won't smile for photographs," Pam says, "because it's against his personality." They talk about checking my oil and other fluids in my car. "I'd hate to see you broke down along the road somewhere," he says.

Rachel Johnson Bray

> Rachel was my longed-for baby sister. Until I was six years old, I only had big brothers. I was the outsider. I longed for a baby sister. My eccentric Grandma Smith told me I could order a baby from the Sears catalog. I would look the babies over, decide on one, and cut the pictures out. Grandma would help me put them in an envelope and we would send it away ... and I would wait ... and wait ... for my baby sister. I think we started doing this when I was around three years old. Well, a few years later, while on birth control pills (that were later taken off the market), my mom was pregnant!!! Finally!!! My order from Sears arrived!—Angela Johnson Blankenship

Angela had arranged for the two of us to stay at her sister Rachel's house while we conducted interviews with family members regarding Melungeon ancestry and possible identity. I remembered Rachel as the doted-on younger sister, not the beautiful blue-eyed woman I would find inside. We went through the front door of a newer house with a landscaped yard in a subdivision in Kokomo, Indiana. The house was a cheerful collection of antique tea pots, over-stuffed leather furniture, and bright colored children's toys. The carpet was littered with pink sparkly princess accessories and bright colored Power Ranger figurines. A somber faced four year old looked past me as he tried to see his longed for Aunt Gigi, his name for Angela. His large brown eyes crinkled and lit up when he saw her, yet he hesitated, unsure of what to do. His olive complexion captured my attention right away, when a beautiful little vision with long wavy hair came into view. She was peeking from around the side of a large fifty-gallon aquarium filled with fish and brightly colored tank accessories. She, too, had large dark eyes and a mischievous grin. Where Colten was a serious young man, articulate and intelligent, Olivia was vivacious, self-assured, and strong-willed. She reminds me of stories I've heard about her mother.

"We fished and went wading in the creek," Angela says about Rachel while recalling their childhood, "we poured dirt on our coon dog's head. She used to tag along fishing with Dad and me. She would be playing with the night crawlers, giving them names and voices. She was such a funny and bright little girl," Angela says wistfully. "I swore she was born with chocolate on her face and her shorts were always twisted sideways. She was a bit of a ragamuffin little girl."

This evening would be spent visiting, catching up, and getting acquainted once again. I would enjoy several books that Olivia would "read" to me throughout the evening. She warmed up enough to lean against my chair and chatter, but not enough to sit on my lap. Colten showed me his Power Ranger toys and card holder but held fast to his aunt lest she disappear. Rachel convinced her husband John to make a donut run to the local bakery, but I was exhausted and went to bed before the donuts arrived. I would soon understand the incentive to stay up and have a Dirty Dan's Donut fresh from the oven as a late night indulgence.

In the morning, we gathered with coffee at the high kitchen table and ravaged the bakery box. I got out my trusty recorder, set it on the table, and watched the light blink as it captured the sounds of a lively, loving, and tightly knit family. Rachel sat biting her nails and directing children. The Keurig single cup coffee maker is set to hissing as our day begins. Angela brought up the research right away as we chatted about the skin color of the family in general and Rachel's kids specifically. "We have a different tint to our skin," said Rachel. "Even if it is light, the color is just different. When Colten was a baby, we took him to get his picture taken," she explained. "The photographer said her boyfriend was Puerto Rican and that her children were mixed. Then she asked if Colten was mixed, too. I've had lots of people ask that." She raises one eyebrow and grins. Her blue eyes, described as soulful by her sister, shine this morning while she relaxes and enjoys this visit with her sister and best friend.

Colten is sitting at the table with a donut, listening and playing. He asks his Aunt Gigi, a hairdresser, if she will put some "stuff" in his hair to make it stick up in front. She assures him she will as she refills her coffee and slides back onto the chair beside me. "It is so hard for us to find makeup in the right shade," Rachel says. "It's always too pink, orange, or yellow," Ang agrees. The conversation is stilted, interrupted by children's requests for milk, or a donut, or someone's attention. Olivia is running around in a pullup that refuses to stay put so Rachel and Ang are constantly tugging at it to twist it back into place,

Rachel (Johnson) Bray with her children in 2014.

and I grin, recalling Angela's descriptions of Rachel. Every so often Colten reminds the adults of the promised hairstyling, and a dog begs to come in or go out. After a while, I convince my upscale hairstylist friend to lower her standards and help me put a supermarket box of hair color on my gray roots. Rachel goes into the laundry room and returns with a plastic tote filled with hair care and styling products—evidence that Aunt Gigi has done hair in this kitchen before. Angela digs through the tote and finds a black cape. While wrapping it around me, she says in amusement, "I wondered what happened to this cape, I forgot I left it here. Wonder what other stuff is in that tote." Still sitting at the table, we continue talking, drinking coffee, and doing hair. Angela notices that Colten's recent haircut from a local salon chain has a few mistakes so she asks for a pair of scissors and repairs them, too. The two sisters commiserate about their mother's activities and actions in a way only family can understand and relate. They are finishing each other's sentences or talking in fragments, communicating as much with facial expressions and gestures as they are with words.

"I've heard the stories from Grandma Johnson about having Indian in us," says Rachel. "Finding out more about the Melungeon connection would explain a lot. It would also be good to know if there are diseases that would be attributed to a certain population, so you could tell your doctor, you know?" I ask if there is anything else she would like to know about as I am doing research and working on their family tree. Rachel suggests, "I guess it would be good to know causes of death, too." Colten starts tapping Angela on the arm, "Hey, Aunt Gigi, you forgot to put that stuff in my hair." "I didn't forget, honey," Ang puts her cup down and helps him into the chair next to her, "I'll do it in a bit. We're talking right now, okay?"

Olivia climbs up onto her mother's lap as the conversation continues. "You don't know what question to ask until you find out about something," Rachel says, explaining her lack of questions as very different from a lack of interest. "The repetition of names through time—did we do that intentionally? You see the same first names used over and over—or is that because of our heritage?" She asked. "It would be kind of cool to find out that we actually belong to anything, but it doesn't change who we are, where we've been or where we're going," she pauses a moment. "Unless there are scholarships involved," Angela finishes for her, laughing. The coffee maker happily hisses, keeping up with our coffee demands, as I sit with dye on my hair, waiting for time to be up so I can wash it off. Colten, once again, asks again for his hair paste, and Olivia chimes in asking for Aunt Gigi to put some in her hair, too, to "make me pretty," she says. Aunt Gigi, realizing her four-year-old nephew has been exceptionally patient in his request for her styling expertise, takes the kids to the bathroom so they can stand on the toilet and watch as she styles their hair. Olivia proudly emerges from the bathroom with a tiny bit of makeup as well. Angie gives Rachel a wink and says, "We were bonding."

The house is buzzing with all sorts of noises, and Rachel is intermittently wiping sticky fingers and doling out hugs or discipline as needed. "Some people's ancestry has gotten them somewhere in life, a kickstart. It could have been worse for us, I guess," Rachel admits. "I'd love to know where Grandma Smith's name came from, Cooprider, it's not a common name. I have some Coopriders come in to the store," she says, referring to her job in an area pharmacy. "They look like they still belong in Gateway," she says, referring to the income-based apartments in Kokomo that are now known for their poverty and crime. It is the same income-based apartment complex where their mother was raised. "It used to be mostly hardworking, poor people. It wasn't the cesspool it is now," Angie tells me. It is called something else now, but the locals still refer to it as Gateway, and the name is used as a euphemism for "poor, dirty, ignorant, and down trodden."

Both women wonder what else might be in their background that explains psychological behaviors of some relatives and diseases, such as

Family discussions circa 2013: Rachel (Johnson) Bray is holding the infant, and in cap is Logan Johnson.

Grandma Johnson's connection to a medical condition associated with a Mediterranean ancestry. Anxiety runs in the family as evidenced by several family members who refuse to drive a car. I glance over at Rachel and catch her biting her nails again.

Westley Logan Keith Johnson

Logan was very excited when I told him of your research, maybe because he, more than the rest of us, questions how he came to be about. I explained to him about Melungeons. I also told him that one of our ancestors had been buried a "negra" and he laughed and said, "Well, that explains my nose! And everybody thinks I'm black anyway." When I said, "She may have been Indian, though." That brought us back to laughing about Colten's birthday party last year when he and I got into a frosting fight and called a truce by "attacking" Dad with the brightly-colored frosting from the birthday cake. We smeared it on Dad's face in "traditional Indian" style and started calling him "Chief Diabetes" and declared he had finally returned to his Indian roots. Dad just sat and blinked at us while we did it. We laughed so hard we cried, but we were prepared to run if Dad made any sudden movements!! I later found Logan and Dad teamed against me and I was tossed into the kids' wading pool. The whole time I screamed that Logan was a "traitor." The little shit just smiled and winked at me!—Angela Blankenship, 2013

Logan's story isn't complete without reading the rest of the family's portraits. He is open and sincere and, more than anyone in his family, is longing to understand where he fits in the dynamic of family relationships. He was the mistress's child and has always longed to feel accepted. He sometimes tries too hard to be one of the Johnsons but at twenty-six years old is coming into his own identity. Ironically, he and Connie's relationship define the family as much as any ancestry or biology.

"Have you heard this?" Logan asks me, referring to how he was introduced to the family. "Dad brought me over to Connie's with a curdled bottle, drunk as shit. Connie could have killed me, and maybe a lesser woman would have. Then she called her husband's mistress and said what a bastard he is and that the baby is staying there," he explains, as he recounts Connie's next words. "He is drunk as hell and he's not taking this baby anywhere."

"Mom may be crazy, but in that moment she was a very big person," adds Angela as we sit around Rachel's table talking. Logan's wife, Samantha, and daughter Lillian add to the overall chaos at Rachel's. The Keurig one cup at a time coffee maker is still frantically hissing, and the laughter and children's voices continue as a backdrop to the conversation.

Angela lived next door and across the alley from her mom and dad in a teeny upstairs apartment. Her brother Keith, his wife, Gina, and son Boo (Keith III) lived in the apartment above her parents. "I was in my apartment when Rachel, who was about thirteen at the time," Angela takes up the conversation, "came running up the stairs that led to my living room. She animatedly exclaimed, 'Sis, Dad brought the baby home! He's drunk! Mom wants you!'"

Logan Johnson holding a young one, Connie (Smith) Johnson and Angela (Johnson) Blankenship in 2013.

When she got to her parents' home, her mother was standing in the hallway, holding the phone receiver with her chin and shoulder. In one arm she was holding a baby of about five months old; in the other hand, she had a bottle of medicine and was trying to read its label. "She was talking to the baby's mother, my father's mistress, on the phone," continues Ang. "She hung up the phone, looked at me and said, 'Angie, your dad brought the baby here. He is drunk as hell and passed out. The baby is sick, the formula bottle he brought is curdled, and this baby's sleeper is too little for him. Look at his little toes: they're all bent back and it's pulling his shoulders.'" Fortunately, Angela's second son was a couple of months older than Logan so she ran home for some baby supplies. Keith II came down from the upstairs apartment, and for a while the siblings all stood looking at the baby. Logan seems relieved to have his two sisters help recount the tale of "how he came to be" as he calls it. He still seems a bit uncomfortable with the story but resigned to its place in the family lore. Unfortunately, this story has defined a large part of Logan's existence.

Logan has a light complexion but African features: full lips, wide nose, and kinky hair. It has not been his skin color that has caught the attention of people in the community but his facial features. "When I first went over to the other factory, KTP," he said, "these guys said 'Are you black?' I said, 'I don't know what I am, I'm just a mutt.' I explained what I knew of the family and stuff. He looked over at another dude and said, 'He's cool, he's one of us,'" Logan says with a deep laugh, "You can't make that shit up." He's been asked if he was Samoan, if he was black, and if he was mixed. Being a big man, trained in boxing, he hasn't had many confrontations—but lots of questions.

While we are at Rachel's, Logan describes his childhood for me. His sisters interject frequently to explain, clarify, or support his remarks and to nod in agreement as he tells his story. "Dad was always drinking. It got to where I'd know, if George Jones was playing it was going to be a bad day, it meant dad was drinking," he explains, laughing, and starts everyone into a knowing chuckle. "'Cause then Dad's gonna start happy, then sad, then mad, then anger, and in the end, Dad is gonna be mad and Mom's gonna be out in the yard screaming, 'Why does he always have to be such a bastard?'" Angela chimes in, "Then Pam's gonna take off in the truck, and Dad's gonna chase after her and jump in the back and hit his head and be bleeding...." She trails off, leaving everyone in stitches.

I ask the siblings what it would mean to have a "good family." "Well," Ang says, with a shake of her head, holding her coffee with one hand and gesturing with the other. "It'd be good to come from a family where George Jones isn't gonna dictate the kind of day you're having."

After the laughter dies down and the coffee refilled, Logan says more seriously, "I don't think we came from a bad family, I think we mean well." Then Logan grins a lopsided grin, and his eyes flash, "Yep, we're poor white trash! You know for a fact you can call your daddy up—and here comes Daddy eight hundred miles in that old truck, cussing and carrying on, but he's there. Or, 'Oh Daddy, John can't fix the heater, can you?' ... and here he comes. He means well," Logan says teasing his sisters about calling on their father and him dropping everything to come help. "Or, 'Oh Daddy, I just wrecked your truck cause I was drunk," he says, as an admission, while they laugh and nod in agreement.

"But, poor white trash we are. Good-hearted poor white trash. We might hate each other and fist fight in the yard—but if one of us needs something we're there for each other," explains Logan. "I don't think you'll find a perfect family. All these things that supposedly make a good family: money, education, a nice house—and they still cheat on their wife," he says. "You will find flaws in every family."

"We try to be there for family," admits Angela. "When somebody is dying in our family, you never leave them alone. You would go there and be with them. They would never be left alone in a hospital room. You can't go with 'em, but you can walk 'em to the edge," she explains. "You just never left them alone."

"Ironic, how people are with their family," Angela continues. "But when Grandpa was dying and he would hit his roughest points and they thought it was nearing the end, he'd always say, 'Go get the kids, I need to see them one last time.' We'd get the phone call saying to get the kids ready, 'Dad wants to see the kids one last time, so I'm coming to get 'em,' Dad would say. I didn't realize how much he loved his grandkids. Then on his death bed, the last thing he wants to see is his grandkids. He was never left alone. It's cool," Ang continues, "such a strong testament to just how much he did love us. We would all stand around the bed and touch him, and tell him how much we loved him—then he would make it through the night and we'd get the call again to get the kids ready, he needed to see the grandkids one last time."

"One of the things that has stuck with me," begins Logan, referring to his maternal grandfather, "we was just getting close. He wasn't in my life, and as I got older and started hanging out with him more, he would give me stuff. Then when he got sick, we would sit up all night and he would be talking crazy shit. He'd want to get up, so I'd get him out of bed, then he'd want to go back. He died on a Saturday and I was gonna go up that night to see him and I'm beating myself up a bit cause I didn't want to necessarily deal with it," he admits. "He would just know stuff, you wouldn't have to tell him, he'd just know. One time I went up there and said, 'Got something to tell ya, Grandpa.' 'Samantha's pregnant,' he told us. And I said, 'How did you know?' And he said, 'I just know, boy.'"

"Now Grandma thinks a good family means you have money, and a famous person, not like a movie star—like a famous politician or attorney or doctor," Angela says, referring to Grandma Johnson. "Marilyn Monroe would mean nothing to her—just a tramp. Now a cousin killed another cousin in our family, but she never mentioned it to you, did she? There was a pile of pictures with Travis in 'em and she started scooting them away." Travis was the cousin that killed Keith II, who is Angela, Rachel and Logan's oldest brother. Keith's family had gone years not speaking to their grandmother when Angela called a truce. "I told Grandma this is the deal, if I'm gonna have a relationship with you, I don't want to hear about him. I don't want to hear how wonderful he is. There is some distortion about the way people remember a lot of things too. Maybe out of respect or time," Angela explains, "some things you just don't talk about. Some *truths*—you just don't talk about it."

"My first experience with Grandma Johnson," says Logan, "was a strange lady coming into Olan Mills to get our picture taken together— with this lady I never met. Mom said she was my grandma, and I thought the hell it is. I must have been around three years old. See, if you were to talk with Grandma, she would tell all about picking me up when I was sick, and taking care of me," he explains, "and I don't remember her getting me—she did come to Grandparents' Day, but remember I'm the bastard that tore the family apart." Logan says this while laughing, but his sisters just smile and exchange glances. The moment is awkward for me, but true to her loyalty to truth and family, Angela jumps in with an important insight.

"The initial thing was Dad being disloyal to our mother," she explains, describing the feelings she had upon learning of Logan's impending birth. "We knew of you," she says. "The thing about it was, that we all dealt with—we knew when you was born, Keithy was at the bar and the bartender said, 'You know Pam had the baby.' So you find out your brother is born by a barmaid. Keith said, 'I don't give a fuck.' It's like you know you're gonna hear about it, but ... why..." she starts, "you hear in a bar?"

"It was not about me, nothing against me," says Logan, trying to understand and to convey that to me. "It was more against Dad than your mother,"

Ang explains. "Here's the whole thing too," explains Logan. "Connie knew, you guys knew, Mom knew–Poppa was a rolling stone. He was a whore, that's just what he was, we all knew that. It is really hard for us too," he says defending his mother. "The night that I was born he was back and forth to the bar—and ended up drunk as shit."

"Then months later he comes over to Connie's," Logan continues, "and says 'This is my son.'"

"It speaks volumes for the level of bigness and good family qualities," Rachel adds. "None of us wanted to hurt Logan." Logan laughs. "None of us are like 'get this kid out of here!'"

"I think that's where I say that's a good family quality," Logan, realizing his own revelation. "Like Connie, no matter what—there's always a special part in my heart for Connie. I love the lady, she's not my mom, but I'll still give her a kiss and a hug. I tell her I love her."

"It wasn't until my later teens that we would become more like siblings," says Logan. "My favorite memory was at her [Rachel's] apartment. One time, we're all rough housing and I flip Rachel upside down and Angie is saying 'Put your sister down,'" he says laughing, and again his sisters laugh with him, recalling the event. "Maybe now as an adult we can feel it more now," he says referring to the family closeness. "'Cause we can go home."

Logan describes the family dynamics, and how he has come to terms with the unusual roles and structure of the Johnson family. His mother, Pam, and Angela's and Rachel's mother, Connie, will often find themselves at family gatherings and holidays together. They are friendly to one another, in no small part due to Connie's innocence and acceptance. One instance is described to me with great hooting and laughing: Connie was at Rachel's visiting, and Pam stopped by with Keith to help with a project, most likely. They started to compare notes with Pam, asking Connie if Keith had an annoying habit when she was married to him. "Mom and Connie were talking and saying when you were married to him did he do, blah blah blah," Logan says describing the event. "'Hell yeah, and let me tell you what else he has done' ..... and then Dad said, 'Fuck this shit, I'll be in the garage.'" The siblings all laugh boisterously, nodding their heads in agreement. "They've got a lot in common," Rachel says still chuckling.

Rachel's husband has come home from work and is sprinkling the conversation with additional observations. Side conversations continue among the siblings and spouses. As sippy cups are being filled and handed to children, the conversations are briefly interrupted so an adult can remind the child to say "thank you," someone is digging in the refrigerator for leftover avocado dip that Rachel made the night before, and toys are swept to the center of the table so that the children can eat. As one child crawls off a lap, another climbs up to occupy it. Logan says, "Even with all this dysfunction, we are still loyal. The loyalty is there. The rest of the shit just doesn't seem so extreme. There's a very humane side to us as well—you just don't treat people bad, and no matter how we're connected—in some fucked up way, they're family. When shit gets real, we will do everything for each other."

My next visit with Logan was at his house when his father and Pam were there for dinner. His house is diagonally across the street from Grandma Johnson's, and Logan is telling his father about his latest run-in with David, Travis's brother. He had heard Grandma's dog crying and went over there to check on her. He is worried about some of David's recent behavior, such as yelling at neighbors and calling the police on Keith.

"I had to get my fuckin' pistol to go over to Grandma's," he says with disgust, lowering his head and shaking it just like Keith. "It's a shame I have to grab a gun to check on my Grandma," he says. "David is fifty years old now—he is one of those people that has an inappropriate kind of love for his grandma."

"He's crazy," says Keith. "Always saying stuff he remembers about me that never happened, that never fucking happened! He was saying his dad, my brother, kicked my ass in some fight. We got in a fight, and I knocked him down and was choking him with my forearm," Keith says, describing the altercation with his brother. "He hit me with a beer bottle then his old lady came out and hit me over the head with a vase. That's how it went down."

Logan continues to explain the constant tension and fighting that he has experienced. He describes how David takes advantage of his grandmother, living in one of her houses rent-free for over twenty years and bringing his laundry to Grandma's to do it. When Grandma says something about it, or suggests he pay the rent, David will get belligerent, and she'll threaten to call Keith. "David said to Grandma 'I you want to see Keith dead, just go ahead and call him!'" Logan tells me about the most recent screaming match.

"But his fucking brother can kill my son," yells Keith. "I'll put my pistol in his mouth and pull the trigger. I'll fucking kill the son of a bitch." I look at Logan, then Pam. They're not shocked. This is a never-ending theme in their lives.

"This has been my whole fucking existence, dealing with this dumb shit!" says Logan. "You know, I am one year old when my brother is killed, then I spend my entire life around a brother of the man that killed my brother. He has ruined my entire lineage! Grandma's worried about who was a doctor and this and that, but not about keeping a son and a mother from having a healthy relationship."

"Him and his brother killed my fuckin' son," Keith continues. "I've had it. He's yelling at Logan, calling him a faggot. I told her, 'Why have you enabled him? You have raised him.' He'd go out, get a job and turn around and quit the job."

"She is the matriarch of the family," Logan says, "she should set a tone for the family. She said, 'Well, there's just so much hate in the family,'" he says, mimicking her voice and mannerisms. "And she just keeps picking at it," Keith responds. "She used to keep talking about Travis, and I told her 'I don't want to hear about it, Mom, the son of a bitch murdered my son!!'" Keith says, raising his voice again and looking at me. His eyes are defiant, the pain evident as if it's been only a week instead of twenty-five years. "I can't figure what the hold he has on her—he's lied to her, he's cheated her, it could be fear," he suggests. "My sister hates him."

A smoke break ensues while we all head outside to clear the air and our heads. I was surprised how quickly the chatter turned to children and gardening and whether Grandma's lights were still on. The laughter and camaraderie were still there—the tension was completely gone. I had to wonder if what I considered an awkward moment was really the norm for Logan, Keith, Pam, and Samantha. I thought about Angela's observation that there are some things you just don't talk about, and I wondered if it held true for everyone in the family or just with Grandma.

We talk about ancestry, family trees, and my research. I explain as honestly and completely as I can the various definitions of Melungeon that I have encountered. Something so complex and emotionally-laden to some is clearly easier for others to accept and internalize. "Do you think you're Melungeon?" I ask Logan. "Probably," he says, flashing a grin and laughing. "Do I care? No," he says referring to the possibility of Indian, black, and Middle Eastern or Spanish contributions to his ancestry. "It would mean I'm *di-ver-si-fied*," he says proudly, puffing out his chest and laughing. "It would mean I've got a background not everybody's got, YAY." We all laugh, looking around at each other and taking it all in.

"You hit it on the head the other day," Logan explained, reminding me of our conversation the day before at Rachel's. "You started looking at what's a Melungeon and after a while you started realizing it is nothing,

Logan Johnson in 2011.

this is just stories, people. We're not Greek or Hispanic or Melungeon, we're people who have had poor times, good times, and bad times. It's how *their* stories are *our* stories. For a lifetime, it gives your brother a voice, it gives your son a voice, and your daughter a dream," he says poignantly, crediting me for much deeper thought than I recall sharing.

"Them people had hard times, they was dirt poor, dirt floor poor, and hated by every single person they encountered. A lot of people want to be purebreds, but the best dog you can get is a mutt!" Keith exclaims. "If I'm black I don't care, if I'm half black I don't care, if I'm Indian I don't care. It doesn't matter to me—I just see through the bullshit, and the whole system in this country is bullshit. The capitalist system in this country is a system for the rich people to be rich.

"It doesn't matter what my great-grandpappy did, I can't change any of that. I still have to wake up every morning, put one foot in front of the other and provide for my daughter and my wife. It doesn't matter, you know. If I was the mistress's child, illegitimate, it doesn't matter. I'm here now. Of course it was hard, but it doesn't matter anymore. When I was younger, sure it bothered me, that's one hell of a way to come about, hearing these stories—it was hard. Through the years, I had to accept it. It is just the way it was. Ang, Rachel, Shawn, they were siblings, and Connie was Connie. I didn't know any different cause that's the way it was. It did bother me at times, because of not feeling connected or accepted, but then Angie was always there—she would come get me and take me to church camp, Rachel would come get me and take me places. When you're fourteen and friends would say they saw Logan in the mall with some hot girl," he stops at the implications and laughs. "I'm the mistress's child, though—that's real."

CHAPTER 5

Other Portraits

William Isom

We must act, white supremacy is still fucking everybody.

In May of 2013, I made it to Knoxville, to The Birdhouse to find William sitting outside in the backyard at a table with a sign announcing "fish fry, $5" taped to it. He sat with two women next to the table, a large fryer directly behind him. On the table was a large stainless steel buffet pan with fresh fried catfish, some plastic tubs of coleslaw, and a box of homemade snickerdoodle cookies wrapped in small plastic bags and tied with ribbons. Baked beans were available in a large tinfoil pan as well as a package of dinner rolls. All of the folks had a beer, and a pint of Crown Royal sat on the table next to a dry washcloth used as a potholder. There were tongs for the fish, and condiments sat on a side table: mustard, hot sauce, and ketchup, along with a package of white bread. Most of the people who did purchase a dinner ate the fish with hot sauce and mustard.

William is the volunteer coordinator at The Birdhouse in Knoxville, Tennessee, a community space preserved and maintained for and by the people of the neighborhood to collaborate on common projects and concerns. According to their website, The Birdhouse is a project of the Neighborhood Center, an open community space in the historic 4th and Gill Neighborhood of Knoxville. It is an all-volunteer-run effort, funded only by the people—a completely unique enterprise where the whole region comes together to create, build, eat, garden, dance, learn, share and organize with and for each other.

The organization partners with the community "in providing community space where active skill sharing, DIY workshops, gardening, participatory media production, historical documentation, and artistic creation, performance and exhibition can contribute to the life of the immediate community and the general public." The Birdhouse is a cause about which Isom is passionate. I had asked him what he would advise for the Melungeon communities of Hawkins and Hancock counties in Tennessee. "Create a space like this," he said, gesturing to the yard and house that is The Birdhouse.

William was smoking the stub of a cigarette while nursing his beer, when we started talking about Melungeons. He wore a red ball cap, a dark shirt and jeans, then added a hooded sweatshirt as it was rather cool and spitting rain. There was a large umbrella over the table, and above a canopy of trees helped block the rain. As we talked, people would come up to pay for a dinner; William would chat and help them and then return to our conversation. Groups would mingle, often standing with their plate, or go back inside where the loud music of several bands was wafting out of the house into the yard every time the door opened.

The little yard had a small garden in a corner with a hand-painted sign that said "tators." The grass was not recently mowed, but was at a reasonable length, and a little paved path about a foot wide wound through the yard from the gate I entered to the table where we were sitting. He introduced me to the people by saying "Everyone, this is Tammy, and Tammy this is everyone." A larger man with short hair and glasses, wearing a dark t-shirt and shorts, with tattoos going down his lower leg and arm, shifted his beer to his left hand to shake my hand and say, "Nice to meet you, I'm everyone too." We chuckled, and I returned my attention to William.

An easy-mannered man in his late thirties, William and I had been introduced by a mutual friend and Melungeon scholar Darlene Wilson. He is a community organizer, filmmaker, leader, mentor, activist, and father of two. We had enjoyed a telephone conversation, several emails, an interview, and conversation at the Appalachian Studies Association Conference in Boone, North Carolina. William had been sitting behind a table, also. He is a founding member of Hands Off Appalachia and was sitting at a long table with information about the dangers of mountain top removal and the impact of large banking conglomerates like UBS. A donation box was available for collecting funds for the campaign against UBS.

Isom was born in Hamblin County, Tennessee, in 1973 to parents with several children already. Grandparents and neighbors also welcomed the dark haired boy into the community located in the Appalachian Mountains. He grew up hearing the word Melungeon, not realizing that for many, Melungeon was an odd thing, until he traveled outside of the area. "Then I realized, oh, not everybody knows about Melungeons—it was just something growing up that people knew about and talked about [here]. It was matter of fact, nothing mysterious—like, you know so and so the Melungeon guy over [on the next ridge]," he explained. He had a young friend Joey, and they were almost inseparable. Growing up, the friend identified as Melungeon. "We was best friends, he was from Hancock family. My family didn't identify as Melungeon, and

William Isom, circa 2010.

his did. But we were always together as families, and people equated us as being brothers or kin."

Our conversation continued as I asked about what his family would say about Melungeons and how he was socialized to understand the term. He explained about going hunting with his father and some other older men in Prospect up on Newman's Ridge. The older men would tell stories about Melungeons, leaving a young Isom to understand that many had their own theories of "who" they were. "My dad would say it was nothing but Indians, runaway slaves, and whites all mixed together. Another guy said they was mixed Indians." The younger folks would have a different way of explaining their ancestry, "People my age would say, 'well, I can't drink that, you know, cause I'm Indian, I'm liable to get wild,'" Isom explained.

In the community where he lived, he recalls that labeling someone a Melungeon was definitely a racial thing. For the most part, however, if you were just describing someone, it wasn't derogatory. But if you were attacking someone, "or as a kid, like if you called somebody—another kid—to their face, a damned Melungeon, that meant that you really, really, hated that person to the core of their being. You could call them anything else, but that was the worst thing you could say or call someone." This was not an accepted identity by William or his family—yet.

Isom began to understand the complexity of Melungeons a bit more after Brent Kennedy's book came out: *Melungeons: Resurrection of a Proud People.* He had already been working on his family genealogy when he discovered his mother was Kennedy's second cousin. "I looked in his book and found my mom's family tree—so I thought, well that is something."

William has a somewhat swarthy complexion, with dark eyes that sparkle with mischief. He has black hair, trendy glasses, and a full beard with no mustache. He grins more than smiles, and while he is easy to talk with, he is very difficult for me to read. As people come to the gathering at The Birdhouse, a music festival of sorts, he greets them all and asks about their lives and activities, demonstrating a personal interest in each individual. He is personable, well read and articulate, while using a vocabulary that I would describe as "down to earth" or "homey." I want to know so much more about this man, but am not even certain of the questions I can ask. I get the impression that trust is not easily won, and I am nervous about asking anything that might mar the relationship. He has been extremely generous with his time and information, especially with intimate personal knowledge, and he assures me that I cannot offend him.

As I begin the line of questioning that I am exploring for this research, I examine his face for signs that I have overstepped a boundary. I start by asking which box he checks for race on any forms or documents. "I check 'em all," he says as he flashes a grin. I chuckle a bit as I reveal that my son refuses to check any of the boxes, and I wonder if the difference means anything. Then I ask him about his parents. He is thoughtful, choosing his words carefully. "Well, my mom checks the white box, and my dad probably checks the black one," he says.

We discuss his genealogy, learning more about the impact of race and how it relates to Melungeon families. His mother's side was from Wise County, Virginia, where her parents were "white enough to go to town and get a job." Isom discusses the benefits of families whose skin tones are light enough to "pass" and assimilate into white culture. It made the difference between being hired for the town jobs or having to stay secluded and subsist on part-time employment, farming, and odd jobs for the community. His maternal grandparents had already assimilated by the time his mother was born. On the other hand, his father's family had *stayed* Melungeon, meaning that they didn't assimilate into the greater society and they intermarried with other mixed, Melungeon, or Indian families (non-white).

Isom describes a point in his grandparents' lives where they had to make a choice to seek lighter mates or "stay" in the community. His father's family consistently married into the darker skinned community that excluded them from the town jobs that could have lifted the family out of poverty. While he sees the difference between Appalachians and Melungeons as racial, he also acknowledges "but then that becomes murky, as white as people are from the mountains, if you're in a holler and you're poor you're still not white enough to go into town and get a job. If you were Appalachian and had dark skin, then that would exacerbate your problems. If you had dark skin, that's all it took, you were not welcome down with the town folks. Life experiences like day to day racism, had big influence on people of color's life in America. One of the most important things then leading to pockets of Melungeon people was being a place where who you find camaraderie and build community. My dad would say, 'Why in the hell am I gonna go where I know they don't want me? I'm not gonna go where I'm not wanted!'

"A community of supportive and accepting people fortifies and gives foundation to your identity," says Isom. "I don't know about more specific things that formulated a Melungeon identity: in my mind, it was a broad range of life experiences that have combined and added to it. If you get to the point when you are comfortable with who you are and what you're made up as. Brent's book is one of the things you could point to as adding to that identity."

As people from southern Appalachia became more impoverished due to lack of tillable land, increases in population, and limits on growing tobacco, families began to move north where no one knew of their family ancestry and where industrial and automobile jobs were plentiful. A couple of uncles moved north for auto jobs, but Isom's parents were able to make a living where they were. The uncles went to Cleveland, got a job at Ford, and retired there.

Soon began many a conversation with family and friends, including Darlene Wilson, about the meaning and implications of a Melungeon identity. It became a personal quest for Isom's mother, sister, nephew, and the rest of the family to learn what they could. The conversations led to a critical view of who is researching this particular population and the implications of such research. Isom's experiences and responsibilities as an activist lend a unique perspective on the current dichotomy between documentary evidence as proof of belonging or common experience leading to identity.

"I think there is a group of people, like scholarly people, that believe there is a core group of Melungeons up on Newman's Ridge that represents the original Melungeons. But that just seems like an academic or white supremacist way of looking at things. To assume there is one core group seems rather arrogant, arrogance rooted in white supremacy. I think there is any number of families that are Melungeon that are not traceable to that group. And I know that there are a number of people today that have not assimilated and run afoul of the power structure pretty regularly," he says with a chuckle.

He admits he is not comfortable discussing his racial or Melungeon identity with strangers; it depends on why they want to know and in what context. He also cautions researching this topic from a [emotional or cultural] place far removed from Appalachia. Melungeons are leery of the tourists who are making their homes and communities into attractions. Their families have been represented in ways that have been offensive.

We talked further about this as I noted that I had been to the recent Melungeon Union sponsored by the Melungeon Heritage Association. Held in Big Stone Gap, Virginia, the attendance and agenda at the "meeting" was only a tiny flicker of its former self. Controversy and infighting has taken a huge toll on the once thriving association. I had looked around at the thirty or so attendees, noting that several sitting there were also presenters. I seemed to be sitting in a sea of middle-aged white people, who were excited about the speakers on DNA. I asked about the lack of Hancock County residents attending the gathering when he said, "You don't see poor people at a conference on poverty either." It is part of the power structure where the representative group of an academic conference has been dehumanized. As an activist, Isom believes that "the people" know what they need, what will work, and what will not to help their communities. For someone from outside the group to determine meaning and implications is more than ineffective—it objectifies the population, making them an item of study instead of a group of individuals with their own experiences, feelings, and family traditions.

He notes that there are real racial problems and the Melungeon people don't want their lives documented. He explains the history of socialization whereby elders passed along the sentiment that, "Yes, we might be Melungeon but at least we ain't black. You could say we're Portuguese, or Phoenician, or from Mars—just don't say we're black because then we're done for—there is no way we can assimilate." For those who have assimilated, both racially and economically, and can pass for white, some of these older people have the mindset that "no, we don't have any black in us" since they know what the consequences have been. "A lot of people today that live in this area don't go to the courthouse unless they just *have* to—it's not good, it's a place where people got in trouble, or it cost you."

Thanks to Walter Plecker and racial purity laws, there are gaps in genealogical and accurate historical research. By avoiding the courthouse, registering births, deaths, and marriages, they could at times protect their loved ones from the legal ramifications of the law. "People wouldn't say they were black, or Indian or whatever. Yeah, you'll find that a lot, especially black or Native American ...with my great-great-granddad, there was no death record, we found the tombstone out in the woods somewhere kind of by accident." He describes the trek he and other family members made into a forgotten burial ground where there were a few old headstones. Some were nothing more than markers, and others had weathered to the point of being illegible. He ended up stumbling unexpectedly across a half-buried stone covered with leaves and other debris from the past several decades. As he brushed the dirt aside with his hands, he discovered the name Isom on the stone and excitedly dug it from the earth. He had found the headstone of his ancestor Kelson Harrison Isom.

Unfortunately, burial places, family photos, and many oral histories were lost because people stopped talking and sharing family stories. "Because of Plecker, we lost a lot of documentation as well as the stories," Isom lamented. "There's no difference, to me, between being Appalachian and being Melungeon. Melungeons seem to be, after the Indians, the foundation of Appalachian culture and lifestyle. Being Melungeon, now, just fortifies my Appalachian identity. It provides a broader narrative for resistance to the white supremacist capitalist structure that continues to extract from our region. But, in all honesty, being Melungeon is still not something that's talked about with just anyone. It's still something I hold close."

I asked William if he considered himself Melungeon today. "I do—it depends on what the situation is—and the atmosphere of how that is brought up—but, yes I do identify as Melungeon, among other things. It means, to me, descended from historically mixed-raced families in southern Appalachia."

As the son of a sharecropper, and a trucker himself, Isom's father instilled a strong work ethic in his children. His mother encouraged an idealist passion for those

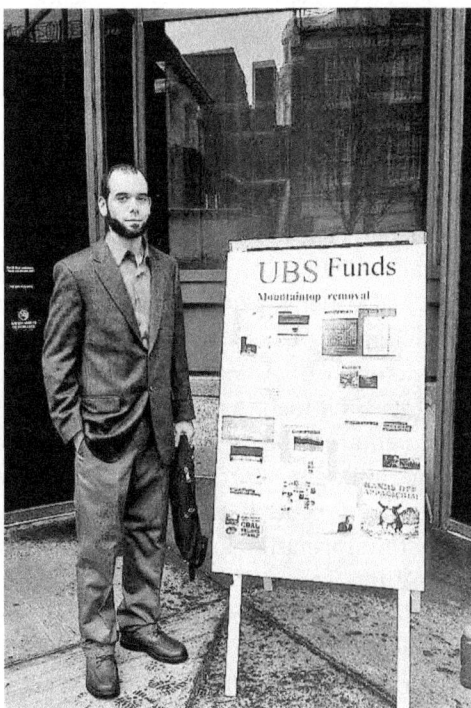

William Isom, circa 2012.

less fortunate. He credits both of his parents for his dedication to activism and social justice. He is not comfortable with the status quo and leads others into protests against larger corporations and banks that continue to oppress and marginalize the working people of Appalachia. Distrust of authority and fierce independence are also part of being Melungeon and Appalachian. bell hooks called it a natural anarchy that comes with life experiences; one's community dictates one's life with the outside world.

William Isom insists he has a responsibility to understand his place in history and that it is important to *remember and resist.*

Joanne Pezzullo

As far as whether you—myself—or anyone has "Melungeon" ancestors you must answer the question—"clearly and concisely"—"what is a Melungeon"—I believe that I have. In 1848 they told the country who they were—Portuguese who had mixed with the Indians and then went to Tennessee where they mixed with the Indians, blacks and whites. Not only documents, but DNA is supporting exactly what they said. There are many surnames in early records and histories that were "Portuguese" and there are others that record some as Indians. In the long run, I believe it is up to each family line—not just because they are a Gibson, Collins, Goins, etc., to find their family history—each one is different.

"I can't claim any Melungeon heritage—and never have—I don't claim any whatsoever," Joanne told me during our first conversation. I had met Joanne while working on genealogy. We both were researching our Gibson lines when I asked her for help. I noted that she was a regular contributor to many Melungeon websites, including her own, "Melungeon Indians," and I had hoped for some clarification on my own ancestry. We eventually concluded that our Gibsons were not related to each other. When I began my doctoral work, I looked her up again, and we reconnected. During my pilot research Joanne provided me with a telephone interview to use in a documentary to be presented at the Appalachian Studies Association conference in Boone, North Carolina. While we have not been able to connect in person, Facebook and the telephone have provided effective avenues to share information and become co-researchers.

While Joanne's passion and commitment to Melungeon and genealogical research is evident in her postings and contributions on relevant websites, it was really prominent in her voice and word choice when I interviewed her. I had my trusty recorder going with the phone on speaker as I sat up with my notepad and articles on the dining room table of my home. Her voice is clear and assertive, her understanding well-researched and analyzed. My family was home at the time and couldn't help but be drawn to the conversation, stopping at the table and listening. Their facial expressions were a delight to watch as they heard someone else as excited and intrigued as I was over the subject matter. We swapped out phones once as the battery died and kept the tape going for almost four hours.

Joanne cautions me to be careful when collecting information and reading books, considering their motives and what information the authors were invested in and out to prove. She spoke with confidence born of inside knowledge about the early DNA studies and the various perspectives of different researchers trying to show Jewish, Turkish, or Native American connections or to eliminate an African-American contribution to the bloodlines. She chuckled more than laughed, and the indignation in her voice was obvious as she talked about one researcher looking for a "real" Melungeon to test. "She was trying so hard to prove what she wanted that she ended up taking this person out of the project," Joanne explained. Another prominent researcher and author "has done the same thing, mostly from the female lines—they were taken out of the project with no explanation—none whatsoever," she says. "Because I am so vocal of my criticism on the DNA project, I get emails from people saying that they were denied being a part of the project or were kicked out of the project," she exclaimed. "I could go on for years and years about this stuff and it gives me a headache." Then we both laughed.

I was well aware of the controversies that had played out publically on the Melungeon-L genealogy website. Joanne doesn't mince words, calls a spade a spade, and lets the chips fall where they may. Strong and opinionated, Joanne had told me she had thick skin as a result of being one of

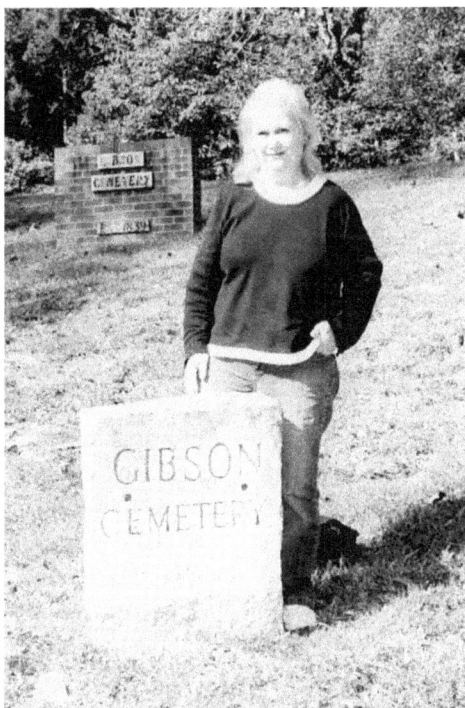

Joanne Pezzullo, 2013.

seven siblings. However, a couple of posts on Melungeon-L show glimmers of hurt feelings over challenges and mean-spirited responses to her posts. Usually she could give as good as she got, but in the early years of the discussion, her strong critiques of research would instigate a rash of personal critiques that were shocking.

"I started with a few other people, all researching together," she explains, "then I would show one of them where his genealogy was flawed and he insisted on printing his version." She was incredulous that anyone would stick with a line of thinking when the evidence pointed to something else. "Nobody really knows who they were speaking of when they were calling people Melungeon. For instance, in 1856 the Virginia newspapers were full of references of Melungeons, they were like a powerful group—like a political group that were supposedly a mixed race. Henry Wise, the governor of Virginia, is the one that popularized this term—they were the Melungeons of Virginia, and another article said they were in Alabama—and they were there when the Virginia County first started. They were called Melungeons, where did these people really come from? People want to claim the "word" and they don't even know."

Joanne argues that no one has seen the original transcripts of the Stoney Creek Church minutes. The often-referenced document is quoted from a transcription, "and if it is a bad transcription—sometimes they're awful with all kinds of mistakes," she says. "The person who wrote it was Nevil Wayland, and he was married to a Gibson and either his mother or his wife was a Melungeon. Why is it only mentioned once? Emory L. Hamilton was supposed to be the first person to write the history of Virginia and never mentioned that the Melungeons were in the Stoney Creek Church. Isn't that odd that Hamilton, who wrote all kinds of well-received history books, never mentions that?" she asks. "You can't pin a whole people's history on that one piece of paper transcribing the Melungeon paper at Stoney Creek Church. It doesn't mean anything if there is only one paper," she insists. I am writing fast, trying to list my questions, resources, and the spelling of names.

"Like I said, I had never heard of this word Melungeon, but my family were Gibsons. They came from Morgan County Kentucky, but they were not dark, always listed as white, which is why I have always doubted their kinship to Melungeons who were sometimes listed as white but very often listed as Black or Mulatto. Our Gibsons are haplogroup I [Vikings]. The Gibson who were neighbors in Morgan County were the Bryson Gibson family which were very dark, African haplogroup," Joanne explains. "There are five distinct DNA groups for the Gibsons, but [the people on the discussion boards] will still call them all Melungeons if they are a Gibson."

"My mother threw such a fit when I started doing the research, she would get enraged when I discussed doing research on the family. It's like there was always a secret and no one wanted to talk about it, and a hint that there might have been someone black in the family, you know what I mean? Families are scared, and angry." Joanne recounts, "My grandfather, grandson of Elizabeth Gibson, insisted he was 100% Irish—but at one time he said he was Portuguese and laughed. My grandmother said 'Now Bill, don't go telling those stories' and that was the extent of it. So there may have been a hint. Those 'other Gibsons' were certainly known to have African roots but also called Indian."

"So what makes me angry," says Joanne, "is all the angry words I had with my mother over the family history was all for naught because in the long run, they were not related. They were stereotyped—their name was Gibson."

I study the photos on Facebook, looking for snippets of the woman behind the research. There is one photo of Joanne by herself, standing on the porch of Jack Goins's cabin in Tennessee. Her hair is pulled back from her face with wisps of silvered brown backlit from the sun. Her face glows, and her dark brown eyes look open and inquisitive. She wears a dark sweatshirt with the saying, "Who are these kids and why are they calling me Mom?" on it. Chains from a porch swing are visible behind her, and her arms hang casually at her sides. More photos from the same trip show her roaming through cemeteries and posing in front of a stone engraved "Gibson Cemetery." Her face is unlined, leaving one to guess her age at anywhere from fifty years and up.

"I don't think there is an easy answer," Joanne responds to my questions of why someone would want to identify as Melungeon. "You have probably found that out already. There are many reasons different people want to be Melungeon." Our first conversation identified two camps of people that Joanne has noticed coming to the discussion boards. She would later add a third. "Anyone who is drawn to the Melungeon research is brought there because they suspect there is some African in them— half come to prove it isn't there. The other half knows that it's there and want to be special," she surmises, "they belong to this mysterious group." A pair of researchers that Joanne spent a lot of time with wasted many hours arguing about the African DNA. "You don't know where it came from," she says, "they could have come in the 1500s with Pardo's group as slaves and then mixed with Indians. Then wouldn't they be Indians by 1800?"

"Then there was the Hamilton County Melungeons, we fought and fought about whether to include them in the core Melungeon group,"

Joanne says, referring to her collaboration with several other prominent researchers. "There are court records and how can you not include them?" she asks. "They are saying you have to sweep them under the rug. Yet the court documents are calling them Melungeons, their neighbors are calling them Melungeons. They said it's a problem, it's a big problem—one individual said 'they're fake Melungeons,' and refused to consider anything else." In the end, the researchers rejected them from the project.

Joanne referred me to the court transcripts of the Hamilton County Melungeons posted on her website. Dedicated to primary source documents, she has discovered many articles and posted them in their entirety on both her site and the Melungeon-L site. She is angered when she sees pieces of articles pulled out of context without links or references for people to make their own decisions on the content. The court case referenced is one of a young girl who had proven to the satisfaction of the court that she was Moorish and not black, in order to claim her inheritance. Joanne has traced many of the Melungeons to the Pee Dee River area of South Carolina and uses this area as a reference point in identifying Melungeons. Solomon Bolton was involved in the above case: his father was in the Revolution, filed for a pension, and said he was born on the Pee Dee River in 1730 or '35. "There are people in the transcripts saying they knew him and knew he was Portuguese," says Joanne.

"Robert Thomas was a Cherokee," she adds. "He was the author of *Cherokee Communities of the South* [Burnette, 1889]. He says in his paper that the Pee Dee River is where everybody went home. It was where all the tribes came to congregate." Another piece on her website is a letter written by Lawrence Johnson in 1889 in response to an article on ophthalmic diseases. "Johnson was an educated man; when he read the article by Burnette, he wrote a letter to the editor and said that he knew who those people were and that they originated on the Pee Dee River. He knew the records were in the library in Charleston in 1890 and about the ships that came in and where the people came from. He knew the word *Melungeon* and knew it was referring to the Portuguese people that lived on the Pee Dee River," Joanne says, sounding exasperated. "So why can't people believe these eye witnesses to history? I have uncovered all these documents and no one wants to believe them. I mean, why would this man have written this? He was a geologist. They believe the 1856 papers, but don't want to believe these? They want them to be mysterious, or the information just doesn't fit with their stories," Joanne exclaims. One prominent Melungeon author said, "The Bolton case was court records and court records aren't facts." "What do you mean?" Joanne cries, "It's a court record! They are sworn under oath!"

Joanne chuckles again as we discuss the variety of people searching for their Melungeon roots. "Do some people just want to belong so bad that they cling on to it and don't do the research or listen to the research when someone else finds it?" she wonders. "The people said they were Portuguese—then they mixed with the Indians—then they came to Newman's Ridge and mixed with the Indians, blacks, and whites. Why would they lie about it? The Goins said they mixed with the blacks—they've known that. They told Dromgoole the same thing—they said they were Portuguese, Indian and black." By now I look around the dining table and find the rest of my family transfixed as she talks. Joanne's ability to hold an audience captive without any visual aids was impressive.

"The one thing that really astounds me, is that you can accept that the Cherokee can say this is Turtle Island and that their world started with little people. Would anyone ever make fun of their legends or family stories, or say they don't believe them? No—no scholar would EVER do that," Joanne argues. "The other thing I can't understand is with the African DNA. Even if they were slaves and they came over here in 1618 and mixed with the Indians, after three hundred years, aren't they Indian?" She asks. "Nope, they say if they have African DNA they are African. There are card-carrying Cherokee Indians on the reservation with African DNA and would anyone ever say they are not Indian? Never!"

The idea of DNA testing, along with the interpretations, has been a thorn in her side for years. Joanne is amazed that anyone with any sense at all would think you could truly provide a valid Melungeon DNA test. "There is no Melungeon DNA test," she says, echoing other researcher's sentiments. "One author started a DNA company and said they could find your Melungeon family. They are really, really exploiting people," she says. Joanne articulates an understanding of the historical context and social contributions to the meaning of race but also contributes to the old argument against the "one drop" rule. She is truly flustered with pinpointing when the contribution of identifiable DNA trumps years of lived culture.

Joanne, however, is "absolutely glad she got her DNA tested." I had asked her why, what did it tell her? "Okay, well—well—I did it with Family Tree DNA first and was disappointed because I got 400–500 matches ... wrote to one hundred people and no one responded. One group had nineteen people who descended on the same ancestor and only one wrote me back. They are probably doing a one name project," she explains.

"The Ancestry.com test, that is connected through your family tree," she tells me. "When you get your results back and you do match someone, it goes right to their tree and it says you have a common ancestor. *And* the people on ancestry are interested in the genealogy or they wouldn't even be there. I had two families I had wrong that I was able to straighten out with the DNA." Excitedly she tells me about helping others as well as learning more about her own family. "Constantly today I am getting emails that help me prove or disprove my lines. I am absolutely thrilled with it!"

Joanne is a fixer and a caregiver. Besides raising her own several children, she took in two nieces and raised them for twelve years; she is currently helping her son with her grandchildren. When her first grandchild was born, she lived with Joanne for six years while her mother, Joanne's daughter, served in the Iraq war. The photos on her Facebook page include weddings, birthdays, memorials, and even grandchildren visiting their grandfather in the hospital. Family is more than just important; it appears to define the day-to-day activities of her life. Several historical family pictures reveal commonalities in the eyes and set of the mouth. Many of her profile pictures through the year have been artists' renditions of Victorian women. You can tell a lot about a person through their photo collections, I realize. Memes with patriotic themes are scattered throughout the collection along with other little sayings about the power of prayer. I wonder if her assertiveness is really a protective measure born of self-reliance and years of protecting others. I also wonder if she is brutally honest in her words in hopes that others will return the favor. I get the sense that trust has been misplaced in the past and she won't let it happen again. She is a smart cookie.

I ask Joanne if she is Melungeon. She doesn't answer immediately. "Hmmmm, I wouldn't think so," she says, "but I'm open, I'm still looking. My families were all around. There are Ivys involved in the 1812 court records, then the Perkins, they were in the Johnson City, Tennessee, court in 1858 where someone was trying to take their land saying they were Africans and couldn't own it. Then the Collinses who went to Indiana and the Chavis family that went to Cherokee area in Alabama. The Shoemakes got 640 acres or something like a small reservation at Little Crow Creek in Jackson County, Alabama. All these people were from the Pee Dee River area." She describes the Hall family experiences: "Thomas Hall got a race affidavit after 1836 in Tennessee to say he was Portuguese. He went to Arkansas on the White River, and from there he went to Missouri. He had to use the affidavit to prove he wasn't black and make the public schools accept his children who were thrown out for not being white."

While the evidence seems overwhelming to me, clearly Joanne isn't willing to declare herself Melungeon. "What would it take?" I ask her. "I would have to find something," she explains. "I can't find any documents connecting my relatives to the Pee Dee River or to the other groups called Melungeons. For one thing, our DNA matches descendants of Valentine Gibson of Louisa County who went to Stokes County, North Carolina. Most of his sons married Quakers and the Quakers did not allow for mixed-race families in their memberships."

"But remember, I'm not out to prove anything, one way or another," she says. "Whatever way it goes, I'm open to. I'm just trying to research my family. You know how these boards are, if you said you were a Melungeon they would be all over you, you know, all over you," Joanne says sardonically. "That's how these boards are, they'd say you're not a Melungeon." I tell her about my meeting with Brent Kennedy in 2001 when he looked at my mother, sister, nephew, and me and pronounced us Melungeons. "It sure seemed easy to be a Melungeon then," I say, laughing. Joanne is delighted with the memory and laughs. "That just tickles me," she says.

"This will probably knock your socks off, it will really surprise you," Joanne says preparing to reveal a stressful time in her Melungeon research. "It started out so innocently. I want to say this first: I really, really, really liked Brent Kennedy," she says emphatically emphasizing every word. "We had many, many private emails. I was there from the beginning. After these first people started the picnic, Brent Kennedy hijacked it and he invited all the people from Turkey to come over. I followed along for quite a while, and I believed it all for a long time, and I followed Brent. Then he went to Washington D.C., and went before some committee, and there was this fiasco." Being well-read and informed, Joanne was shocked and disappointed at a few Kennedy statements she came across and chose to post on the Melungeon-L discussion board. In part (forgive me, Joanne, for not including the whole post), she said:

> This is about the fact that items such as this was printed in newspapers and posted to this list;
>
> "Melungeons number several thousands, and recently have acted as one with the Turkish lobby. They have contributed to denounce a bogus bill that is being pushed by hatemongers in the Armenian community."
>
> This article implies, as does a number of others, that SEVERAL THOUSANDS of Melungeons are taking a *POLITICAL* stand.
>
> Perhaps if the MHA board along with the several thousands of Melungeon descendants would write to some of the webmasters we might get some of this stuff removed. The Turkish-Armenian subject is still a very newsworthy item. You need only go to google-news and type it in to see how newsworthy. I did not introduce these articles and this subject to this list to embarrass ANYONE or a WITCH HUNT—I seriously want this stuff like this below removed from the internet.

MELUNGEONS EXTEND FULL SUPPORT TO TURKEY WASHINGTON
D.C.—While the discussions continue whether to take the draft law on so-called
genocide on Armenians into agenda of the local senate of Virginia state, Melungeons who introduce themselves as Americans of Turkish origin, announced on
Friday that they extend full support to Turkey.
    Prof. Brent Kennedy, one of the leaders of Melungeons society, who partici-
pated in the meeting of the Assembly of American-Turkish Associations (ATAA)
said that they support Turkey regarding the issue of the draft law on so-called
genocide on Armenians [Pezzullo, 2008].

The above comments from Joanne are a response to a political move by
the Turkish government to deny any involvement with the Armenian genocide and Brent Kennedy's support of Turkey. The family of Brent Kennedy
brought a lawsuit against Joanne. Eventually acquitted, Joanne spent two
years and hundreds of dollars fighting the suit that she calls "ridiculous."
"I criticized Brent on the boards for his support of Turkey in this political
mess and his insistence on Turkish origins, and these other guys were dis-
tasteful and nasty in their remarks about Brent," she said. Not wanting
Brent to speak for her or all members of the Melungeon Heritage Association, Joanne demanded that the remarks be publically retracted and
any connection between MHA and the Turkey contingency be severed.
"It went on for almost two years—I had to hire an attorney, it cost me lots
of money. What they were trying to get me for, and they brought the FBI
in for, they were saying that I was printing stuff out of his book without
his permission," she said, referring to Kennedy's second book with Joseph
Scolnick (2004). "They didn't know the emails I had from Brent, giving
me permission to publish anything I wanted," she explained.

    "The hostile environment at the M list seriously never bothered me,"
Joanne rationalized. "As you read the messages, I think you will probably
begin to see there are probably like three groups. There are the Brent
Kennedy followers, then there are the Newman's Ridge only group. The
descendants from Newman's Ridge want to hold tight to the 'mysterious'
aspect of the Melungeons—and want to consider themselves a small,
exclusive club. So this is where the third group comes in that I mentioned:
the researchers. The ones who are actually looking for answers, not
because they want to know they belong to this 'mysterious' group of people, but because they want to know who their families really were," she
explains.

    Over twenty years of genealogical work and almost as much investi-
gation on Melungeons informed Joanne Pezzullo on historical context,
migration patterns, and DNA analysis and limitations. "I've talked to a lot
of people over the years and I think many of them felt they were doing

this for their ancestors—because of the way they were treated or described," explains Joanne. "You know, when I started doing this research—it wasn't like I wanted to *be* something, but I wanted to prove something. Like I said, my mother was absolutely enraged that I was doing this research on the family. My dad and his parents and the stories they had explained some things. They went to egg rolls at the White House, fought with Custer, some came over on the Mayflower. However, on my mother's side my grandmother came from Bath County, Kentucky, and told me that her father was three-quarters Susquehanna. I read that they were long extinct and thought 'Why would she even know about them, why would she say that? Why not Cherokee or something familiar?'" she said passionately. "I wanted to prove or disprove what I had heard." Incredibly for Joanne, "Pretty much everything I heard has been truthful, although some exaggerated," she laughs, "so I can't say I was looking to 'be' somebody, but to prove something."

"I really am rather a 'behind the scenes' person," Joanne says as we wrap up the call. "When I first started my website in 2002, I didn't put my name on it for a long time. I don't know why I didn't either. I did find posts on L where they were speculating that Pat Elder was probably the author. In fact, they were sure 'it couldn't be Joanne.' Pat and I had a good laugh over that," she says, "I'd just say I'm a good researcher."

"But seriously," I ask her, "if you could wave a magic wand and do your own study—what would YOU do?"

"A study on the studiers would be fascinating," she says with a chuckle.

Jack Goins

In gratitude, I recognize the ones now deceased.... The stories told to me in the early 1950s by my grandfather, Henry Harrison Goins, and the great memory of my parents, McKinley and Ona Arrington Goins.

Jack Goins was sitting at a table in the dark room of the Hawkins County Archives. Long dated conference tables crowded the center of the room that was lined with volumes of books, binders, and boxes. "I wasn't sure you were coming," he said softly, "I didn't hear from you." I had called Jack earlier in the week from Michigan to set up an interview. We agreed to a place and time for the coming Saturday at the Hawkins County Archives in Rogersville, Tennessee, an eleven hour drive from my home. We found the one story brick building and walked through the heavy side door. It had been drizzling all morning and there was quite a chill. He looked up as we walked in and removed his cap but left the lightweight navy jacket on.

He smiled as I shook his hand and his steely blue eyes warmed just a bit. His lined face represented the passing of several seasons, but his countenance was hard to read and unnerved me just a bit. "Well, where do you want me?" he asked as I began setting up my small video camera and checking the batteries in my audio recorder. He seemed to be all business as I positioned him across from the large windows typical of old post offices or government buildings. The natural light would be helpful for video and pictures.

Jack looked directly ahead most of the time sitting straight, with his hands on the table in front of him. "This is Hawkins County Archives," he said by way of explanation of our meeting place and without any gestures. "I started this, we got the records from the court house, it was in oh-five, January I believe, with a whole bunch of people helping. We cleaned and indexed the records then the Mormons came here and stayed almost two years," he says chuckling. "Brent [Kennedy] helped me here about as much as any one person when I started these archives. We ended up with a new Dell computer and printer and everything from his work, and $1,000 to get things started. 'Course we needed it, those acid free folders are twenty-five cents apiece and we used ten thousand of them. The county owns the building and pays the water and electric but we operate on donations." He talked slowly, scratching the top of his head every so often. A pen was visible in the shirt pocket of his button-up dress shirt. His wire-rimmed glasses provided rectangular frames for his eyes, though he would often look over the top of them.

"I've been researching all my life," he said, "I'll be eighty in April." He smiled, rubbed his chin and continued. "Yeah, I've been around awhile. I started in the '60s, you know, started out at home and worked my way back nine generations on my Goins family. I wasn't interested in writing a book or even about the Melungeons." His face revealed nothing but his hands fiddled with the green-colored cover of the book he authored sitting on the table. Looking at the variety of census and court records on the shelves behind him, it was easy to believe that the family history had gotten him hooked.

"My grandpa, when he stayed with us, he would talk about the old things, I guess he got me interested in it." Jack smiled warmly at the recollection. "Well, he wouldn't be talking to *me*, he would be talking to other people. Like, one Sunday he was talking to a neighbor, he was from over in Hancock County, too, I remember Grandpa saying they [Melungeons] were some kind of Indian, that's what he used, some kind of Indian." It seemed to tickle him, the reference to "some kind of Indian," and he laughed shaking his head.

"Of course I was born over there in Hancock County and I didn't know about [Melungeons] then. 'Course Dad and my Grandpa did. When I started, I was researching both my family lines, and I run into the same people in both lines sometimes. Like the Riddles, I have them in both Dad and Mom's line." He went on to explain this part of his line including having relatives involved in the Revolution and as pioneers. He discussed one relative, a Riddle, who was a Baptist minister, converted to

Jack Goins, 2017.

the Mormon faith and went with the Mormons in their march to Utah. John's great grandson wrote a book on his Riddle family. It was 1500 pages according to a descendant. He had a lot of wives, not sure how many. Some of his brothers claimed he just went because they could have more than one wife," he said laughing.

"I had two grandpas killed, one in the Civil War and this one here in the Revolution. He's hung for being a Tory. So you could say I'm lucky to be alive. That's what happens when you research," he said. "You find out all that stuff. I wanted to learn more about it because it was my family." He explained his interest in family and genealogy as almost an obsession. He laughed and emphasized, "I just wanted to know—that's all!"

There was silence again for a bit as he looked through his book and then back at me. "So do you believe you're Melungeon?" I asked in earnest, gaining courage. "I never even thought about it, you know, but I am if the rest of them are," he said sarcastically. "I'm not like Wayne Winkler though, I don't feel like *I'm* a Melungeon, I'm just a *descendant* of them. I don't think there is any such thing today and I told Wayne that." Again he looks directly at me, making eye contact and chuckling. "He sets and claims he's a Melungeon, but he's not!"

"See, the family finder tests shows that all those people are all related. Every one of them," he says, referring to the folks from Newman's Ridge and their direct family members. Jack's project required specific guidelines for acceptance: "a study of males who have proven known Melungeon ancestors, according to old records, and agreed on by some of the top Melungeon researchers," along with a five-generation pedigree, with historical records labeling the family or individual as free colored, mulatto, or black.

"Even the way I done it, there would be some that didn't belong, but there would be few. We had pretty good genealogy to know who they were, we asked for five pedigree haplogroup chart of descendants. "And you want to eliminate all of them that you don't think is Melungeon?" I asked. "I don't want to eliminate them, I just don't accept those who do not meet the requirements as stated in the project. I don't accept them as a Melungeon or even as a descendant," he said. "They want to be something they're not, they think they're left out if there is no handle put on them I guess. Lord only knows. We began with four administrators and our goal was to find the origin of the people that everybody *knew* was Melungeon who had done any research at all. There's nobody who's ever come up with a settlement like that [at Sneedville or Newman's Ridge], and really there's a lot of people there. And all their names are right in that census. So that's how I decided who would be in the project, the descendants of those on the census, well, not only the census, Valentine Collins wasn't on the census, he had already left, but those on the records, the tax records and land records, the church records, I used all that and the revolutionary war records and pension applications.

"The DNA study we presented to a peer review," he states proudly. "Yeah, we did a lot of work. What it is, see, you must request to get on the core Melungeon DNA project. We've got it listed what people needs to list to apply, and if you're kin, we set up another one called Melungeon families, and that's the largest one. We didn't want to eliminate anybody, a lot of them probably have more Melungeon than I have, but that's just the way we done it. It tells you the original race and finds those you match in the FTDNA data base.

"When I receive a request to join the core Melungeon DNA project I read their request and if they descend from a core Melungeon listed in our project I accept their request. If they don't then their request is denied. I reject those who do not follow the rules listed in our project." He is laughing again, shaking his head with incredulity as he explains what they will ask. "'Grandpa said we are Melungeon,' and stuff like that. "I hate to turn people down, but most of the people who ask me to get on I turn away. You wouldn't believe why they want to be on there—they say 'I want to see if I am a Melungeon.' That's the truth," he adds amazed. "*It don't do that*," he said emphatically. "*It just tells you if you've descended from those core Melungeons.*"

"And those two mixing is what ended up being Melungeon," he said referring to blacks and whites. "And that's how them other one's got that too like Brass Ankles, Red Bones, and them. You can't be a Melungeon if you are black or if you're an Indian. See that's what I tell 'em, if you're an Indian you can't be a Melungeon, if you're *all* Indian—'cause they were mixed!"

"Like this Johnnie Rhea, now she was a Melungeon, even today you'd have to say those who stayed and married in the clan would have the dark features of their Melungeon ancestor."

"I'm satisfied who they was and how they spread," he said, his eyes once again hard and direct. "I used tax records, you know, and these were the same people on the tax list in Orange County and that's the grandparents that probably started out as mulatto and you know what that was, and that may be how it got started. Everybody says it's a French word meanin' mixed, so I don't know, could be." The Southern drawl softens the words but doesn't reach his eyes.

So I ask him what makes someone a Melungeon, and he replies "well, what makes them Melungeon is they're a mixture of black and white, I've proved it right here," he says tapping his book. "But I don't look at Melungeons…. I don't look at them as a race. It's an ethnic group, but I don't look at them as a race like an Indian or a Jew or some of them," he says. "It's a name you know, that they didn't like, that was put on them by their white neighbors."

I asked about whether or not he felt the Melungeons were somehow connected to the Redbones or Brass Ankles groups. In his book, Goins states that "Melungeons were formed in a certain time and place in our history."[1] "No," he stated, the firm set of his face and now the telltale sign of looking directly at me said that this point was important. "Those were separate. When Price did that research in the 1950s, he had them listed separately."

He asked for a bit of time to find a specific story from his book. Upon finding it, he looks up smiling, then bows his head and begins to read: "Lewis Jarvis, see, he was a captain in the Civil War. This Jarvis says that they was given this name [Melungeon] by their white neighbors who came here with them." He put down the book. "They both came here at the same time [whites and Melungeons]. You can prove that with those tax records. There's lots you can find out with the tax records. But it was a derogatory name. It was given to them because of the color of their skin. That's the way I view it really, it's a derogatory name which they hated, now everybody wants to be one." His eyes twinkle and his face visibly lightens as he grins and continues laughing.

"So when you back track them, you see that's where Melungeons come from most of the time," he says getting serious. "See, I followed them on the tax records. They come from Orange County [North Carolina] at the Flat River. That church, Flat River Baptist, was the same denomination as Stony Creek and Blackwater, some referred to them as old Hard Shell Baptist. They went first to Stoney Creek, so I went there and took pictures, all that's in this book," he says while once again tapping the book on the table. "Was in the first book too." I felt scolded that I hadn't remembered what was in his books. "They went there, then to Blackwater. They changed their membership from Stoney Creek to Blackwater, and that's where, in those [church] minutes, is where the first Melungeon word is used in the 1813 minutes of Stony Creek Baptist Church."

Jack's purpose and project became clearer as he explained his methods to me. "See, that's the difference in this here story from those other stories, this one you can tell who the people are" he said referring to the story. "You can find them on the census, and the tax records, that's what we did. The standards were just for those people because I wanted to know who those people were, not Kennedy's Melungeons. He'd already been there and done his. I helped him gather some of the Y DNA samples, they were sent to a lab in England to be analyzed. That's when I first found I was African," he says laughing and hitting the table in front of him with his fist. "And I went and had it done again. It said the same thing." His eyes shine mischievously as he hits the table again, laughing.

"The mtDNA that Brent did was everybody. I was involved in it, he didn't even know some of those people, everybody wanted to be in it and what does that prove, it's an Appalachian DNA project that's all it is," says Goins, making eye contact, straight faced.

I asked if there were two groups of Melungeons then, Brent's and these that he was testing. He said "Yeah, if you want to call Brent's 'Melungeons.' Most of them around Wise [County Virginia], they came there from Hancock County during the coal, to mine coal. And a Felix Miner, he's out of my Miner family, he's–I knew all them, he got a great big coal company over there, and he hired everyone who came up there from Hancock County. And that's where they came from. No, he done DNA on every one of his family surnames. His Mullins's aren't related to Mahala or those Mullins. I wanted to know the origin of my Goins line. My great great grandpa's haplogroup was African, ain't no question, and he married a white woman, a European," he says laughing. "DNA proved it.

"See, R1b is the Walmart haplogroup—that's what you are—Walmart, cause that's the largest one," again he seems tickled and revels in the joke since I had told him that my line of Gibsons were R1b. "Now see, I'm E1b, then E1b1a now E-M2, they keep changing the haplogroup identity. When our core Melungeon Y-DNA project began showing a large group with African haplogroups Joanne Pezzullo accused me of padding the results with my Goins and removing men with R haplogroups from the project. At the time five Goins family test results were African but none of them matched each other. We did not remove anyone from the project. We had a Gibson and several Collins and Bunch families whose haplogroup was African. Joanne was not involved in our DNA project she was a member of MHS, Melungeon Historical Society. Wayne [Winkler] was the first president. We formed that group when we found out that MHA became dues paying members of Turkey ATAA organization. All of the MHA members did not leave. I was president when we voted to close MHS because no local people volunteered to help with meetings and yearly reunions."

I asked why the MHA is still hanging on. "There's more people," he states. "More people that wants to be Melungeon than is Melungeon."

* * *

I asked Jack if the people on Newman's Ridge or in Sneedville had any cultural traits or unique behaviors, customs, or traditions. "I think each neighborhood had their own way of doing things," he replied. "Their language is different. One lady came and said 'I can't understand you people.' I told her she had to learn to speak English," he said laughing softly. "They say it was Elizabethan English—I say just mountain hillbilly, I guess."

I asked about squatting or promiscuity, babies out of wedlock, if those were part of being Melungeon. "No," he said, "it's just part of being American, really." Again he laughed. "I don't believe in none of those traits, the Anatolian knot, everybody's got one, just some peoples' is bigger, I don't believe in none of that stuff. Even Brent went and said that his disease isn't a Melungeon disease, and that's the way he was known [Kennedy's

bout with Sarcoidosis was originally claimed to be evidence of Mediterranean admixture and part of the Melungeon condition]."

Melungeon researchers are a relatively small group and often know
one another. Jack was no exception. "I wrote in here what Wayne Winkler
said," said Jack, "that the publicity generated by Brent Kennedy's book and
later development of the MHA led many people to claim a Melungeon
connection, a claim often built on very flimsy evidence. Wayne'd like to
have that back now, I mean, he's on the fence. One time he's on one side
then he's on the other. That's the way it is," Jack said, chuckling and thumbing the corners of the book.

I brought up the controversies that continue to swirl around Melun-
geon literature and research. It seems that much of the original movement
attributed to Kennedy's first book has splintered into several factions.
People join the one that best confirms their own identity and Jack agreed.
Goins continues to explain some of the confusion of Sneedville residents:
"The original Melungeons was all gone before the outside drama, *Walk
Towards the Sunset*, in 1969. Collins was instrumental in getting that. It
was important because it identified [Melungeons], what they were and
who they were. Nobody knew in 1969. There was a story in the *Saturday
Evening Post* where my brother-in-law's mother over there on the ridge
said she can remember Mahala Mullins living out there. However, when
they said 'Melungeons,' she didn't know what that was. When I interviewed
her, she said she didn't even know what they're talking about." His point
was not lost on me. They were the people that others studied. However,
it was difficult if not impossible to recognize themselves in the writings
that followed.

"[Katherine] Vande Brake has two books out. I've never understood
her. Really, I mean I like her, she's a nice lady. She's done all her research
at Vardy, right there in the middle of it and she writes stuff about Melungeons that I don't know nothing about."

Goins, a no-nonsense person, was intelligent, direct, and all business.
"I believe there ain't no Melungeons today, just descendants of 'em. That's
been my message from day one really, people ask if I'm a Melungeon and
I tell them no, but I descended from two of 'em."

CHAPTER 6

What Does This Tell Us?

The information gleaned from Melungeon research has focused on history, origin theories, racial discrimination, and oppression/privilege narratives. These findings helped all co-researchers of this study to better understand the interaction between the internal and external perceptions of *Melungeon-ness*, as well as the meaning each of us attributed to being Melungeon. We explored grand questions and found that identity, both individual and collective, is messy, complicated, and often elusive to define. However, our stories and memories of lived experiences continue to shape and define our perceptions of ourselves and our understanding of how others see us.

In the preceding portraits, I introduced the Johnson family, the Gibson sisters, cousin Anna Partin, and my own family, including mother Sylvia, daughter Kateri, and sister Arlene. I have also included distinctly individual portraits of William Isom, Joanne Pezzullo, and Jack Goins. From their co-constructed portraits, the voices and experiences add to the larger discussion on identity work.

The Melungeon Identity Movement began in earnest with Kennedy and Kennedy's 1997 book *The Melungeons: The Resurrection of a Proud People.*[1] The book was a catalyst for those searching for answers to genealogical questions as well as those looking for answers physical traits or medical issues not easily explained. People were longing for roots, such as those found in Alex Haley's book of the same name, and details about how their ancestors lived, such as those in the internationally released and acclaimed television series *Who Do You Think You Are?* Coupled with multicultural education prevalent in public schools across the nation, the awareness of a racial, ethnic, and cultural identity became more important, albeit controversial, for large populations of mostly white individuals and families.[2] Websites such as Ancestry.com and USGenWeb.org have catered to this population with the latest technology and search engines, including DNA studies to prove one's ancestry.

165

With information on census records and family trees more accessible, more individuals are filling in the pieces of their family puzzle where Granny may have left off. Starting with family narratives and possibly a family Bible, these individuals are constructing a more nuanced and connected identity. Some of the co-researchers in this project took advantage of such access, and others trusted the basic search to me or other family members. Once in possession of the information, it was intriguing to see how these co-researchers integrated the knowledge with their experiences and family stories.

The co-researchers were invited to participate, and indeed recruited to participate, via family connections, social media, and Melungeon websites as well as networking with other Melungeon researchers. Specifically, I recruited my mother's cousins who are still living in the Cumberland Gap area: Anna Reed Partin, Katie Gibson Hillison, and Wilma Gibson King. I encouraged them to be a part of the project while I was doing research on my own family history and trying to determine if there were any Melungeon connections or identity. I did not have a prior relationship with these cousins and had only met one of them once before. Angela Johnson is a friend with whom I have maintained contact for over twenty years. Her father's family was also from the same geographic area, and she had persistent questions regarding ancestry due to her darker skin and more "exotic" features. When she began the project, many of her family members asked to participate. Their inclusion in the Johnson Portraits section gives a more holistic view of each individual member and how each navigated the questions about physical appearance, as well as how each had integrated Grandma Johnson's values, traditions, and stories into their individual and collective identities. My mother, sister, and daughter were a part of the original pilot study and offered a three generation perspective on a "Southern" identity ultimately removed from the mountains.

I approached Joanne Pezzullo to take part due to her extensive research and knowledge of the Melungeon Identity Movement's origins, historical and political contexts as a group, and the impact of various leaders within the movement. She was identified by her well-articulated and passionate posts on Melungeon blogs and discussion boards. William Isom was referred to me by Darlene Wilson, a Melungeon scholar and author. William is a local activist from the Cumberland Gap area, participates in and leads groups in popular education, and identifies as Melungeon.

Of the co-researchers, only William positively identified as Melungeon. Katie accepted Melungeon ancestry due to her previous readings and family research. Wilma was intrigued, had heard of it and Katie's acknowledgment of the connection, but wasn't sure. Sylvia and Kateri would love to be able to claim a Melungeon identity, but they are not sure what evidence they need. Arlene believes she is a Melungeon descendant, yet she is not sure what that means in her life. Joanne is open to the idea, extremely well-versed in the research, but has not discovered any evidence to indicate that she is descended from Melungeons. Jack says he has descended from two Melungeons and has spent considerable time researching his family migration patterns and genealogy, including DNA. The Johnson family knew nothing of Melungeons and had never heard the term before. Grandma Johnson identifies as part Native American, and the other family members are hopeful and think they "probably" are Melungeon, given the amount of information I've been able to give them. Anna Partin had not heard the word before and has no real interest in this idea, but she was excited to learn more about the family and was hopeful that I could help fill in blanks in the family tree.

As I read back through the portraits, several themes seemed clear: family loyalty, poverty, generalized geographic location of ancestors in the Cumberland Gap area, acceptance of family narratives related to ancestry, storytelling as a means of expressing self and as evidence of belonging, resistance to dominance, respect for education, and informal means of grassroots leadership. I will discuss each theme and the related narratives as they correlate with the themes I presented in the literature review.

Correlations with Historical Documents

Genealogy

Several co-researchers have constructed family tree documents with various degrees of complexity and detail. Joanne Pezzullo utilizes Family Tree Maker and Ancestry.com to keep track of her family trees. With her passion for primary source documents and historical records, Joanne has included migration patterns to outline where her family has moved and with which groups of people. She has coupled that with books and publications from local historians and historical societies. Pezzullo has located and shared original documents that had been inaccurately transcribed and often repeated, with their inaccuracies, in Melungeon publications and at Melungeon presentations. She has spent considerable time researching newspaper articles in often-forgotten archives detailing uses of the term Melungeon, along with their association with Lumbee Indians.

Connie Johnson had kept not just her own Bible full of birth announcements, obituaries, and wedding invitations, but also her mother's. When we completed her interviews, she had piles of documents, photographs, and other tidbits of life. Keeping the envelopes because of a loved one's handwriting was common for her as well as for Wilma King and Grandma Johnson. Anna Partin had a large envelope full of Ancestry.com documents that she could locate right away and was eager to show me. Logan Johnson's mother, Pam, (Keith Johnson's current wife) had also kept a folder with all of the Johnson genealogy. Specific photos were meaningful to several family members, including Keith Johnson, who relied on a picture of himself wrestling a bear as evidence of his experience. These documents and photographs served as verification, or proof, of the things they were telling me.

DEATH AND BIRTH CERTIFICATES

Angela Johnson's great-great-great-grandmother Mary Hughes Arms was buried in 1924, and her death certificate lists her as "*negra.*" Her daughter, Mary Arms Bunch, was buried in a spring in Tennessee in the path of the Tennessee Valley Authority's Norris Dam project. When Hughes Arms was disinterred to be moved, comments from onlookers claimed she "still looked like the old Indian she was." Coincidently, although she was buried in Tennessee, the Racial Purity Act of 1924 enacted in Virginia would influence the coroner's responses on the document. She had been listed as white in all census records and marriage records, but had the misfortune of dying in the midst of the political and racial turmoil. It did bring an element of doubt and mistrust of sanctioned officials, historical documents, and certified records.

Another ironic twist was the impact of Plecker's 1912–1946 reign as first registrar of Virginia's Bureau of Vital Statistics on my own family. Born in 1943, my mother's birth was not registered until 1954 along with her brother's 1945 birth. This was thought to be compelling evidence that Plecker's influence was far reaching. Plecker had written letters to the clerks in neighboring states reminding them of the importance of accurate reporting or consequences of not accurately reporting an individual's race on government records. He referred to surnames that were likely of mixed bloodlines, names that researchers use today as part of the evidence of possible Melungeon connections.

While doing research in the Bell County, Kentucky, courthouse, we also had difficulties finding birth records on any of my grandmother's siblings or her parents. There was a large gap in death certificates picking up again in the 1950s. Once more, the lack of documentation gave us pause.

GOVERNMENT AND LEGAL DOCUMENTS

Census records were important to most families and researchers in locating where people were living during life events such as birth or death so one could determine which courthouse might hold their records. Coupled with other tax records, church minutes, and wills or other legal documents in courthouses, you could trace migration patterns and find additional family members living nearby. By painstakingly computing ages of individuals and their children within those records, we could include or eliminate other relatives with similar names. If one is lucky enough to find a will, it may very well list all children and property including land records.

Often entire families were found where siblings would name their children after their brothers and sisters, complicating the research process. The Moses Ball family in Lee County, Virginia, included five brothers who named their sons after each other, leaving a tangled mess of Moses, Georges, James, and Johns living in the same area. Common given names were noted by Angela Blankenship and her sister Rachel Bray as we looked through family records and official documents. The tradition of naming children after a beloved grandparent or sibling continued in their family, often times by giving children two middle names.

Cemeteries also proved fruitful in locating unnamed spouses or what may have happened to children who no longer showed up on a census. One could also gather clues about family connections depending on where family members were buried, the name of the cemetery, and who may be lying nearby. Grave rubbings using tin foil and a soft brush revealed much of the engravings allowing us to make out names and dates.

PHOTOGRAPHS

As documentary evidence, photographs were kept by all co-researchers and their families. There were photographs of ancestors and formal portraits with family members peering out from the ages unsmiling. Funeral pictures were also popular, documenting practices of in-home services and the laying out of the deceased. Most of the old photographs had handwritten captions on the back identifying the subjects, year, and location. Nicknames were often used which provided clues to characters in family narratives, and spelling of names was clarified when written in the mother's hand. Besides documenting individuals, photographs were also used as evidence of furniture, homes, pets, and events. They also acted as prompts for memories and discussions and could reveal personality and relationships upon close examination. Grandma Johnson had recently copied hundreds of photos for her grandchildren and had taken the time to write the details of the image on the back of each copy.

Social Construction of Knowledge

As is noted in identity work literature, organizational leaders are in a unique position to espouse a particular ideology through their access to a number of members. Leaders play a vital role in framing movements and identity, giving structure and context to the organization. The competing identities represented by various Melungeon research groups have been disrupted by the varied agendas of leadership. As noted by Vande Brake in earlier correspondence and interviews, leadership became split along the lines of who may qualify as a Melungeon (according to an organization or group) and by what evidence. From a social-psychological perspective, one could frame these factions and varied commitments as subcultures. Examining the intergroup relations requires perspective. Viewing Melungeons as a subculture of Appalachia is but one view. Viewing the various factions of Melungeon groups as subcultures of "Melungeons" might prove useful in the sharing of resources and research between groups.

Competing websites, blogs, and discussion boards further define the factions. Followers of the different groups are loyal to the ideology of the leader even in the face of contradictory evidence, due to an identity congruence supported by that leader.[3] Yet, this can be explained by the cultural lenses through which each group is viewing not just the Melungeon research, but their individual goals and objectives as well.

Family History

Family stories are strong reminders of belonging to a group that has had shared experiences, meaning, and discourse, amongst the co-researchers. Kateri was not the only co-researcher to indicate that hearing other family members recount the same stories she had heard from her grandmother was validating. She plans to tell her children the same stories of her grandmother's early years in Kentucky. Listening to the Johnsons individually and in groups found the same stories told and retold with minor variations. Even the story of Logan's introduction into the Johnson family as the mistress's child was told by several of the family members as a testament to Connie's disposition, to Keith's philandering, and even to sibling relationships. Memories of kidnapping their father played out in stories for both Wilma and Katie as they retell the story of taking a very sick Arbie Gibson to the hospital in the nick of time.

While discussing the darker complexion of the Gibsons and Johnsons, stories of a Native American ancestor are repeated almost verbatim from one family member to the next. In fact, this seems to a popular experience in all of the Melungeon related groups, blogs, and gatherings. The memories of Grandma's stories are being told over and over as each teller explains where he or she fits into the family continuum. Mary Hughes Arms, Angela's ancestor that was buried as a *negra* was identified not as an ancestor but as her great-great-great-grandmother. Where co-researchers could not verify or make connections between the stories and their own understanding, the meaning of Grandma's stories were more difficult to integrate into their lives. Connie tells how her grandmother explained their heritage of being Black Dutch, and Sylvia told a story of how her grandmother explained to the census takers that she was Black Irish.

These last areas of photographic evidence, genealogical documents, family notes, wills, and bibles, may attest to oral histories where government control was not trusted. When authority doesn't believe one's own identity construction (i.e. Plecker changing birth, death, and marriage records), people search for additional evidence to provide as proof. This is another area that could use further research in light of reliance on DNA as proof of identity.

COMMUNITY

The most poignant data on social construction comes from William Isom. He explains how a variety of people in the community in which he grew up defined Melungeons: "My dad would say it was nothing but Indians, runaway slaves, and whites all mixed together. Another guy said they was mixed Indians. [Today if I was at a party], people my age would say 'Well, I can't drink that, you know, 'cause I'm Indian, I'm liable to get wild,'" Isom explained, laughing.

While hiking through numerous graveyards, Arlene noticed that there were often people with familiar surnames buried right outside the actual cemetery. A little research and local lore explains them as the "colored folks" who were not allowed to be buried in the proper cemetery alongside white folks.[4] This effectively created a social construction of race hierarchy in the area. Anna and Sylvia noted the oddity of their grandmother having both a white and black preacher at her funeral. In the original telling to me, Sylvia explained how strange it was for the times (1959). Anna, another relative, noted that the black preacher had to stay in another preacher's home outside of town and come in just for the service.

Several times I was fortunate enough to participate in family discussions with the Johnsons and the Gibson cousins (Anna, Katie, Wilma, and Sylvia) when stories and memories were discussed and clarified and a consensus achieved about the accepted rendering of the tale. Often, once out of earshot of other family members, individuals would revert to their own story with the comment, "I didn't remember it that way." This appears to be a recognized process according to McAdams whereby the "sharing of personal experiences functions as a major mechanism of socialization and helps to build an organized personal history from a growing base of autobiographical memories."[5] It appears that at times there were family narratives as well as the personal.

From value of knowledge to college degrees, education remained valued in the people I interviewed. Joanne's research and need for primary sources, William's activism and work with popular education, including the Highlander Institute, and Grandma Johnson's collection of history books specific to her place of origin all speak to the role that education plays in their lives. Keith Johnson regaled me with stories of beloved books and his favorite author Jesse Stuart. It was a connection with his deceased son that was important, a mutual love for the Appalachian author.

Angela is currently enrolled in college and planning to obtain a degree in social work to advocate for those less fortunate, those without a voice. Katie had returned to get a Child Development Associates degree, while her sister Wilma had finished three years of college with glowing grades. Sylvia had taken classes in occupational therapy upon her divorce twenty-six years ago.

Kateri's experiences with NHD, National History Day, along with her formal education in the public schools and the example set by her mother who pursued higher education throughout Kateri's young life, have all helped her articulate a nuanced explanation of research and responsibility: "You've always stressed the importance of having extremely educated people who have dedicated large parts of their lives to researching this one topic. You stressed over and over that those are the credible sources," she says making air quotes. "I wouldn't want someone not very educated to tell me this is what a Melungeon is—I'd wonder, do you have the resources [for extensive research]? But then, I don't want someone extremely educated making all the decisions because they weren't there, they don't know, they didn't live it," she insists.

Experiences of Identity and Belonging

More than what is revealed in the portraits, those items I was asked to remove speak to family loyalty. In fact, one person left the project completely so family members wouldn't be hurt or upset by what was said. Stories of children playing in the creek naked and other humorous antics were deleted to protect cousins not spoken to in years. By far the most powerful illustration of family loyalty came from Angela Blankenship. We had talked to so many of her family members, mother, father, sister, half-brother, that she indicated it didn't feel right not to include portraits of the rest of her family members, hence the inclusion of the portraits of brother and Grandma Johnson.

I was struck by the Johnson's definition of who was included as family and who was not, particularly one day when I was meeting with Connie and Logan came to visit, the son of her ex-husband who was born while Connie and Keith were still married. They hugged, Connie welcomed Logan and his wife, and we continued chatting. As Logan had noted, "Even with all this dysfunction, we are still loyal. The loyalty is there. The rest of the shit just doesn't seem so extreme. There's a very humane side to us as well—you just don't treat people bad, and no matter how we're connected—in some fucked up way they're family. When shit gets real, we will do everything for each other."

Sylvia recalls how this loyalty was broadened to include nieces, nephews, cousins, and other extended family: "Mom helped out each one of my cousins, each one of them lived with us at one time." We reminisced about her mother and brother also moving in with us when they needed a place to stay. Married with her own children, my mother Sylvia would also take in any family members that needed a place to stay, often for months at a time.

William Isom notes in his portrait that poverty is a "hell of an equator, bonding people together in their common experiences of struggle and survival." Anna describes a similar sentiment, noting that as a child she didn't know any different because everyone was poor. "There was no water in the house, no toilets, just outside toilets, no rugs on the floors, newspaper for wall paper," she says. "That's how we's brought up—but the whole neighborhood was poor, that's how we was all brought up."

As a small child Sylvia hadn't seen many automobiles, and certainly no one in the immediate vicinity owned one. The appearance of a shiny new vehicle meant that somebody important had come to the mountain. The couple from the vehicle walked arm in arm up the lane, both of them dressed elaborately for the area. "I ran to my grandma and told her I thought the king and queen was coming and grandma just cracked up," Sylvia recalled. "She thought that was so funny. When she looked from the porch she said, 'law's sake, girl, that's your mother.'"

Katie Hillison recalls one of the biggest shocks of being sent to Henderson Settlement, a home for needy children that included a school and dormitories: "I had just turned twelve when we got there," said Katie. "It was my first ever birthday cake and ice cream. We never celebrated birthdays, hardly ever even had a Christmas tree. And we sure never had no three meals a day, we didn't know what to make of all that food." Her sister Wilma also recalls their poor beginnings: "The one house we had that had the dirt floors, our grandparents lived in that before we did," she said, describing her early years.

It seems much of Angela's childhood was spent struggling financially, being hungry, not having a family home. The communities she lived in were not made up of families similar to hers. Fathers had jobs, mothers drove kids to events, and families went school clothes shopping, all things lacking in the Keith Johnson household as Angela was growing up. The feeling of stress that pervades a home when children are hungry and jobs are scarce was a common theme for almost all co-researchers.

Being poor wasn't always seen as tragic. "Poor white trash we are," described Logan. "Good-hearted poor white trash. We might hate each other and fist fight in the yard—but if one of us needs something, we're there for each other," he explains. Arlene believes, "There was only two kinds of people, and I'd rather be from that lower class. Yes, I enjoy the hot tub and air conditioning. But, I'd rather be known as the have nots as the haves. Because it makes [the haves] the kind of people I can't stand." A similar sentiment was expressed by Keith Johnson's comment: "The whole system in this country is bullshit, the capitalist system in this country is a system for the rich people to be rich."

Of the people in the project, half were born in the Cumberland Gap area. Of the remaining half, all have descended from the area. Four still live in the area: Anna, Wilma, Katie, and William. Grandma Johnson has a piece of property in Kokomo, Indiana, that the entire family uses and calls the farm. She and Keith call these forty acres their little piece of Tennessee. The connections to place are evident in several conversations that recalled a pull to the mountains and land of the area. It still held a place of fondness in their hearts.

Swinging on grapevines seemed to be a favorite pastime of children in the area, as well as playing in creeks and running on the mountain. Sylvia remembers swinging on the grapevines and playing in the creek. "I wonder if it was my family or the times," Sylvia said. "I remember using my imagination and learning things by discovering them, the best way to learn. We'd play in the creek catching crawdads, us girls would all play together and Billie and Wayne would play together. What one wouldn't think up the other one would." "Opal would swing on grapevines pretending she was Tarzan," said Katie, "we all did." The co-researchers shared similar stories of acting out life events with their toys, being innovative with playthings, and getting into mischief that bonded one to another.

Another common experience was a connection to the coal mines. Brownlow Reed, Anna's father, worked in the coal mines: Capito, Garmeada, wherever he could get a job. "One time when I was sixteen years old, he got a job in Fort Wayne, Indiana, cause he couldn't get no job in the mines," she explained. "My grandfather had bought up four or five coal mines with the idea he would pass them along to his children," Sylvia described. "My dad tried it out," she says referring to her biological father, "and he didn't particularly like it, so that was given back to my grandfather. I think maybe Uncle Arb worked in the coal mines, too." The appearance of coal trucks, box cars loaded with coal, and many picking up pieces of the black fuel were common images.

Isolation was another memory that came up often. Anna recalls being kept at home, not able to visit or play with anyone outside the family. "When we was growing up, we got almost confined up on that mountain," she said. "We didn't get to go play with those kids in the camp, you know, they called it a camp. That's what made it so hard when we got grown. We didn't get to be around people." She recalls the stresses of interacting with others after being isolated for so much of her life. This was similar to the experiences of Wilma and Katie before going to Henderson Settlement and of Sylvia before moving to Michigan.

Sewing clothes, canning and preserving, farming, and cooking were activities that defined many of the women in the project. "We got clothes sometimes from Ad who would come down and bring clothes in for the kids," said Anna. "It's 'cause of her I learned how to sew. Because of that, at twelve years old I could sew them clothes up real good, make 'em fit us," she said. "I've been sewing ever since." Preserving food and cooking and being self-reliant were also common amongst the group. "We kept our food in the creek, or you killed your own chickens right on the spot and ate them right then," Anna explained. "You canned, you picked berries, it had to been living like the Indians."

I asked Kateri what made her identify with a Southern way of life. "Doing the stuff Grandma taught us. Canning, baking, sewing, the garden, stuff like that," she said. Her posting on Facebook regarding a family dinner illustrates her values. It read, "I just love living in a family where just about everything is homemade." After using my twenty-five-year-old sewing machine to make her boyfriend a quilt, we bought her first machine for Christmas the year she was eighteen.

"I realized I wasn't like most women," Sylvia said, referring to the differences she noticed between herself and other housewives in Michigan. "I did things that they just didn't do. Things like garden and canning, sewing and homemade dinners ... it was those kinds of things, what made me *me*, what made me a woman, a wife, a mother." Cooking and baking were a labor of love, something special to give one another. The time spent was just as much a gift as the food itself.

"Remember what the canning room would look like in fall?" Arlene asked. "All the jars would be lined up in rows on the shelves in the basement, the beets and peaches, the green beans, tomatoes, and applesauce. It was gorgeous, I wish I had a picture of how that looked," she said.

"And the part that interests me—it is *very* interesting," says Arlene, "is about people having the same experiences in that community. That's what interests me—what my family and ancestors have gone through, it is all about stuff that builds character, it is about the challenges and hardships they endured that gives me admiration for those people. I think it is the altruism of it all—giving selflessly to see someone enjoy just a few minutes 'cause you took the time to make them feel special."

William has a swarthy, tan complexion, a legacy of African-American ancestry and a symbol of his mixed-race parentage. He did not discuss any personal discrimination or limitations due to his looks but shared sentiments his father expressed when describing why he wouldn't go into town. "My dad would say, 'Why in the hell am I gonna go where I know they don't want me? I'm not gonna go where I'm not wanted!'" According to William, the small community in which he was raised was a comforting place for his father's family. "A community of supportive and accepting people fortifies and gives foundation to your identity," says Isom. He reinforces the social construction of race and cultural values.

"We have a different tint to our skin," said Rachel. "Even if it is light, the color is just different. When Colten was a baby we took him to get his picture taken," she explained, "the photographer ... asked if Colten was mixed. I've had lots of people ask that."

Many co-researchers also lived with their grandparents for extended periods of time. "I spent a lot of time with my grandparents," Connie Johnson explained. "Mom was working at Delco she was still nursing me so she would run home on her lunch hour, nurse me, then go back to work." Eventually her mother left the factory to stay home and care for her mother as she died. "Then after Grandma died, I stayed with Grandpa," she explained. Sylvia recalls vivid memories of the day her mom left, leaving her with her grandparents. "She packed a little brown suitcase, wrapped Billie in a receiving blanket, and I watched her go."

Angela recalls her time with her grandparents fondly, especially her relationship with her beloved Scramps. She describes her grandfather as a good-looking, handsome man who was loving and calm. While Arlene never went to live with her Mamaw, Addie came to live with her family when she was a child, staying for months at a time and sharing a bedroom with her three grandchildren. Playing guitar, singing, and dancing jigs, Addie would entertain the children while smoking her unfiltered Pall Malls and telling them she was their Granny Grunt. I continued the tradition having my mother, Sylvia, live with our family for a time. Kateri remembers a constant presence full of family stories and constant cooking.

Keith also spent long weeks in Tennessee with his grandparents after the family moved to Indiana. "I never really felt like I left Tennessee because every year we'd go back down there for weeks. Stayed with Granny Blackmon." He tells about his dad saying that he didn't realize the kids were so sad to leave Tennessee. "I told him, 'Dad, if I'd thought you would turn that car around I would have really turned on the tears,'" he told me.

Sylvia expressed a very powerful desire to hold an identifiable ancestral identity. "It would mean I belong somewhere, I belong some place, that I *am* someone," she said. Katie Hillison acknowledges the desire some people have to be distinct or special, and that could be the driving force behind so many people claiming a Melungeon identity. However, she felt that being Melungeon is too distinct, too special, "because no one really knows what it means," she said, explaining that telling someone you're part Indian is easier for them to understand. Rachel expressed her thoughts, saying, "it would be kind of cool to find out that we actually belong to anything, but it doesn't change who we are, where we've been or where we're going."

Logan is excited about the probability of such an identity. "It would mean I'm *di-ver-si-fied*," he said proudly. "It would mean I've got a background not everybody's got, YAY." Kateri also expressed delight in the idea. "Now there is something else, there is something exciting, there's not just the boring ol' Whitehall girl I thought I was my whole life," she said.

Ways of Knowing and Being

This section explores how the co-researchers constructed their knowledge and how they performed their identity roles in day-to-day life. Culture organizes experience in three ways: by providing a set of ways that "we" do things, determining a higher goal or "mission" that drives decision-making and determining what we do when there are no clear directions to deal with a specific event; find similarities or connections, find differences or categorize, or find order.[6] These ways of knowing and being contribute to their salient identity, either group or individual.

For many, the family narratives and behaviors of grandparents and extended family were congruent enough for them to integrate the knowledge into their sense of self. For others, enough questions remained that the use of extensive research became a foundation of their knowledge. For those seeking documents and research outside the family, the investigation supported and validated family narratives. Stories of Native American grandmothers were often validated by the mere presence of photographs that showed physical characteristics that co-researchers associated with the population. For others, cultural practices of applying poultices, fishing with a bow and arrow, playing music, dancing, and living in commune with the mountain environment were the evidence they needed. For all members of this project, an amalgamation of all information was integrated into what they knew and enacted in their daily lives.

"I've heard the stories from Grandma about having Indian in us," says Rachel. "Finding out more about the Melungeon connection would explain a lot. It would also be good to know if there are diseases that would be attributed to a certain population, so you could tell your doctor, you know. I guess it would be good to know causes of death too."

All co-researchers practiced storytelling as a means of expressing beliefs and providing evidence of self-identity. When asked about possible racial composition of their families, individuals pointed out stories to illustrate what they knew. Angela describes the following experiences by way of explanation: "My mother's mother was very dark skinned, and I look the most like her. Here's another part of it, I don't know much about that part of the family—far as we know they only came from Indiana. My great-grandfather lived in the black neighborhood, not like it is today, but go back to the 70s—where the blacks and whites were in very different areas. He was the only light-skinned person in the black neighborhood. My grandmother would take me with her twice a day to help him with groceries, make meals, and stuff like that. I grew up as a small child playing in the streets with the black kids. Before I started school and during the summers. No one really knew why he lived there," she says. "What made him choose that?"

Katie also told a story by way of answering my inquiry. "I remember Daddy saying he was taken to visit at a family reunion and there were black children there. He asked why they were there and was told they were his kin," she said.

"Talking to everyone down [in Middlesboro, Kentucky] about Gibsons made me believe I was at least a small part Melungeon, add that to the [geographical] area and it just adds up," Arlene explains. "For me, I just want to know, I have nothing to gain or lose from it. It won't change anything if I am 80% sure or 99% sure. I still have the same ancestors," she says. "The family stories were *very* interesting and went a long way to telling me who I am."

Personal experiences and observations were also integrated into co-researchers' knowledge and ways of learning, noting headstones outside the cemetery fence, for example. Being asked, "What are you?" in reference to their physical characteristics led many to know that they looked different and that the difference meant something to the person asking. Noting the segregation of black and white communities and the presence of the Ku Klux Klan also contributed to the body of knowledge and the understanding the community had of various populations.

Reminiscing about relatives dancing traditional Appalachian jigs, playing guitars, and preferring to fish or hunt rather than work allowed for family systems to jointly, or socially, construct their agreed upon meaning of behaviors. Several of the families discussed illegitimate children and infidelities, norming the practice amongst their relatives. Keith discusses his grandfather's "rambling ways." Logan describes his father as "a rolling stone," and Katie described her father and grandfather in much the same way. "You know Daddy and Grandpa was like that," she said. "They all was messing around. You wouldn't know just how many children Grandpa had there around Middlesboro." Sylvia tells a now familiar story about her father: "Mom said she caught Daddy in a motel room with another lady and that she went in and beat the tar out of both the lady and Daddy and then tore the hell out of the motel room."

Often the behaviors observed within family groups resembled a complex dance. First one would bring up a remembered event, then another would add to that if the first part was accepted as happening as told. The individuals would continue adding to the story while others either nodded their approval and moved to the next piece of the tale or corrected the earlier version. By the end of the conversation, there would be a tacitly agreed upon and jointly constructed family narrative. That's not to say that individuals wouldn't disagree in private, but they had agreed to the public version of the telling.

Resistance to dominance was also discussed, sometimes overtly and sometimes a bit more subtly. Keith explained to his son that the TVA (Tennessee Valley Authority) came into the area to build a hydroelectric dam on the Clinch River. "They practically stole that land, according to Mom," he said. "I heard they didn't give 'em much more'n $25 an acre."

Another time Keith says, "Like I said I don't care if I'm part black, but I'd rather be Indian—'cause they're the most down trodden people on this earth. 'Cause I always hated the establishment and that just gives me an excuse to hate 'em more." During the occupation at Wounded Knee, Keith was busy raising his family. "If I'd have known about Wounded Knee in the '70s, I'd have had my rifle and been with them. Because they've been screwed forever …what they did to the Indians, you talk about genocide, like Buffalo Bill, fuck him—he shoots all the buffalo from a train, eliminates all their food then the government diverts all their water. I just see through the bullshit, and the whole system in this country is bullshit." Logan added his thoughts, "I think that's the story of our family: we just want to go where no one can bitch at us."

William, a founding member of Hands Off Appalachia, participates in frequent protests about the dangers of mountain top removal and the impact of large banking conglomerates like UBS. Familiar with the popular education movement espoused at the Highlander Institute, founded by Myles Horton, he had some powerful thoughts regarding how scholarship can further oppress populations. It is part of the power structure where the representative group of an academic conference has been dehumanized. As an activist, Isom believes that "the people" know what they need, what will work, and what will not help their communities. For someone from outside the group to determine meaning and implications is more than ineffective— it objectifies the population, making them an item of study, instead of a group of individuals with their own experiences, feelings, and family traditions.

"Because of Plecker, we lost a lot of documentation as well as the stories," William lamented. "Being Melungeon, now, just fortifies my Appalachian identity. It provides a broader narrative for resistance to the white supremacist capitalist structure that continues to extract from our region." He explains his view by describing a responsibility to understand his place in history, and that it is important to "remember and resist."

Grandma Johnson believes in things "Made in America" and unions. These two things are what provided for her family. They are what allowed her to have small luxuries, explains her granddaughter Angela. "She is loyal to the UAW and her country. She had small luxuries, but gave up the big ones to help her family. She has bailed grandsons out of jail, paid medical bills, and allowed her grandchildren to borrow her vehicles indefinitely," Angela describes whom she calls the leader of the family. "She has provided and continues to provide for family members. She makes no apologies for her choices and doesn't expect sympathy for her life circumstances. She will quietly say, 'That's just what you do.'"

Angela continues, illustrating the same leadership skills passed down to her. "If my phone displays "Unknown" on the screen, I know it's from my brother and we will only have fifteen minutes to talk. He will have to wait thirty minutes before he can make another call. I will often excuse myself from whomever I'm with and say, 'It's my brother who's in prison. I have to take this call.' In the beginning, I didn't think how people might take it. It surprised me to see nervous smiles appear on their faces." Using personal lessons, Angela advocates for those less fortunate by subtly educating her clients. "Now, I actually have fun with it! I love to say it in front of those who pride themselves on being open-minded, non-judgmental, and socially aware. Sometimes I will make a point later by saying, 'Every person in prison has a family.'"

William is the volunteer coordinator at The Birdhouse in Knoxville, Tennessee, a community space preserved and maintained for and by the people of the neighborhood for grassroots collaboration and action. Joanne cautions me to be careful when collecting information and reading books, considering the authors' motives and what information the authors were invested in and out to prove. She believes in empowerment, finding and sharing the fruits of her investigations in public forums. She is angered when she sees pieces of articles pulled out of context without links or references for people to use to make their own decisions on the content. She has also received much grief for comments she has made in response to a political move by the Turkish government to deny any involvement in the Armenian genocide and Brent Kennedy's support of Turkey. "I criticized

Brent on the boards, for his support of Turkey in this political mess," she said, explaining some of the conflict on the Melungeon-L website on RootsWeb. Not wanting Brent to speak for her or all members of the Melungeon Heritage Association, Joanne demanded that the remarks be publically retracted and any connection between MHA and the Turkey contingency be severed.

Additional Themes

Anger

A recurrent theme I did not anticipate but was not surprised at was that of anger. Several co-researchers remain angry at the turn the Melungeon identity movement is taking. Looking at who belongs and by what evidence has frustrated those who seek the identity, those who desire to understand the identity, and especially those who have been ascribed such an identity. As Arlene has declared, "Who decides who's a Melungeon and who ain't?" she asks, "and why do they get to decide"? The whole idea of what makes research credible and the idea of some scholar writing a book or article and using that power to define someone's identity makes her blood boil: "It's not like it gets you anything, does it?"

"I just can't get past the idea that someone could say that you're not good enough to be a Melungeon because you don't have this documentation, when the neighbors on both sides of you are Melungeon and going through the same stuff. How can they say you aren't also experiencing it?" Arlene continues with a poignant statement regarding her own identity, "Ultimately, it comes down to who you *want* to be," she explains. "I don't want anyone to walk away from my house feeling unwelcome. The idea that you can have nothing and still be happy, take care of your family, and still welcome someone into your house as if they are part of your family and have them feel that way and truly believe they are welcome, that's who I am, who I want to be, how I want to be remembered. I don't need some piece of paper or documentation telling me that's what I am."

Growing stronger in her admonishments, Joanne is frustrated not just with a movement that seeks to determine who belongs and who doesn't, but also with colleagues and researchers who deliberately skew data collection (she alleges) to promote a particular agenda. "She was trying so hard to prove what she wanted that she ended up taking this person out of the project," Joanne explained. Another prominent researcher and author "has done the same thing, mostly from the female lines—they were taken out of the project with no explanation—none whatsoever," she says. "Because I am so vocal of my criticism on the DNA project I get emails from people saying that they were denied being a part of the project or were kicked out of the project," she exclaimed. "I could go on for years and years about this stuff and it gives me a headache."

Even though she claims no Melungeon heritage, Joanne belonged to several Melungeon websites, blogs, and organizations and even started her own Melungeon website called *Melungeon Indians*. She responds to other researchers, shares her discoveries, and helps with genealogical research. "I started with a few other people, all researching together," she explains, "then I would show one of them where his genealogy was flawed and he insisted on printing his version." She was incredulous that anyone would stick with a line of thinking when the evidence pointed to something else. "Nobody really knows who they were speaking of when they were calling people Melungeon," she says, referring to the first references of Melungeons in newspaper articles and church minutes.

As researchers strayed further from inquiry into international politics, she demanded that a closer look at leadership be conducted. Just who had given Brent Kennedy the right to speak for the Melungeon Heritage Association? My investigation has not found an answer to this question. Yet a scathing discourse ensued regarding the direction and purpose of the group on the Melungeon-L website. Joanne responded,

> Perhaps if the MHA board along with the several thousands of Melungeon descendants would write to some of the webmasters we might get some of this stuff removed. The Turkish-Armenian subject is still a very newsworthy item. You need only go to google-news and type it in to see how newsworthy. I did not introduce these articles and this subject to this list to embarrass ANYONE or a WITCH HUNT—I seriously want this stuff like this below removed from the internet.
> MELUNGEONS EXTEND FULL SUPPORT TO TURKEY WASHINGTON D.C.—While the discussions continue whether to take the draft law on so-called genocide on Armenians into agenda of the local senate of Virginia state, Melungeons who introduce themselves as Americans of Turkish origin, announced on Friday that they extend full support to Turkey.[7]

Joanne was particularly bothered that someone would dare speak for the entire group of Melungeons within the MHA without proper authority as the official leader of the group. The whole idea of who could speak for who continues to frustrate and infuriate her: "Whatever way it goes, I'm open to. I'm just trying to research my family. You know how these boards are, if you said you were a Melungeon they would be all over you, you know, all over you," Joanne says sardonically. "That's how these boards are, they'd say you're not a Melungeon."

William was stronger yet in his statements of Melungeon researchers. "I think there is a group of people, like scholarly people that believe there is a core group of Melungeons up on Newman's Ridge that represent the original Melungeons. But that just seems like an academic or white supremacist way of looking at things. To assume there is one core group seems rather arrogant, arrogance rooted in white supremacy. I think there is any number of families that are Melungeon that are not traceable to that group. And I know that there are a number of people today that have not assimilated and run afoul of the power structure pretty regularly," he says with a chuckle.

RACIAL CONCERNS

It became obvious through many portraits that co-researchers were more desirous of a Native American connection rather than African-American. I became intrigued with the stories that were removed and the participant that chose not to be associated with the project as well as that individual's references to black admixture in ancestry. In fact, I got the sense that although some believed in the merits of DNA studies for geneal-ogy and ethnicity, many kept their distance from such a procedure as it may prove a sub-Saharan admixture in their family lines. "If I was to get genetic testing right now, I would be fine, okay," explains Angela, "but you don't know what the climate is going to be in fifty years. If it is docu-mented, would I be able to hide if things changed? Especially if we have proof—you don't know what is ever to say we won't ever face that again," she says, referring to the Native American removal of 1834 or the Holo-caust during World War II.

When talking to Keith Johnson, I explained that his mother doesn't seem to be upset about being Indian, "but I get the impression she wouldn't be too pleased to find out she was part black."

"You'd have the right impression," he said plainly. "And I wouldn't like blacks no better if I was one. I haven't got much use for black people, in fact most black people. Hell, I used to belong to the NAACP," says Keith. "Like I said, I don't care if I'm part black, but I'd rather be Indian ..."

"I have Indian and dark-skinned people on my mother's side, too," Katie explained. "Melungeon wasn't always black, they were just dark-skinned." In another conversation on Facebook she said, "I'm glad you did take it off, though," she said, referring to a documentary I had posted on

YouTube, " because some people might get a little bent out of shape over the Melungeon side of it.... I don't know why ... to me it didn't mean having African American in the family it meant people with a darker skin color, not Black, but darker toned ... but for some reason ... even now ... they want to hide it."

Katie had done research before meeting me on the Melungeons. "That's how I know it is something people don't want to be associated with. It isn't just African Americans, it was a foreign race of people or Indians, just people with darker skin. Around here, I don't recall ever seeing a black person, period, they didn't associate with white people unless they were the help. Here you will find, not like up north, people still, especially in this area here—they still have the KKK, the Klan and race things in Barbourville. It still goes on. They'll come in and hold a meeting there." Racial tensions were still very high in the Cumberland Gap area. While people who had out-migrated to other areas could explore their ethnicity or racial ancestry in relative safety, people still living in the area experienced overt racism on a regular basis. It was a part of the local vernacular. Terms like "sweating like a nigger at an election" or "someone had a nigger in the woodpile" were common phrases that were expressed often.

RESILIENCE

Almost all co-researchers revealed intimate hurts, tragic events, and embarrassing moments. Although reactions varied, only once was I asked to leave out a story to protect a family member from emotional distress. From adultery to molestation, drinking and killing, the stories told were as much a part of the co-researchers' identities as the place they lived and the food they ate. A strong illustration of this phenomenon was mentioned by Arlene Walsh as she fussed over receiving her son's school pictures. "They took his moles off," she said in exasperation. "I never pay for the touch-ups, never," she said, "and they always take his moles off his face. Two little spots, but that's him—that IS my son. Why do they hafta do that? Do they get to decide what looks good?" she asks, referring to the photographer.

According to Carol Fullerton (2004) "the telling of these experiences can bridge generations and cultures and provide an important avenue for us to learn about resilience in the face of trauma."[8] The strength of character shines through the tragedies presented. The individuals who shared their tragedies faced them openly, changed future decisions and behaviors because of them, and incorporated those events to construct their identities as survivors. Interestingly, these facets of their identities were not the most salient, but neither were they hidden or refused. "I'm the mistress's child," said Logan. "But, that's not all you are," Angela says quickly, "you're a brother, a father, a son, a friend." They defined one another as much by relationships as events. And as noted earlier, and as evidenced by Fullerton, the sharing of stories may very well prove therapeutic to the author as well as educational to the listener.

Upon further examination of the portraits, other researchers or investigators may uncover additional themes.

CHAPTER 7

Implications for Activism

Within the many and varied Melungeon systems, leaders have waxed and waned with interest in the movement, and the number of participants has decreased in some while growing in others. With the portraits of co-researchers in this project we have illustrated a desire for identity, informal leadership, direction, and answers. We are looking for the defining traits that one can use to authenticate membership in the group claiming a Melungeon identity. What much of the research has encouraged to date is looking at origin theories and defining what a Melungeon is. Leaders and scholars in the field of Melungeon research differ in their thoughts and ideas, offering a different prototype of a Melungeon with each theory. Followers are reviewing these theories to discover which one is giving the clearest definition that would include them and enhance their own sense of power and self-esteem by association.

According to Hogg, "when individuals identify with a certain group, they are likely to be attracted to the most prototypical member of the group, the one who embodies the aspirations, attitudes, and identity of the group."[1] Considering the rise in interest since the rendering of Brent Kennedy's first book, I posit that participants of the movement assigned the prototypical traits of Kennedy to the group. This effectively made Kennedy the leader and the original participants in the movement his followers. This contributed to his assuming a leadership position, authorizing him to speak for the Melungeon Heritage Association regarding the Turkish killing of Armenians.

Kennedy was a charismatic man, charming and gracious. He spoke eloquently and often was very inclusive in his investigations (much to the chagrin of subsequent investigators). I still recall his warm hospitality and gracious demeanor when, as a graduate student, I asked to meet with him to better understand his perspective. I had brought my mother and sister to Wise, Virginia, with me in early September 2001, and they waited in the car for me as I went in to speak with him. When he found out that they were waiting in the parking lot, Brent came out with me to introduce himself and to meet them. I keep thinking he was just so kind. He looked at my mother and my nephew, felt the backs of our heads, explained a thing or two about eye folds, and pronounced us all Melungeons. "Oh yep, yep, see there," he said, feeling my mom's head.

I was just learning about cultural anthropology and melding that with a degree in family studies. Every educational step I have taken has been with one or another family member holding my hand, pushing from behind, or carrying me, and this experience was no different. I didn't realize then the tragedies that would befall Brent before I could speak with him again. A series of strokes have challenged his already fragile physical condition. Like many researchers before me, and more that will come later, Brent's books will be quoted and critiqued.

I discovered that once a person has gained a sense of membership, integrated it into their sense of self, and enacted what they believe to be a Melungeon identity in their lives, it becomes a matter of survival when that sense of self is challenged by others. Scholars, researchers, authors, and social media participants did exactly that, perhaps in an effort to stem the tide of new members and to maintain their own distinctiveness within the group. They were the "real" Melungeons and the rest of us were wannabes or frauds.

Brewer points to an optimal spot on a continuum between blandness and distinction that this identity would provide for researchers.[2] This point would indicate the right amount of distinction to feel special, raise self-esteem, and allow one to associate with a particular person or group. Being too different, however, would not allow the esteem one desires. One's cohort must understand the value of the uniqueness in order to give the required admiration for being different or distinct. The discussion between ethnic blandness and Optimal Distinctiveness Theory can contribute greatly to identity work and social movements. It is why in Michigan I can claim "Southern roots" and feel an optimum level of being unique amongst my peers. But being "Melungeon" would be too outside the realm of my peer set to offer any benefit to my esteem. However, if living in the Southern states, claiming a "Melungeon" identity or ancestor might offer the "bragging rights" that my nephew Devon spoke of.

"Optimal distinctiveness motivates people to belong to groups that optimally satisfy people's contrasting needs for assimilation and inclusiveness on the one hand and for differentiation and uniqueness on the other."[3] Since many of the co-researchers seek a distinguishing element to separate them from the "white bread" view of Americana, I understood what extinguishing this distinctness could mean.

Motivation to belong to a particular group is varied and complex. Uncertainty reduction, self-esteem, and optimal distinctiveness are three triggers for motivating social identity. These motives can largely determine how relationships within a group and amongst competing groups interact. Consider the groups competing for respect amongst those desiring a Melungeon identity: the uncertainty about which documents provide evidence may push adherents to find well-defined groups with clear traits and expectations for behavior. If one's family devalues African Americans, determining which camp eliminates them from the mixture will preserve and raise self-esteem while providing an explanation for physical traits and family rumors. For some co-researchers, this uncertainty was not worth facing without support. Angela explained the conundrum with this analogy: "It's almost like religions that broke off from the Catholic church during the Reformation. Different factions start collecting their weapons— in this instance the weapons become documents, or DNA, or some other power thing. Then they make their own rules like statements of faith or doctrines to outline how members are supposed to believe or behave. So people start joining the church that lets them believe what they want to."

This project found the following:

1. Some co-researchers desired to be distinct and special, leading them to contemplate a Melungeon identity.
2. Some hoped that being Melungeon or having Melungeon ancestors would explain physical characteristics and certain behaviors. They hoped it would also explain gaps in a family tree or secrets. ** Groups 1 and 2 also are divided into two subgroups: (a) those who are Melungeon via common experiences (internal locus of control), or (b) those who are Melungeon via approved evidence (external locus of control).
3. Group 3 knew little of the term, ran across it while researching, and thought it was interesting. If they were to come to the conclusion that they were Melungeon or had Melungeon ancestors, great; if they did not, it was no big deal. They were not invested in the idea as part of an ongoing identity.
4. Group 4 has been ascribed the identity by their community. It comes with no choice. This group is often still living in the area and stands to lose the most through discrimination or objectification.

The four groups and subgroups can and do overlap and interact with one another as a dynamic and fluid system. As discussed earlier, it is the intersection of roles that helps determine the differences in how identity is developed and integrated. Individuals live and change, grow and develop. As one co-researcher put it, "It's like a mini identity crisis every time I get a new piece of the puzzle, or discover something new about my family." Yes, identity work requires an acceptance and integration of knowledge—identity congruence. Whether challenged by others, calling our identity into question, or coming across documents or research that conflicts with what we "know" to be true, a decision must be made. Does the information support or challenge our values, our goals, our sense of self? More importantly, how do the changes in identity salience contribute to behaviors?

This project points to ways that Melungeon-ness is enacted, accepted or rejected, as well as how it is researched amongst a few individuals. Some are searching within a family system, illustrating how different components within the system impact others and the system at large. This could be useful to other groups seeking to understand and integrate many roles within an identity, such as Native Americans, the Pan-Asian collective, and institutions seeking to change the culture and identity of an organization. In order for individuals to integrate and enact an identity, they must first seek to understand what the identity is, and what evidence is required to accept or reject that identity for themselves. The team, or family, is also impacted when one or more members accept or reject the identity for themselves—or challenge the authenticity of a team member or family member's identity claim. As social identity theory posits, one must first understand oneself on a deep psychological level before one can accept institutional roles, such as leadership or team member.

Identity is such a complex and messy thing as well as a vital part of one's being. De Quintal's dissertation on Native Americans finds that "maintaining one's identity in a world in which other(s)... deny your identity's authenticity can be traumatic. [People] are reluctant to share other parts of their ancestry for fear of being called frauds."[4] The same can happen in organizations and other systems where one's role is called into question and challenged. The ability to effectively enter a system and fulfill one's duties to a culture or entity requires identity work, personally and collectively.

Angry and hurt, Melissa [NLI] relates how she feels when people question her heritage: "Mostly, it's because I have been asked so many times by other Native

Americans, 'Well, can you prove who you are? Well then, how can I believe who you are? You can just be fibbin'. Tell me your history, tell me your story.' One girl even said, 'You have no proof.' That bothered me. It was insulting for me. It would be insulting for anyone to tell someone else, 'You aren't who you are.'"[5]

The above quote is from a dissertation on Native American identity and fits well with the trauma many Melungeon descendants face in today's movement. Joanne expressed much the same when she stated, "I'm just trying to research my family. You know how these boards are, if you said you were a Melungeon, they would be all over you, you know, all over you," she said. "That's how these boards are, they'd say *you're not a Melungeon*," (emphasis added).

To be studied like an intriguing artifact instead of the collective experiences of individuals is not only tragic but also unprincipled in today's understanding of sound scholarship and ethical practice. I urge all researchers of populations to empower the group to lead interpretation and analysis of studies that impact them. Self-identified Melungeons should also take responsibility for responding to questionable research and insisting on a place at the proverbial table. Then, and only then, will the Melungeon research move forward in effecting positive change for a population still marginalized and objectified. With collective action born from within, Melungeon researchers can become activists, illustrating how together they can find strength in numbers, instead of being divided and conquered—again.

Analysis of data in this research project also points to practical applications in other areas of investigation and disciplines:

1. It is imperative to understand how important it is for followers of social movements to identify with the leader for him or her to have influence on behaviors. Indeed, it is crucial that leaders understand the intersectionality, the complexity, and the salience of all identities. Without this shared understanding, groups lack the motivation to engage in activities toward changing the distribution of justice.

2. To encourage and sustain change within a system, fostering a relationship built on trust and sincerity via Resonant Leadership is required. Boyatzis suggested that a "deeper self-awareness of their leadership behavior and enhance their capabilities to be more effective change agents and relationship managers[...]. The program is anchored in the principles of emotional intelligence, resonant leadership and holistic balance and encourages

participants to become more mindful of their leadership behaviors."[6]

3. Challenges remain in communities that rely on adherence of values, beliefs, and doctrine to sustain their boundaries and existence, in the process, resisting efforts at change for self-preservation.

4. Intersectional research provides researchers with a more complex understanding of identity and meaning-making via those intersections. This is an area of research that should be explored further in Melungeon studies regarding identity. To comprehend the difference between generations, geography, experience, and phenotype amongst those claiming or considering a Melungeon identity would add greatly to our understanding.

5. When subgroup identity distinctiveness is perceived as being threatened, effective leaders will espouse a collective identity through trust, support, and empowerment of followers.

When conducting any research, whether investigating one's own family, an identity, or academic scholarship, it behooves one to ask the question, "Who stands to gain power from this information?"

To salvage the Melungeon Identity Movement, Melungeon researchers, scholars, communities, and authors must determine what the objectives or goals are and build a strategy or map to achieve them. The prevalence of distrust of authority and leadership positions within many Melungeons (in all groups) has challenged the movement in general and different leaders and scholars specifically. It is my hope that the power differential between various factions of Melungeon researchers will dissipate. I am heartened by a statement on the MHA website encouraging "increased understanding and harmony, certainly between nations but also between races, ethnic groups, cultures, and most certainly between those who call themselves Melungeon."

When individuals explore where they belong or what identity is salient in a particular situation, they should consider the intersection of diverse roles which will give them a deeper and more holistic picture of motivations and behaviors. Without compartmentalizing one's self, an individual should consider how one's own motives determine the lens we see others through. Each of us is researching our roots to answer different questions, aligning our views and data in our own self-interests to preserve our identity.

It is my hope that Melungeon identity leaders, scholars, activists, and participants continue to research and debate what being a Melungeon means. It is impressive that such a large number of authors and activists from the "in-group" instead of from the universities and labs are making progress in self-identification and preservation. An inclusive atmosphere, even as a subgroup identified within the larger community, can provide sufficient numbers to collectively organize and make a difference in the way Melungeons are being portrayed and analyzed and can serve as a model for other communities with similar challenges and politics. By not considering alternative ways of being, researchers will privilege the ontology surrounding familiar discourse.

Allowing the power to identify to rest in the hands of a select few, without accountability to a collective, holds the potential of relegating the Melungeon movement to a passing fad, a way for white people to assuage white guilt at the expense of tragedies and oppression perpetrated on their ancestors. Sustained social change requires committed authentic leaders who are in tune with the group and willing to define a collective identity that is sustainable amongst subgroups within the larger community. It is not up to the academy to determine rules of membership.

Chapter Notes

Introduction

1. N.B. and R.V. Kennedy, *The Melungeons: The Resurrection of a Proud People: An Untold Story of Ethnic Cleansing in America* (Macon, GA: Mercer University Press, 1997); E.T. Price, "A Geographic Analysis of White-Negro-Indian Racial Mixtures in Eastern United States," *Annals of the Association of American Geographers* 43, no. 2 (1953): 138–155; M. Schrift, *Becoming Melungeon: Making an Ethnic Identity in the Appalachian South* (Lincoln: University of Nebraska Press, 2013).

2. N. Berkovitch and S. Helman, "Global Social Movements," in *Companion to Gender Studies*, eds. P. Essed, D. Goldberg, & A. Kobayashi (Maldan, MA: Wiley Blackwell, 2009): 266–279.

3. D. Wilson and P. Beaver, "Transgressions in Race and Place: the Ubiquitous Native Grandmother in America's Cultural Memory," in *Neither Separate Nor Equal: Women in the Political Economy*, ed. B.E. Smith (Philadelphia: Temple University Press, 1999).

4. M. Omi and H. Winant, *Racial Formations in the United States: From the 1960s to the 1990s* (London: Rutledge, 1994), 56; P. Essed, *Understanding Everyday Racism: An Interdisciplinary Theory* (Newbury Park, CA: Sage, 1991); R. Frankenberg, *White Women, Race Matters: The Social Construction of Whiteness* (Minneapolis: University of Minnesota Press, 1993); D.T. Goldberg, *The Racial State* (Malden, MA: Wiley-Blackwell, 2002); bell hooks, *Black Looks Race and Representation* (Boston: South End, 1992); David Roediger, *Working Toward Whiteness: How America's Immigrants Became White: The Strange Journey from Ellis Island to the Suburbs* (New York: Basic, 2005).

5. Omi and Winant, 1994, 54–55.

6. Essed, 1991; Frankenberg, 1993; Goldberg, 1993, 2002; hooks, 1992; Omi and Winant, 1994; Rabinow & Rose, 2006; M.

Sommer, "DNA and Cultures of Remembrance: Anthropological Genetics, Biohistories, and Biosocialities," *BioSocieties* 5, no. 3 (2010): 366–390.

7. A. Coleman, "'Tell the Court I Love My [Indian] Wife': Interrogating Race and Self-Identity in Loving v. Virginia," *Souls: A Critical Journey of Black Politics, Culture, and Society* 8, no. 1 (2006): 67–80.

8. *Ibid.*, 70.

9. Goldberg, 2002, p. 243

10. *Ibid.*, 245

11. M. Anglin, "Erasures of the Past: Culture, Power, and Heterogeneity in Appalachia," *Journal of Appalachian Studies* 10, no. 1&2 (2002): 73.

12. David Roediger, *The Wages of Whiteness: Race and the Making of the American Working Class* (New York: Verso, 1999).

13. K. Hilson in discussion with the author, December 30, 2012.

14. Marsha Rice, *The Great White Lies: Dr. Walter Plecker, Eugenics, Melungeons, and Virginia Genealogy* (Self-published, 2013).

15. Schrift, 2013.

16. D. Snow and D. McAdam, "Identity Work Process in the Context of Social Movements: Clarifying the Identity/Movement Nexus," in *Self, Identity, and Social Movements*, eds. T. Stryker and R. White (Minneapolis: University of Minnesota Press, 2000): 47.

17. A. Puckett, "The Melungeon Identity Movement and the Construction of Appalachian Whiteness," *Journal of Linguistic Anthropology* 11, no. 1 (2001): 131–146.

18. Jimenez, 2010; Tatum, 1997.

19. Puckett, 2001, 132.

20. Eva Garroutte, *Real Indians: Identity and the Survival of Native America* (Oakland: University of California Press, 2003), 6.

21. Valentine, 2015, p. 2.

22. Jimenez, 2010; Tatum, 1997.

195

23. D. Walsh in discussion with the author, November 24, 2012.

24. P. McIntosh, "White Privilege: Unpacking the Invisible Knapsack," *Independent School* 49, no. 2 (1990), 31; Tatum, 1997.

25. R. Fivush and C.A. Haden, *Autobiographical Memory and the Construction of a Narrative Self: Developmental and Cultural Perspectives* (New York: Psychology, 2003).

26. A. Woollett and A. Phoenix, "Deconstructing Developmental Psychology Accounts of Mothering," *Feminism & Psychology* 7, no. 2 (1997): 275–282.

27. Sommer, 2010, 378.

28. Jack Goins in discussion with the author, February 18, 2017.

29. D. Rast et al., "Leadership Under Uncertainty: When Leaders Who Are Non-Prototypical Group Members Can Gain Support," *Journal of Experimental Social Psychology* 48, no. 3 (2012): 646–653.

30. F.O. Walumba et al., "Psychological Processes Linking Authentic Leadership to Follower Behaviors," *The Leadership Quarterly* 21, no. 5 (2010): 901–914.

31. Jimenez, 2010, 1759.

32. *Ibid.*, 1769.

33. Wilson & Beaver, 1999, 51.

34. T.K. Williams and M.C. Thornton, "Social Construction of Ethnicity Versus Personal Experience: the Case of Afro-Amerasians," *Journal of Comparative Family Studies* 29, no. 2 (1998): 255–267.

35. R. Fivush, "Co-Constructing Memories and Meaning Over Time," in *Emotion and Memory in Development: Biological, Cognitive, and Social Considerations,* eds. J.A. Quas and R. Fivush (New York: Oxford University Press, 2009).

36. M. Barreto and N. Ellemers, "The Effects of Being Categorized: the Interplay Between Internal and External Social Identities," *European Review of Social Psychology* 14, no. 5 (2003): 139–170; D. Sanchez and J. Garcia, "When Race Matters: Racially Stigmatized Others and Perceiving Race as a Biological Construction Affect Biracial People's Daily Well-Being," *Personality and Social Psychology Bulletin* 35, no. 9 (2009): 1154–1164; S. Townsent, H. Markus, and H. Bergsieker, "My Choice, Your Categories: the Denial of Multiracial Identities," *The Society for the Psychological Study of Social Issues* 65, no. 1 (2009): 185–204.

37. Jimenez, 2010.

38. Rabinow and Rose, 2006 p. 207.

39. Sommer, 2010, 378.

40. *Ibid.*

41. B.F. Williams, "A Class Act: Anthropology and the Race to Nation Across Ethnic Terrain," *Annual Review of Anthropology* 18 (1989): 404.

42. Wilson and Beaver, 1999.

43. Anglin, 2002, 73.

44. Puckett, 2001, 134.

45. Pinker as cited in Sanchez and Garcia, 2009, 202.

46. Puckett, 2001, 136.

47. Puckett, 2001, 135; Garroutte, 2003.

48. Beaver, 1992; Puckett, 2001.

49. Puckett, 2001, 136.

50. Fivush and Haden, 2003.

51. A. Kuhn and K. McAllister, *Locating Memory* (Brooklyn: Berghahn, 2006), 6.

52. Puckett, 2001, 138.

53. Roediger, 2005.

54. Jack Goins in discussion with the author, February 18, 2017.

55. R.A. Heifetz, *Leadership Without Easy Answers* (Cambridge, MA: Harvard University Press, 1994).

56. R.E. Boyatzis et al., "Developing Resonant Leaders Through Emotional Intelligence, Vision, and Coaching," *Organizational Dynamics* 42, no. 1 (2013), 21.

57. D. Goleman, R.E. Boyatzis, and A. McKee, *The New Leaders: Transforming the Art of Leadership Into the Science of Results* (London: Little, Brown, 2002).

58. Tatum, 1997; K. Vande Brake, *How They Shine: Melungeon* (Macon, GA: Mercer University Press, 2006).

59. C. Sturm, "Blood Politics, Racial Classifications, and Cherokee National Identity," *American Indian Quarterly* 22 (1998), 243.

60. M. Heidegger, *Being and Time* (New York: Harper and Row, 1962).

61. T. Alexander and C. Berry, "Who is Appalachian? Self-Reported Appalachian Ancestry in the 2000 Census," *Appalachian Journal* 38, no. 1 (2010): 46–56.

62. M. Barreto, N. Ellemers, and S.T. Fiske, "'What Did You Say, and Who Do You Think You Are?' How Power Differences Affect Emotional Reactions to Prejudice," *Journal of Social Issues* 66, no. 3 (2010): 477–492; A. Bazuin-Yoder, "Positive and Negative Childhood and Adolescent Identity Memories Stemming from One's Country and Culture-of-Origin: A Comparative Narrative Analysis," *Child & Youth Care Forum* 40, no. 1 (2011): 77–92.

63. M. Barreto and N. Ellemers, "Current Issues in the Study of Social Stigma: Some Controversies and Unresolved Issues," *Journal of Social Issues* 66, no. 3 (2010): 431–445; R.E. Johnson, C. Chang, and C.C. Rosen, "'Who I Am Depends on How Fairly I'm Treated': Effects of Justice on Self-Identity and Regulatory Focus," *Journal of Applied So-

cial Psychology 40, no. 12 (2010): 3020–3058.

64. F. Heylighen, *Epistemology*, 1993. http://pespmc1.vub.ac.be/EPISTEMI.html.

65. J. Badagliacco and C. Ruiz, "Impoverished Appalachia and Kentucky Genomes: What is At Stake? How Do Feminists Reply?" *New Genetics and Society* 25, no. 2 (2006), 209–226; P. Brodwin, "Bioethics in Action and Human Population Genetics Research," *Culture, Medicine, and Psychiatry* 29 (2005): 145–178; K. Hackstaff, "Who Are We? Genealogists Negotiating Ethno-Racial Identities," *Qualitative Sociology Review*, no. 2 (2009): 173–194; S.P. Hanna, "Representing Appalachia: Appalshop Films and the Politics of Regional Identity," PhD diss., University of Kentucky, 1997; C.N. Hickman, "'What to Throw Away/What to Keep': Mobilizing Expressive Culture and Regional Reconstruction in Appalachia," PhD diss., University of North Carolina at Chapel Hill, 1999; C. Lenz, "Genealogy and Archaeology: Analyzing Generational Positioning in Historical Narratives," *Journal of Comparative Family Studies* 42, no. 3 (2011): 319–327; C.A. Massey, "The Responsibility of Forms: Social and Visual Rhetorics of Appalachian Identity," PhD diss., Ohio University, 2009; W.G. Roy, "Aesthetic Identity, Race, and American Folk Music," *Qualitative Sociology* 25, no. 3 (2002): 459–469; R. Rubin, "'What Ain't Called Melungeons is Called Hillbillies': Southern Appalachia's In-Between People," *Forum for Modern Language Studies* 40, no. 3 (2004), 259–278; K. Stroebe, M. Barreto, and N. Ellemers, "When Searching Hurts: the Role of Information Search in Reactions to Gender Discrimination," *Sex Roles* 62, no. 1 (2010): 60–76; R. Tutton, "'They Want to Know Where They Came From': Population Genetics, Identity, and Family Genealogy," *New Genetics and Society* 23, no. 1 (2004): 105–120.

66. Heylighen, 1993.

67. Anglin, 2002; Barreto and Ellemers, 2003, 2010; N. Ellemers and M. Barreto, "Collective Action in Modern Times: How Modern Expressions of Prejudice Prevent Collective Action," *Journal of Social Issues* 65, no. 4 (2009): 749–768.

68. S. Lawrence-Lightfoot and J.H. Davis, *The Art and Science of Portraiture* (San Francisco: Jossey-Bass, 1997).

69. Puckett, 2001.

Chapter 1

1. K. Vande Brake in discussion with the author, August, 2012.

2. M.B. Brewer, "Optimal Distinctiveness Theory: Its History and Development," in *Handbook of Theories of Social Psychologies*, eds. P.A.M. Van Lange, A.W. Kruglanski, & E.T. Higgins (Thousand Oaks, CA: Sage, 2012); Darlene Wilson, "Some Reflections on Appalachian and Melungeon History," *The Coalfield Progress* (Norton, VA), June 25, 1996.

3. W. Winkler in discussion with the author, June 25, 2012.

4. W. Winkler, *Walking Toward the Sunset: The Melungeons of Appalachia* (Macon, GA: Mercer University Press, 2005), ix.

5. *Ibid.*, x.

6. W. Brownlow, "Impudent Melungeon," *Jonesboro Whig and Independent Journal* (Jonesboro, TN), October 7, 1840: 3.

7. K.J. Lyday-Lee, *Select Mountain Literature of Will Allen Dromgoole* (Knoxville: University of Tennessee Press, 1982), 78.

8. P. Elder, *Melungeons: Examining an Appalachian Legend* (Blountville, TN: Continuity, 1999).

9. W. A. Plecker, *The New Family and Racial Improvement* (Richmond: Bureau of Vital Statistics, State Department of Health, 1928).

10. C. Beale, "American Tri-Racial Isolates," *Eugenics Quarterly* 4, no. 4 (1957): 187–196; C. Beale, "An Overview of the Phenomenon of Mixed Racial Isolates in the United States," *American Anthropologist* 74 (1974), 704.

11. N.B. Kennedy and R.V. Kennedy, *The Melungeons: The Resurrection of a Proud People: An Untold Story of Ethnic Cleansing in America* (Macon, GA: Mercer University Press, 1997).

12. M. Schrift, *Becoming Melungeon: Making an Ethnic Identity in the Appalachian South* (Lincoln: University of Nebraska Press, 2013).

13. D. Wilson, 1996.

14. D. Wilson in discussion with the author, June 27, 2012.

15. R.J. Estes, et al., "Melungeons: A Multiethnic Population," *Journal of Genetic Genealogy* (2011), http://www.jogg.info/pages/72/files/Estes.pdf.

16. J.D. Hill, *History, Power, and Identity Ethnogenesis in the Americas, 1492–1992* (Iowa City: University of Iowa Press, 1996).

17. G. Sider," Identity as History: Ethnohistory, Ethnogenesis and Ethnocide in the Southeastern United States," *Identities* 1, no. 1 (1994): 109–122.

18. D.D. Davis, *A Case of Identity: Ethnogenesis of the New Houma Indians* (Durham, NC: Duke University Press, 2001); J.H. Dor-

mon, "Louisiana's 'Creoles of Color': Ethnicity, Marginality, and Identity," *Social Science Quarterly* 73, no. 3 (1992): 615–626.

19. A. Coleman, "'Tell the Court I Love My [Indian] Wife': Interrogating Race and Self-Identity in Loving v. Virginia," *Souls: A Critical Journey of Black Politics, Culture, and Society* 8, no. 1 (2006): 67–80.

20. P.A. Lombardo, *Miscegenation, Eugenics, and Racism: Historical Footnotes to Loving v. Virginia* (Davis: University of California Press, 1988), 451.

21. Eva Garroutte, *Real Indians: Identity and the Survival of Native America* (Oakland: University of California Press, 2003), 6.

22. C. Sturm, "Blood Politics, Racial Classifications, and Cherokee National Identity," *American Indian Quarterly* 22 (1998), 243.

23. J. Fraley, "From Hillbilly Power Riots to Protected Class Status by Ordinance: A History of Appalachian Discrimination," *Conference Papers—Law & Society* 1 (2009), 2.

24. W.L. Adamson, *Hegemony and Revolution: A Study of Antonio Gramsci's Political and Cultural Theory* (Berkeley: University of California Press, 1980).

25. bell hooks, *Belonging: A Culture of Place* (New York: Routledge, 2009).

26. A. Puckett, "The Melungeon Identity Movement and the Construction of Appalachian Whiteness," *Journal of Linguistic Anthropology* 11, no. 1 (2001): 131–146.

27. J.C. Scott, *Domination and the Arts of Resistance: Hidden Transcripts* (New Haven, CT: Yale University Press, 1990).

28. E. Goffman, "The Presentation of Self," in *Life as Theater: A Dramaturgical Sourcebook*, eds. D. Brissett and C. Edgley (Hawthorne, NY: Aldine de Gruyter, 1990).

29. K. Vande Brake, *How They Shine: Melungeon* (Macon, GA: Mercer University Press, 2006), 1–2.

30. L.D. Tugman-Gabriel, "Seeking Roots in Shifting Ground: Ethnic Identity Development and Melungeons of Southern Appalachia," PhD diss., Fielding Graduate University, 2011.

31. D. Jenkins, "Common Law, Mountain Music, and the Construction of Community Identity," *Social and Legal Studies* 19, no. 3 (2010), 351.

32. C. Kenny and T. Ngaroimata-Fraser, *Living Indigenous Leadership: Native Narratives on Building Strong Communities* (Vancouver: University of British Columbia Press, 2012), 4.

33. V. DeMarce, "'Verry Slitly Mixt': Tri-Racial Isolate Families of the Upper South:

A Genealogical Study," *National Genealogical Society Quarterly* 80, no. 1 (1992): 5–35.

34. Kennedy and Kennedy, 1997, xv.

35. M. Sommer, "DNA and Cultures of Remembrance: Anthropological Genetics, Biohistories, and Biosocialities," *BioSocieties* 5, no. 3 (2010): 366–390.

36. E.C. Hirschman and D. Panther-Yates, "Peering Inward for Ethnic Identity: Consumer Interpretation of DNA Test Results," *Identity: An International Journal of Theory and Research* 8, no. 1 (2008): 47–66.

37. R.W. Belk, *Handbook of Qualitative Research Methods in Marketing* (Northampton, MA: Edward Elgar, 2006), 424.

38. P. Brodwin, "'Bioethics in Action' and Human Population Genetics Research," *Culture, Medicine, and Psychiatry* 29 (2005): 145–178.

39. Estes, et al., 2011.

40. R. Tutton, "'They Want to Know Where They Came From': Population Genetics, Identity, and Family Genealogy," *New Genetics and Society* 23, no. 1 (2004): 105–120.

41. K. Vande Brake in discussion with the author, July 12, 2012.

42. B. Belton, "'Weak Power': Community and Identity," *Ethnic and Racial Studies* 36, no. 2 (2013), 289.

43. *Ibid.*, 293.

44. R. Van Veelen, S. Otten, and N. Hansen, "Linking Self and In Group: Self-Anchoring as Distinctive Cognitive Route to Self-Identification," *European Journal of Social Psychology* 41, no. 5 (2011): 628, 637.

45. Brewer, 2012.

46. N. Tasdemir, "The Relationships Between Motivations of Intergroup Differentiation as a Function of Different Dimensions of Social Identity," *Review of General Psychology* 15, no. 2 (2011): 125–137.

47. R.K. Dhamoon, "Considerations on Mainstreaming Intersectionality," *Political Research Quarterly* 64, no. 1 (2011), 238.

48. McDowell & Hernandez, 2010, p 93.

49. J.J. Podber, *The Electronic Front Porch* (Macon, GA: Mercer University Press, 2007).

50. B. Davies and S. Gannon, *Doing Collective Biography* (New York: Open University, 2006).

51. Vande Brake, 2011.

Chapter 2

1. C. Beale, "An Overview of the Phenomenon of Mixed Racial Isolates in the United States," *American Anthropologist* 74 (1972), 704; S. Brooks, "Coming Home: Finding My Appalachian Mothers Through Emma Bell

Miles," *NWSA Journal* 11, no. 3 (1999), 157; E.T. Price, "A Geographic Analysis of White-Negro-Indian Racial Mixtures in Eastern United States," Annals of the Association of American Geographers 43, no. 2 (1953): 138–155; K. Vande Brake, *How They Shine: Melungeon* (Macon, GA: Mercer University Press, 2006); W. Winkler, *Walking Toward the Sunset: The Melungeons of Appalachia* (Macon, GA: Mercer University Press, 2005).

2. R.E. Stake, *The Art of Case Study Research* (Thousand Oaks, CA: Sage, 1995), xii.

3. S. Lawrence-Lightfoot and J.H. Davis, *The Art and Science of Portraiture* (San Francisco, Jossey-Bass, 1997).

4. J. Russell, "Time Sharing: Women's Changing Relationship with Computer Science," EdD diss., University of Vermont, 2004.

5. A. Nayak, "After Race: Ethnography, Race, and Post-Race Theory," *Ethnic and Racial Studies* 29, no. 3 (2006), 247.

6. *Ibid.*, 427.

7. T.K. Williams and M.C. Thornton, "Social Construction of Ethnicity Versus Personal Experience: the Case of Afro-Amerasians," *Journal of Comparative Family Studies* 29, no. 2 (1998): 255–267.

8. Lawrence-Lightfoot and Davis, xv–xvi.

9. *Ibid.*, 99 and 122.

10. *Ibid.*, 103.

11. P. Elder, *Melungeons: Examining an Appalachian Legend* (Blountville, TN: Continuity, 1999); T. Hashaw, *Children of Perdition: Melungeons and the Struggle of Mixed America* (Macon, GA: Mercer University Press, 2007).

12. Lawrence-Lightfoot and Davis, 58.

13. B. Dicks, B. Soyinka, and A. Coffey, "Multimodal Ethnography," Qualitative Research 6, no. 1 (2006): 77–96; Lawrence-Lightfoot & Davis, 1997; J. Sprague, *Feminist Methodologies for Critical Researchers: Bridging Differences* (Lanham, MD: Rowman & Littlefield, 2005).

14. N.K. Denzin, Y.S. Lincoln, and L.T. Smith, *Handbook of Critical and Indigenous Methodologies* (Los Angeles: Sage, 2008).

15. B. Tedlock, "Participant Observation to the Observation of Participation: The Emergence of Narrative Ethnography," *Journal of Anthropological Research* 47, no. 1 (1991), 69.

16. M. Strathern, *Partial Connections* (Lanham, MD: AltaMira, 2004).

17. Denzin et al., 2008; Strathern, 2004.

18. Lawrence-Lightfoot and Davis, 1997.

19. E. Husserl, *The Crisis of European Sciences and Transcendental Phenomenology* (Evanston: Northwestern University Press, 1970).

20. L. Finlay, "Introducing Phenomeno-logical Research," Dr. Linda Finlay, 2008, http://lindafinlay.co.uk/phenomenology/.

21. Husserl, 1970.

22. Finlay, 2008.

23. Finlay, 2008; Stake, 1995.

24. Stake, 1995.

25. *Ibid.*

26. Dicks, et. al, 2006.

27. J. Warin, Y. Solomon, and C. Lewis, "Swapping Stories, Comparing Plots: Triangulating Individual Narratives Within Families," *International Journal of Social Research Methodology: Theory & Practice* 10, no. 2 (2007): 121–134.

Chapter 5

1. Jack Goins, *Melungeons: Footprints from the Past* (Self-published, 2009), 228.

Chapter 6

1. N.B. and R.V. Kennedy, *The Melungeons: The Resurrection of a Proud People: An Untold Story of Ethnic Cleansing in America* (Macon, GA: Mercer University Press, 1997).

2. J.A. Banks, "Multicultural Education: Historical Development, Dimensions, and Practice," *Review of Research in Education* 19 (1993): 3–49.

3. D. Snow and D. McAdam, "Identity Work Process in the Context of Social Movements: Clarifying the Identity/Movement Nexus," in *Self, Identity, and Social Movements,* eds. T. Stryker and R. White (Minneapolis: University of Minnesota Press, 2000).

4. Phil Cheeks in discussion with the author, August 2012.

5. D. McAdams, "Identity and the Life Story," in *Autobiographical Memory and the Construction of the Narrative Self,* eds. R. Fivush and C. Haden (Mahwah, NJ: Lawrence Erlbaum, 2003).

6. D. Oyserman, "Culture Three Ways: Culture and Subcultures Within Countries," *Annual Review of Psychology* 68 (2017): 435–463.

7. Joanne Pezzullo, "[Melungeon] Everyone," *RootsWeb,* February 2, 2008, http://archiver.rootsweb.ancestry.com/th/read/melungeon/2008-02/1202039442.

8. Fullerton 2004.

Chapter 7

1. M.A. Hogg, "Social Identity and the Psychology of Groups," in *Handbook of Self*

and Identity, eds. M.R. Leary and J.P. Tangney (New York: Guilford, 2012), 511.

2. M.B. Brewer, "Optimal Distinctiveness Theory: Its History and Development," in *Handbook of Theories of Social Psychologies*, eds. P.A.M. Van Lange, A.W. Kruglanski, & E.T. Higgins (Thousand Oaks, CA: Sage, 2012).

3. Hogg 2012.

4. D.A. De Quintal, "Race, 'Face,' and American Indian Nations: Native American Identity in Southern New England," PhD diss., University of Chicago, 2012, 178.

5. Dwanna Lynn Robertson, "Card-Carrying Indian: The Social Construction of an American Indian Legal Identity," MA thesis, Oklahoma State University, 2010, 77.

6. R.E. Boyatzis et al, "Developing Resonant Leaders Through Emotional Intelligence, Vision, and Coaching," *Organizational Dynamics* 42, no. 1 (2013), 17–18.

Bibliography

Adamson, W. L. *Hegemony and Revolution: A Study of Antonio Gramsci's Political and Cultural Theory*. Berkeley: University of California Press, 1980.

Alexander, T., & Berry, C. "Who is Appalachian? Self-Reported Appalachian Ancestry in the 2000 Census." *Appalachian Journal* 38 (2010): 46–56.

Anglin, M. "Erasures of the Past: Culture, Power, and Heterogeneity in Appalachia." *Journal of Appalachian Studies* 10 (2004): 73–84.

Badagliacco, J., & Ruiz, C. "Impoverished Appalachia and Kentucky Genomes: What is at Stake? How Do Feminists Reply?" *New Genetics & Society* 25 (2006): 209–226.

Banks, J. A. "Multicultural Education: Historical Development, Dimensions, and Practice." *Review of Research in Education* 19 (1993): 3–49.

Barreto, M., & Ellemers, N. "Current Issues in the Study of Social Stigma: Some Controversies and Unresolved Issues." *Journal of Social Issues* 66 (2010): 431–445.

_____. "The Effects of Being Categorised: The Interplay Between Internal and External Social Identities." *European Review of Social Psychology* 14 (2003): 139–170.

Barreto, M., Ellemers, N., & Fiske, S. T. "'What Did You Say, and Who Do You Think You Are?' How Power Differences Affect Emotional Reactions to Prejudice." *Journal of Social Issues* 66 (2010): 477–492.

Bazuin-Yoder, A. "Positive and Negative Childhood and Adolescent Identity Memories Stemming from One's Country and Culture-of-Origin: A Comparative Narrative Analysis." *Child & Youth Care Forum* 40 (2001): 77–92.

Beale, C. "American Tri-Racial Isolates." *Eugenics Quarterly* 4 (1957): 187–196.

_____. "An Overview of the Phenomenon of Mixed Racial Isolates in the United States." *American Anthropologist* 74 (1972): 704–710.

Beaver, P. D. *Rural Community in the Appalachian South*. Lexington: University Press of Kentucky, 1986.

Belk, R.W. *Handbook of Qualitative Research Methods in Marketing*. Northampton, MA: Edward Elgar, 2006.

Belton, B. "'Weak Power': Community and Identity." *Ethnic and Racial Studies* 36 (2013): 282–297.

Berkovitch, N., & Helman, S. "Global Social Movements." In *Companion to Gender Studies*, edited by P. Essed, D. Goldberg, & A. Kobayashi, 266–279. Maldan, MA: Wiley Blackwell, 2009.

Brewer, M. B. "Optimal Distinctiveness Theory: Its History and Development." In *Handbook of Theories of Social Psychologies*, edited by P. A. M. Van Lange, A. W. Kruglanski, & E. T. Higgins, 81–98. Thousand Oaks, CA: Sage, 2012.

Brodwin, P. "'Bioethics in Action' and Human Population Genetics Research." *Culture, Medicine, and Psychiatry* 29 (2005): 145–178.

Brooks, S. "Coming Home: Finding My Appalachian Mothers Through Emma Bell Miles." *NWSA Journal* 11 (1999): 157–171.

Boyatzis, R. E., Smith, M. L., Van Oosten, E., & Woolford, L. "Developing Resonant Leaders Through Emotional Intelligence, Vision and Coaching." *Or-

ganizational Dynamics 42 (2013): 17–24.

Burnette, S. "A Note on the Melungeons." *American Anthropologist* 2 (1889): 347–349.

Coleman, A. "'Tell the Court I Love My [Indian] Wife': Interrogating Race and Self-Identity in Loving v. Virginia." *Souls: A Critical Journal of Black Politics, Culture and Society* 8 (2006): 67–80.

Davies, B., & Gannon, S. *Doing Collective Biography*. New York: Open University Press, 2006.

Davis, D. D. *A Case of Identity: Ethnogenesis of the New Houma Indians*. Durham, NC: Duke University Press, 2001.

Delle Donne, C. *Federal Census Schedules, 1850–1880: Primary Sources for Historical Research*, General Services Administration, Reference Information Paper, no. 67. Washington, D.C.: National Archives and Record Service, 1973.

DeMarce, V. "'Verry Slitly Mixt': Tri-Racial Isolate Families of the Upper South: A Genealogical Study." *National Genealogical Society Quarterly* 80 (1992): 5–35.

Denzin, N. K., Lincoln, Y. S., & Smith, L. T. *Handbook of Critical and Indigenous Methodologies*. Los Angeles: Sage, 2008.

De Quintal, D. A. "Race, 'Face', and American Indian Nations: Native American Identity in Southern New England." PhD diss., University of Chicago, 2012.

Dewey, J. *Experience and Education*. New York: Macmillan, 1938.

Dhamoon, R. K. "Considerations on Mainstreaming Intersectionality." *Political Research Quarterly* 64 (2001): 230–243.

Dicks, B., & Mason, B. *Hypermedia and Ethnography: Reflections on the Construction of a Research Approach*. London: Sage, 1998.

Dicks, B., Soyinka, B., & Coffey, A. "Multimodal Ethnography." *Qualitative Research* 6 (2006): 77–96.

Dormon, J. H. "Louisiana's 'Creoles of Color': Ethnicity, Marginality, and Identity." *Social Science Quarterly* 73 (1992): 615–626.

Elder, P. *Melungeons: Examining an Appalachian Legend*. Blountville, TN: Continuity, 1999.

Ellemers, N., & Barreto, M. "Collective Action in Modern Times: How Modern Expressions of Prejudice Prevent Collective Action." *Journal of Social Issues* 65 (2009): 749–768.

English, F.W. "A Critical Appraisal of Sara Lawrence-Lightfoot's Portraiture as a Method of Educational Research." *Educational Researcher* 29 (2000): 21–26.

Essed, P. *Understanding Everyday Racism: An Interdisciplinary Theory*. Newbury Park, CA: Sage, 1991.

Estes, R. J., Goins, J. H., Ferguson, P., & Crain, J. L. "Melungeons: A Multiethnic Population." *Journal of Genetic Genealogy* (2011). Accessed at http://www.jogg.info/72/files/Estes.pdf.

Finlay, L. "Introducing Phenomenological Research." Dr. Linda Finlay, 2008. http://lindafinlay.co.uk/phenomenology/.

Fivush, R. "Co-Constructing Memories and Meaning Over Time." In *Emotion and Memory in Development: Biological, Cognitive, and Social Considerations*, edited by J. A. Quas & R. Fivush, 343–354. New York: Oxford University Press, 2009.

Fivush, R., & Haden, C. A. *Autobiographical Memory and the Construction of a Narrative Self: Developmental and Cultural Perspectives*. New York: Psychology, 2003.

Frankenberg, R. *White Women, Race Matters: The Social Construction of Whiteness*. Minneapolis: University of Minnesota Press, 1993.

Fraley, J. "From Hillbilly Power Riots to Protected Class Status by Ordinance: A History of Appalachian Discrimination." Paper presented at the annual meeting of the Law and Society Association, Denver, Colorado, May 25, 2009.

Fullerton, Carol S. "Shared Meaning Following Trauma: Bridging Generations and Cultures." *Psychiatry* 67, no. 1 (2004): 61–62.

Garroutte, Eva. *Real Indians: Identity and the Survival of Native America*. Oakland: University of California Press, 2003.

Goffman, E. "The Presentation of Self." In *Life as Theater: A Dramaturgical Sourcebook*, edited by D. Brissett & C. Edgley, 129–139. Hawthorne, NY: Aldine de Gruyter, 1990.

Goldberg, D. T. *The Racial State*. Maden, MA: Wiley-Blackwell, 2002.

_____. *Racist Culture: Philosophy and the Politics of Meaning*. Cambridge MA: Blackwell, 1993.

Goleman, D., Boyatzis, R. E., & McKee, A. *The New Leaders: Transforming the Art of Leadership into the Science of Results*. London: Little, Brown, 2002.

Goins, J. *Melungeons: Footprints from the Past*. Self-published, 2009.

Hackstaff, K. "Who Are We? Genealogists Negotiating Ethno-Racial Identities." *Qualitative Sociology* 32 (2009): 173–194.

Haley, A. *Roots: The Saga of an American Family*. New York: Vanguard, 2007.

Hanna, S. P. "Representing Appalachia: Appalshop Films and the Politics of Regional Identity." PhD diss., University of Kentucky, 1997.

Hashaw, T. *Children of Perdition: Melungeons and the Struggle of Mixed America*. Macon, GA: Mercer University Press, 2007.

Heidegger, M. *Being and Time*. New York: Harper and Row, 1962.

Heifetz, R. A. *Leadership Without Easy Answers*. Cambridge, MA: Harvard University Press, 1994.

Heylighen, F. "Epistemology." 1993. http://pespmc1.vub.ac.be/EPISTEMI.html.

Hickman, C. N. "'What to Throw Away/What to Keep': Mobilizing Expressive Culture and Regional Reconstruction in Appalachia." PhD diss., University of North Carolina at Chapel Hill, 1998.

Hill, J. D. *History, Power, and Identity Ethnogenesis in the Americas, 1492–1992*. Iowa City: University of Iowa Press, 1996.

Hirschman, E. C., & Panther-Yates, D. "Peering Inward for Ethnic Identity: Consumer Interpretation of DNA Test Results." *Identity: An International Journal of Theory and Research* 8 (2008): 47–66.

Hogg, M. A. "Social Identity and the Psychology of Groups." In *Handbook of Self and Identity*, edited by M. R. Leary & J. P. Tangney, 502–519. New York: Guilford, 2012.

hooks, bell. *Belonging: A Culture of Place*. New York: Routledge, 2009.

_____. *Black Looks: Race and Representation*. Boston: South End, 1992.

Hornsey, M. J., & Hogg, M. A. "Subgroup Differentiation as a Response to an Overly Inclusive Group: A Test of Optimal Distinctiveness Theory." *European Journal of Social Psychology* 29 (1999): 543–550.

Husserl, E. *The Crisis of European Sciences and Transcendental Phenomenology*. Evanston: Northwestern University Press, 1970.

Jenkins, D. "Common Law, Mountain Music, and the Construction of Community Identity." *Social & Legal Studies* 19 (2010): 351–369.

Jimenez, T. "Affiliative Ethnic Identity: A More Elastic Link Between Ethnic Ancestry and Culture." *Ethnic and Racial Studies* 33 (2010): 1756–1775.

Johnson, R. E., Chang, C., & Rosen, C. C. "'Who I Am Depends on How Fairly I'm Treated': Effects of Justice on Self-Identity and Regulatory Focus." *Journal of Applied Social Psychology* 40 (2010): 3020–3058.

Kennedy, N. B., & Kennedy, R. V. *The Melungeons: The Resurrection of a Proud People: An Untold Story of Ethnic Cleansing in America*. Macon, GA: Mercer University Press, 1997.

Kenny, C., & Ngaroimata-Fraser, T., eds. *Living Indigenous Leadership: Native Narratives on Building Strong Communities*. Vancouver: University of British Columbia, 2012.

Kolb, D. A., Boyatzis, R. E., & Mainemelis, C. "Experiential Learning Theory: Previous Research and New Directions." In *Perspectives on Thinking, Learning, and Cognitive Styles*, edited by R. J. Sternberg & L. Zhang, 227–247. Mahwah, NJ: Lawrence Erlbaum, 2001.

Kuhn, A., & McAllister, K. *Locating Memory*. Brooklyn, NY: Berghahn, 2006.

Lawrence-Lightfoot, S., & Davis, J. H. *The Art and Science of Portraiture*. San Francisco: Jossey-Bass, 1997.

Lenz, C. "Genealogy and Archaeology: Analyzing Generational Positioning in

Historical Narratives." *Journal of Comparative Family Studies* 42 (2011): 319–327.

Lombardo, P. A. *Miscegenation, Eugenics and Racism: Historical Footnotes to Loving v. Virginia.* Davis: University of California Press, 1988.

Lyday-Lee, K. J. *Select Mountain Literature of Will Allen Dromgoole.* Knoxville: University of Tennessee Press, 1982.

Massey, C. A. "The Responsibility of Forms: Social and Visual Rhetorics of Appalachian Identity." PhD diss., Ohio University, 2009.

McAdams, D. "Identity and the Life Story." In *Autobiographical Memory and the Construction of the Narrative Self,* edited by R. Fivush & C. Haden, 187–208. Mahwah, NJ: Lawrence Erlbaum, 2003.

McDonald, M. E. "A Portrait of the Role and Value of Solitude for Educational Leaders." EdD diss., University of Northern Arizona, 2005.

McIntosh, P. "White Privilege: Unpacking the Invisible Knapsack." *Independent School* 49 (1990): 31–36.

Nayak, A. "After Race: Ethnography, Race and Post-Race Theory." *Ethnic and Racial Studies* 29 (2006): 411–430.

Omi, M., & Winant, H. *Racial Formations in the United States: From the 1960s to the 1990s.* London: Rutledge, 1994.

Oyserman, D. "Culture Three Ways: Culture and Subcultures Within Countries." *Annual Review of Psychology* 68 (2017): 435–463.

Pezzullo, J. "Melungeon Indians," 2013. http://historical-melungeons.com/.

Plecker, W. A. "The New Family and Racial Improvement." Richmond, VA: Bureau of Vital Statistics, State Department of Health, 1928.

Podber, J. J. *The Electronic Front Porch: An Oral History of the Arrival of Modern Media in Rural Appalachia and the Melungeon Community.* Macon, GA; Mercer University Press, 2007.

Price, E. T. "A Geographic Analysis of White-Negro-Indian Racial Mixtures in Eastern United States." *Annals of the Association of American Geographers* 43 (1953): 138–155.

Puckett, A. "The Melungeon Identity Movement and the Construction of Appalachian Whiteness." *Journal of Linguistic Anthropology* 11 (2001): 131–146.

Rast, D., Gaffney, A. M., Hogg, M. A., & Crisp, R. J. "Leadership Under Uncertainty: When Leaders Who Are Non-Prototypical Group Members Can Gain Support." *Journal of Experimental Social Psychology* 48 (2012): 646–653.

Rice, M. *The Great White Lies: Dr. Walter Plecker, Eugenics, Melungeons, and Virginia Genealogy.* Self-published, 2013.

Riley, S. "Mixed Race Studies," 2013. http://www.mixedracestudies.org/wordpress/?p=13860.

Robertson, D. L. "Card-Carrying Indian: The Social Construction of an American Indian Legal Identity." Master's thesis, Oklahoma State University, 2010.

Roediger, D. R. *The Wages of Whiteness: Race and the Making of the American Working Class.* New York: Verso, 1999.

_____. *Working Toward Whiteness: How America's Immigrants Became White: The Strange Journey from Ellis Island to the Suburbs.* New York: Basic, 2005.

Rootsweb. "Melungeon-L Archives." Last modified 2017. http://archiver.rootsweb.ancestry.com/th/index/Melungeon.

Rose, N. *The Politics of Life Itself: Biomedicine, Power, and Subjectivity in the Twenty-First Century.* Princeton, NJ: Princeton University Press, 2007.

Roy, W.G. "Aesthetic Identity, Race, and American Folk Music." *Qualitative Sociology* 25 (2002): 459–469.

_____. "'Race Records' and 'Hillbilly Music': Institutional Origins of Racial Categories in the American Commercial Recording Industry." *Poetics* 32 (2004): 265–279.

Rubin, R. "'What Ain't Called Melungeons Is Called Hillbillies': Southern Appalachia's In-Between People." *Forum for Modern Language Studies* 40 (2004): 259–278.

Russell, J. "Time Sharing: Women's Changing Relationship with Computer Science." EdD diss., University of Vermont, 2004.

Sanchez, D., & Garcia, J. "When Race Matters: Racially Stigmatized Others and Perceiving Race as a Biological Construction Affect Biracial People's Daily Well-Being." *Personality and Social Psychology Bulletin* 35 (2009): 1154–1164.

Schrift, M. *Becoming Melungeon: Making an Ethnic Identity in the Appalachian South.* Lincoln: University of Nebraska Press, 2013.

Scolnick, J., & Kennedy, N. B. *From Anatolia to Appalachia: A Turkish-American Dialogue.* Macon, GA: Mercer University Press, 2004.

Scott, J. C. *Domination and the Arts of Resistance: Hidden Transcripts.* New Haven, CT: Yale University Press, 1990.

Sider, G. "Identity as History: Ethnohistory, Ethnogenesis and Ethnocide in the Southeastern United States." *Identities* 1(1994): 109–122.

Snow, D., & McAdam, D. "Identity Work Process in the Context of Social Movements: Clarifying the Identity/Movement Nexus." In *Self, Identity, and Social Movements,* edited by T. Stryker & R. White, 41–67. Minneapolis: University of Minnesota Press, 2000.

Sommer, M. "DNA and Cultures of Remembrance: Anthropological Genetics, Biohistories and Biosocialities." *BioSocieties* 5 (2010): 366–390.

Sprague, J. *Feminist Methodologies for Critical Researchers: Bridging Differences.* Lanham, MD: Rowman & Littlefield, 2005.

Stake, R. E. *The Art of Case Study Research.* Thousand Oaks, CA: Sage, 1995.

Strathern, M. *Partial Connections.* Lanham, MD: AltaMira, 2004.

Stroebe, K., Barreto, M., & Ellemers, N. "When Searching Hurts: The Role of Information Search in Reactions to Gender Discrimination." *Sex Roles* 62 (2010): 60–76.

Sturm, C. "Blood Politics, Racial Classification, and Cherokee National Identity." *American Indian Quarterly* 22 (1998): 230–237.

Tasdemir, N. "The Relationships Between Motivations of Intergroup Differentiation as a Function of Different Dimensions of Social Identity." *Review of General Psychology* 15 (2011): 125–137.

Tatum, B. D. *Why Are All the Black Kids Sitting Together in the Cafeteria?* New York: Basic, 1997.

Tedlock, B. "Participant Observation to the Observation of Participation: The Emergence of Narrative Ethnography." *Journal of Anthropological Research* 47 (1991): 69–94.

Townsent, S., Markus, H., & Bergsieker, H. "My Choice, Your Categories: The Denial of Multiracial Identities." *The Society for the Psychological Study of Social Issues* 65 (2009): 185–204.

Tugman-Gabriel, L. D. "Seeking Roots in Shifting Ground: Ethnic Identity Development and Melungeons of Southern Appalachia." PhD diss., Fielding Graduate University, 2011.

Tutton, R. "'They Want to Know Where They Came From': Population Genetics, Identity, and Family Genealogy." *New Genetics & Society* 23 (2004): 105–120.

Vande Brake, K. *How They Shine: Melungeon.* Macon, GA: Mercer University Press, 2006.

_____. *Through the Back Door: Melungeon Literacies and Twenty-First Century Technologies.* Macon, GA: Mercer University Press, 2009.

Van Veelen, R., Otten, S., & Hansen, N. "Linking Self and In Group: Self-Anchoring as Distinctive Cognitive Route to Social Identification." *European Journal of Social Psychology* 41 (2011): 628–637.

Walumbwa, F. O., Wang, P., Wang, H., Schaubroeck, J., & Avolio, B. J. "Psychological Processes Linking Authentic Leadership to Follower Behaviors." *The Leadership Quarterly* 21 (2010): 901–914.

Warin, J., Solomon, Y., & Lewis, C. "Swapping Stories: Comparing Plots: Triangulating Individual Narratives Within Families." *International Journal of Social Research Methodology: Theory & Practice* 10 (2007): 121–134.

Williams, B. F. "A Class Act: Anthropology and the Race to Nation Across Ethnic Terrain." *Annual Review of Anthropology* 18 (1989): 401–444.

Williams, T. K., & Thornton, M. C. "Social Construction of Ethnicity Versus Personal Experience: The Case of Afro-Amerasians." *Journal of Comparative Family Studies* 29 (1998): 255–267.

Wilson, D. "Some Reflections on Appalachian and Melungeon History." *The Coalfield Progress* (Norton, VA), June 25, 1996.

Wilson, D., & Beaver, P. "Transgressions in Race and Place: The Ubiquitous Native Grandmother in America's Cultural Memory." In *Neither Separate Nor Equal: Women in the Political Economy,* edited by B. E. Smith, 34–56. Philadelphia: Temple University Press, 1999.

Winkler, W. *Walking Toward the Sunset: The Melungeons of Appalachia.* Macon, GA: Mercer University Press, 2005.

Woollett, A., & Phoenix, A. "Deconstructing Developmental Psychology Accounts of Mothering." *Feminism & Psychology* 7 (1997): 275–282.

Index

www.ingramcontent.com/pod-product-compliance
Lightning Source LLC
Chambersburg PA
CBHW031131270326
41929CB00011B/1585